PRAISE FOR TIMOTHY BEAL'S

The Rise and Fall of the Bible

"A very readable explanation of how the Christian Bible became 'the book' it is today, from individual manuscripts on papyrus scrolls to collections of scrolls held by individual Christian communities."
— *Cleveland Plain Dealer*

"An engaging but also challenging re-reading of the sacred texts in the full light of history."
— *Jewish Journal*

"*The Rise and Fall of the Bible* is a succinct, clear and fascinating look at two phenomena: what Beal calls 'biblical consumerism' — in which buying Bibles and Bible-related publications and products substitutes for more meaningful encounters with the foundational text of Western Civilization — and the history of how the book came to be assembled."
— Salon.com

"Smart and conversational, Beal provides the kind of context about the Bible's ancient origins in the Holy Land, and its recent marketing by American entrepreneurs, that anyone who reads it should know."
— *New Jersey Star-Ledger*

"Well-written and engaging . . . A laudable look at the Good Book."
— *Kirkus*

"Remarkably accessible . . . Beal is more than just a debunker; in fact, once evangelical, he still considers himself a Christian. He exhorts readers to see the Bible not as a book of finite answers but as a crucible of questions that provoke, inspire, and even anger those who pick it up. The same might be said about his own book."
— *Booklist,* Starred Review

"This amazing book will make you see the Scriptures in a new light. Beal shows us that the origins of the Bible are messy and shaped by chance, but also that the Bible still can move us and needs to be taken seriously. Thou shalt read Beal."
— A. J. Jacobs author of *The Year of Living Biblically*

"Beal's exciting book offers both fascinating history and a new and insightful way to approach the 'sacred text.'"
— John Shelby Spong, author of *Eternal Life: A New Vision*

"A lot of us know just enough about the Bible to make us dangerous. Tim Beal wants to take us deeper in our understanding — not just about what the Bible says, but about what it is, and how it came to us in its many current forms. Under Beal's instruction, we will lose some of our naivete, but we'll gain maturity of insight that will more than compensate. A needed book from a talented writer." — Brian D. McLaren, author of *A New Kind of Christianity*

The Rise and Fall of the Bible

BOOKS BY TIMOTHY BEAL

*The Book of Hiding: Gender, Ethnicity,
Annihilation, and Esther*

*Esther (Berit Olam Studies in Hebrew
Narrative and Poetry)*

Religion and Its Monsters

Theory for Religious Studies (with William E. Deal)

*Roadside Religion: In Search of the Sacred, the
Strange, and the Substance of Faith*

Religion in America: A Very Short Introduction

*Biblical Literacy: The Essential Bible Stories
Everyone Needs to Know*

*The Rise and Fall of the Bible: The Unexpected
History of an Accidental Book*

The Rise and Fall of the Bible

THE
UNEXPECTED
HISTORY
OF AN
ACCIDENTAL
BOOK

TIMOTHY BEAL

MARINER BOOKS
HOUGHTON MIFFLIN HARCOURT
BOSTON   NEW YORK

First Mariner Books edition 2012

Copyright © 2011 by Timothy Beal

www.hmhbooks.com

Library of Congress Cataloging-in-Publication Data
Beal, Timothy K. (Timothy Kandler), date.
The rise and fall of the Bible : the unexpected history of an
accidental book / Timothy Beal.
p. cm.
Includes bibliographical references and index.
ISBN 978-0-15-101358-6
ISBN 978-0-547-73734-8 (pbk.)
1. Bible — Criticism, interpretation, etc. I. Title.
BS511.3.B43 2011
220.60973'0904 — dc22   2010005734

Book design by Brian Moore

Printed in the United States of America

DOC 10 9 8 7 6 5 4 3 2 1

For MOM

GERALDINE KANDLER BEAL

"rightly dividing the word of truth"

Contents

The End of the Word as We Know It:
A Personal Introduction

I REMEMBER MOM'S BIBLE especially well: the feel and smell of the dark red pebbly leather cover, the heft of it, the delicate paper, gray and silky-soft at the corners from countless careful turns, the way it flopped over her hands when she opened it. Like other Bibles in our home, its value as a holy thing came not only from its quality of materials and craftsmanship, and not only from our familial faith in the words on its pages as the inspired Word of God, but also from years of daily, devotional attention. It seemed both sacred and mundane, a hallowed object, demanding my highest reverence, and an everyday tool, lying open on the kitchen counter like an old phonebook.

Growing up conservative evangelical in the 1960s and '70s, mine was a childhood steeped in biblical devotion. Our two-story house in the foothills of the Chugach Mountains, outside Anchorage, Alaska, was filled with books, good for the long, dark winters. But no book was more treasured than the Bible. It was the cornerstone of our family's spiritual well-being, the go-to source for any serious question we might have, from sex, drugs, and rock 'n' roll to heaven, hell, and why bad things happen to good people.

Mom and Dad were models of biblical fidelity, of daily living in the Word. My strongest childhood memories of them testify to the high value they placed on Bible study and reflection: Mom, awake before sunrise, kneeling before the living room recliner as if it were a prie-dieu, reading her Bible while our cat lay purring and pawing on her warm back; Dad, leaving early for breakfast Bible studies and meetings of the local chapter of the Gideons at Denny's; the two of them, at the end of the day, sitting together on the sofa in the TV room, or lying side by side in bed, propped up on pillows, silently reading their Bibles.

My parents' biblical faith was by no means sentimental or simplistic. It was as seriously intellectual as it was devout. On drives home from church, they discussed the preacher's biblical interpretations in rigorous detail. When we got home, the discussion often continued, with Bibles open on the kitchen table. Mom studied Greek in college, and sometimes she'd pull out her old Greek New Testament to see how else the text might be translated. Stereotypes of conservative evangelical Christians as anti-intellectual notwithstanding, the Bible culture in which I was raised fostered serious, reasoned, critical engagement with the Scriptures. Biblical interpretation demanded all your heart, mind, and strength.

Magic 8 Ball Bible

My own youthful version of biblical faith, however, shaped at least as much by the emerging Christian pop youth culture of the 1970s as by my parents, was considerably less sophisticated. I tended to approach the Bible as though it were a divine oracle of truth, the ultimate Magic 8 Ball. Ask it a question and it would give you God's answer. I'd close my eyes while flipping through it like a dictionary, stop at random, and point my index finger somewhere on the open page, trusting that it would land on the passage I needed to read at that particular moment. This mode of biblical divination remains popular among kids as well as adults to this day. Many people tell miracle stories about how it gave them exactly the life-changing answer they needed. For me, not so much.

"Does Joanne like me?"
Flip, flip, flip. Stop. Point.
"He that is wounded in the stones, or hath his privy member cut off, shall not enter into the congregation of the LORD" (Deuteronomy 23:1).

Eventually I learned to flip far enough through my Bible to avoid the long legal discourses on skin diseases and crushed testicles in Leviticus, Numbers, and Deuteronomy. But I still didn't find what I was looking for.

The biblical Magic 8 Ball game revealed more about me, about my hopes and wishes for the Bible, and especially my *idea* of the Bible, than it did about biblical literature itself. I conceived of the Bible as God's book of answers, which if opened and read rightly would speak directly to me with concrete, divinely authored advice about my life and how to live it.

This way of thinking about the Bible was not just my own private notion. It was, and still is, the most common understanding of the Bible: the literal Word of God, God's own book, The Book of all books, plainly revealing who God is and what God wants me to do and believe, from everyday things like dating and diet to ultimate things like heaven and hell.

Think of the hundreds of instruction books and manuals that are called Bibles, from *The Bartender's Bible* to *The Curtain Bible* to *The Small Game and Varmint Hunter's Bible*. What does it mean to call something "the Bible"? What does this title claim for a book? What does it promise? What is the cultural meaning of "the Bible" that a publisher claims when it publishes something like *The Hot Rodder's Bible*? What does "the Bible" mean?

It means *authoritative*. A book called "the Bible" is the ultimate authority. It is the first and last word on the subject.

It means *univocal*. A book called "the Bible" speaks for itself in one, unified voice, without contradiction.

It means *practical*. A book called "the Bible" promises to serve as a reference manual and a dependable guide for how to proceed along the path its reader has chosen.

It means *accessible*. A book called "the Bible" promises to speak to anyone and everyone clearly and simply, without ambiguity, in terms "even I can understand."

It means *comprehensive*. A book called "the Bible" claims to cover everything human beings may ever possibly need to know about its subject, past, present, and future.

It means *exclusive*. A book called "the Bible" admits no rivals, no alternative perspectives. It is complete unto itself, closed, self-contained within a single book, A to Z, alpha to omega, Genesis to Revelation. Nothing may be added or taken away.

This is what I call the *iconic* cultural meaning of the Bible. And it is this meaning that publishers claim for any book they call "the Bible." The Bible is above all an image of divine authority, the perfect Book by the perfect Author.

Nearly all Americans are familiar with this idea of the Bible, and most endorse it. According to the Pew Forum on Religion and Public Life, 78 percent of all Americans say that the Bible is the "word of God," and almost half of those believe that, as such, "it is to be taken literally, word for word." Polling data from the

Barna Group indicate that nearly half of all Americans agree that "the Bible is totally accurate in all of its teachings" (88 percent of all "born-again" Christians believe the same), and the Gallup Poll finds that 65 percent of all Americans believe that the Bible "answers all or most of the basic questions of life." These statements are shorthand descriptions of the idea of the Bible as God's magnum opus, the first and last word on who God is, who we are, why we're here, and where we go after this — depending, of course, on how well we follow The Book, aka B.I.B.L.E., "Basic Instructions Before Leaving Earth."

The Rise of a Cultural Icon

A cultural icon is different from a traditional icon. A traditional icon is a particular material object that is believed to mediate a transcendent reality, and its power to do so is created and maintained by the various rituals people practice in relation to it. An example might be a Bible used to swear in a new president, or a handwritten Torah scroll presented to a congregation in a synagogue. A *cultural* icon is not so concrete. It is not tied to a particular material object, visual image, or ritual practice. Its outlines are a little vague, hard to define sharply. It's a condensation of what people who identify with it believe in and value. It says something about the culture in which it holds iconic power. The American flag is a cultural icon of patriotism. The four-wheel-drive truck is a cultural icon of American independence, toughness, and, most of all, masculinity.

The Bible is a cultural icon of faith as black-and-white certainty and religion as right-and-wrong morality. It's no accident that the most common visual image of the Bible is that of a closed black book. The cultural icon of the Bible represents religious faith as what closes the book on questions about the meaning and purpose of life. It puts them to rest in the name of God. Faith is about believing the right things, and the Bible is the place to find them.

This idea of the Bible as a divine manual for finding happiness with God in this world and salvation in the next is so familiar to us today that we might well assume it's been around forever, that it's as old as Christianity itself. It's not. In fact, its genesis was in nineteenth-century Protestantism, where the Reformation ideal of *sola scriptura*, "Scripture alone," combined with a popular Protestant evangelistic movement, sometimes described as a new Puritanic Biblicism because of its romantic idealization of that earlier, seemingly simpler form of Puritan Christianity, to promote the Bible as the key to solving all of industrial America's emerging problems. The Bible, it was believed, could integrate immigrant populations in the new big cities. It could heal factions among Protestant churches and denominations. It could keep husbands sober and hold nuclear families together, even under new stresses of urban poverty and isolation. Rooted in nostalgia for the mythical, romanticized image of sixteenth- and seventeenth-century Puritan piety, this movement believed that the Bible was the solution for all modern social, familial, and individual ills.

Writing in 1851, theologian and biblical scholar John W. Nevin described this movement's then-novel idea of the Bible this way:

> In this sacred volume, we are told, God has been pleased to place his word in full, by special inspiration, as a supernatural directory for the use of the world to the end of time; for the very purpose of providing a sufficient authority for faith, that might be independent of all human judgment and will . . . The great matter accordingly is to place the bible in every man's hands, and to have him able to read it, that he may then follow it in his own way. The idea seems to be, that the bible was published in the first place as

a sort of divine formulary or text book for the world to follow . . .
so that the dissemination of its printed text throughout the world,
without note or comment, is the one thing specially needful and
specially to be relied upon for the full victory of Christianity, from
sea to sea and from the river to the ends of the earth.

Nevin's reference to "without note or comment" alludes to one
of the movement's most important organizations, the American
Bible Society. Founded in 1816 and modeled on its British sister
organization, the British and Foreign Bible Society, its sole objective was "to encourage a wider circulation of the Holy Scriptures without note or comment." The society's initial address "To
the People of the United States" is indicative of the missionary
zeal surrounding this new movement to "claim our place in the
age of Bibles."

This is no doubt of the Lord, and it is marvelous in our eyes. But
what instrument has he thought fit chiefly to use? That which
contributes, in all latitudes and climes, to make Christians feel
their unity, to rebuke the spirit of strife, and to open upon them
the day of brotherly accord — the Bible! the Bible!

Led primarily by Christian businessmen who made their money
in the emerging fields of insurance and banking, the American
Bible Society followed the latest industrial business models and
was quick to adopt new innovations in the print industry, especially stereotype plates and steam power. Its highly efficient
methods of management, production, and distribution led to tremendous success in fulfilling its mission to get the Word out,
which its members fervently believed to be the only way to save
American society.

The ABS's stipulation that Bibles be printed "without note or comment" was central. It was an expression of commitment to the Puritanic Biblicist ideal that the Bible was complete unto itself, spoke for itself, and required no supplemental explanations or interpretations.

The fundamentalist movement that emerged in the late nineteenth century was the theological heir of the Puritanic Biblicism championed by the ABS and others. What distinguished it as a new movement was its reactionary character. It was first and foremost a defensive reaction to two intellectual revolutions toward the end of the nineteenth century, both of which challenged any reading of the Bible that treated it as an empirical account of human history or as the literal Word of God. The first, which is well known, was the rise of evolutionary theory in the wake of Charles Darwin's publication of *The Origin of Species* in 1859. The second was the rise of German and British "higher criticism" of the Bible, which championed a deductive, scientific approach. It examined biblical literature not as the authoritative source for history, but as data for reconstructing history. That is, it examined biblical literature in light of history rather than the other way around. The most influential of these early higher critics was the German linguist and historian of ancient Israel, Julius Wellhausen. As notoriously irreverent in his social behavior as he was scientific in his approach to biblical literature, Wellhausen, rumor has it, would time his Sunday-morning stroll to the swimming hole to coincide with the letting out of church. But what most famously provoked the ire of many Bible-believers throughout Europe and the United States was his "documentary hypothesis," which argued that the first five books of the Bible were compiled from four different literary strands or "sources." He dated each of these sources to a different period of Israelite and Judean history, and believed that they had been edited together to form the narratives of Genesis through Deuteronomy at a later time, after the Babylonian exile. It was in reaction to this kind of dissecting and historicizing of the Bible that fundamentalism formed its doctrine of *biblical inerrancy,* which proclaims that the Bible is God's literally inspired Word, entirely without error or contradiction, and therefore entirely authoritative. The Bible, it was asserted, must not be subjected to modern science or historical research. On the contrary, those disciplines must be subjected to it.

At the heart of the biblical fundamentalist movement was the Bible study, a small group of people that gathered in someone's home or at lunch break for Bible reading, sharing, and prayer. Modeled on the "social religious meetings" promoted by the great preacher of the Second Great Awakening, Charles Grandison Finney, as a means of keeping spiritual fires burning after the revival meeting ended, these Bible-study groups facilitated focused reading and discussion beyond what people could get from a sermon, applying biblical truths to the spiritual challenges and moral choices individual group members were facing in their own lives. The idea behind them, again, was the conviction that the Bible, as the infallible and literal Word of God, spoke in clear, unambiguous terms that any "plain man" can understand and apply directly to his life. The Bible-study movement thus brought together fundamentalism's rather dry intellectual commitment to biblical inerrancy and revivalism's emphasis on personal piety and moral uprightness.

Outside the intimate setting of the Bible-study group, conflicts between biblical fundamentalism and the new higher criticism were playing out in high public drama. In the early 1890s, the Presbyterian Church conducted a series of heresy trials against the Reverend Charles A. Briggs, a professor of biblical theology at Union Theological Seminary and champion of the new bibli-

cal critical methods. These highly publicized trials led eventually to Briggs's suspension from ministry and Union's decision
to disaffiliate from the Presbyterian Church. But the most dramatic, and ultimately most humiliating, battle for the fundamentalist movement was its showdown with Darwinian evolution in
the 1925 case *Tennessee v. John Thomas Scopes,* which tried Scopes for
teaching evolutionary theory in his high school biology class in
defiance of state law. Although Scopes lost, the news media surrounding the so-called Monkey Trial succeeded in portraying
the biblical fundamentalist perspective, championed by Presbyterian elder and three-time Democratic presidential candidate
William Jennings Bryan, as narrow-minded and intellectually
backward.

In the aftermath of the Scopes trial, fundamentalism lost
much of its former public respect. It began withdrawing from
mainstream society and adopting a strongly separatist perspective, shunning the "worldliness" of modern liberal American
culture. But it did not go dormant. Rather, it reinvented itself
as a nondenominational grass-roots movement, built around
newly formed Bible colleges and seminaries, radio broadcasts,
Bible conferences, and networks of Bible-study groups, many of
which operated as parachurch organizations, that is, independent Christian organizations that operate outside the structure
and governance of a particular church or denomination. In the
process of reinventing itself, moreover, the movement nurtured
what historian Joel A. Carpenter describes as a deeply paradoxi-
cal sense of identity: on the one hand, they were outsiders, rejected by mainstream American society; on the other hand, they
were the quintessential Americans, whose entitlement had been
usurped by secular liberalism.

Needless to say, fundamentalism did not keep its light hid-
den under a bushel forever. By the late 1940s, it reemerged in the

form of "neo-evangelicalism," a media-savvy parachurch movement that saw American popular culture as its mission field. Still
firmly rooted in the biblical fundamentalism that had always
been its hallmark, neo-evangelicalism denounced separatism and
recommitted itself to engage the mainstream with its mission "to
restore Christian America" by bringing it back to the Bible.

Central to neo-evangelicalism was the Youth for Christ movement, which began as a series of Saturday-night youth rallies that
attracted hundreds of thousands of young people in big cities
across the United States. These rallies were led by young, energetic preachers like Billy Graham (the first full-time employee
of Youth for Christ) and were modeled on the big shows popular in the emerging secular entertainment industry. Organizers
produced slick ads and created media tie-ins with mainstream
radio and television to sell their programs. Some of the evangelists went so far as to adopt the voices and styles of celebrities
like Frank Sinatra. Others, like Graham, soon had found their
own distinctive star power. Thus began a new era for fundamentalism, reinvented as an evangelistic movement that sought to
bring its biblical-theological perspective to a new generation by
meeting young people where they were. "Geared to the times, but
anchored to the rock," as the motto of Youth for Christ mixed-
metaphorically puts it. Rather than rejecting mainstream popular culture altogether, they translated their message into its popular media forms. Same message, new medium. Thus was born
the Christian entertainment industry.

By the early 1970s, neo-evangelical rallies were looking less
like a Frank Sinatra show and more like an Aerosmith concert.
In 1972 Campus Crusade for Christ, another parachurch organization much like Youth for Christ, hosted Explo '72, a weeklong
gathering of high school and college students in Dallas, Texas.
The event culminated in what was later dubbed the Christian

Woodstock, an eight-hour-long Christian rock concert in the Cotton Bowl that drew over one hundred thousand people. Controversial among more separatist-leaning fundamentalists, it is remembered above all for inaugurating rock music as a vehicle for evangelism.

At the same time, the big-rally approach to neo-evangelicalism was being supplemented by a new focus on creating local Bible-study clubs in high schools. Especially successful in this format was Young Life. Begun by a youth minister named Jim Rayburn in Gainesville, Texas, this evangelistic ministry treated neighborhood high schools as parishes, reaching out to kids in their own context rather than trying to bring them into the church. Central to Young Life were its weekly Young Life Club meetings, which integrated fun skits and games with more serious (if brief) prayer, discussion, and Bible reading. Kids who were ready to go more deeply into their faith became part of smaller core groups called Campaigners, who met in the morning or after school for more serious Bible study. Youth for Christ eventually adopted the Young Life model, calling its weekly fun meetings Campus Life Club, and supplementing them with more serious Bible-study meetings with student leaders.

Neo-evangelicalism reinvented fundamentalism by repackaging its fundamentals. It aimed to make its gospel popular — pop fundamentalism, if you will. It revised fundamentalism, but not its Bible. At the heart of this revival was the same iconic idea of the Bible as the literal Word of God that had been born in the Puritanic Biblicism of the early nineteenth century.

The Way of Salvation

This is where my own life in Bibles ties into the larger history of the rise of the Bible as a cultural icon. My dad grew up attending Youth for Christ rallies in Lewiston, Maine, in the early 1950s, and my mom, who was four years younger, became a Christian while attending lunchtime Youth for Christ Bible studies in her high school in Spokane, Washington. After college, in the early 1960s, she served as a full-time Young Life organizer and club leader for high schools in Portland, Oregon. When I was in grade school, she and Dad led weekly Young Life Campaigner groups in our living room. After moving to Anchorage, Alaska, which was Youth for Christ territory, they were closely involved supporters and sponsors of that organization. I was a committed member of my high school's chapter of Campus Life, participating in club meetings, attending weekly Bible-study breakfast groups, and serving as a student staffer on Campus Life on Wheels long-distance bike tours. I also was a leader in our church's youth group, and went on various evangelistic mission trips, including a boat trip to coastal villages in southeast Alaska along with a youth group from Wasilla High School. (For all I can remember, Sarah Palin, who graduated from high school the same year I did, might have been onboard.) All that to say, I was steeped in the neo-evangelical culture and its understanding of the Bible.

Like my peers, I believed that the Bible was God's Word written down for me, answering all my questions about who God is and what God wants for my life, from the mundane to the ultimate. Or at least I knew that was what I needed to believe. But that was not what I found when I actually opened the Bible up and looked around inside. The most famous biblical characters, so often lifted up as models of faith, seemed just the opposite: Abraham, who, unable to trust in God's promise, twice passes off his wife, Sarah, as his sister in order to save his own skin; Rebekah, who plays favorites among her two sons, helping the younger, Jacob, steal the birthright of the elder, Esau; King David, who repeatedly exploits those who love him, who takes whatever he wants, including women (married or not), who shows no remorse until he gets caught, and whose alienated son dies trying to kill him and take his throne; and Jael, Rahab, Ehud, and many other lesser-known biblical heroes and heroines who achieve greatness through trickery and betrayal. Often, "biblical values" struck me as foreign, as if they had come from a radically unfamiliar time and place. Which in fact they had. But that made me anxious. It worried me that I couldn't get beyond the Bible's strangeness to discover its purportedly timeless relevance.

Moreover, it didn't seem like the Bible was always saying the same thing. One psalmist proclaims absolute confidence that all is right with the world and God is on his throne, while another cries out in despair, seeing nothing but chaos and divine absence (and that's the kind Jesus quotes from the cross). One passage lays out a moral universe in which goodness is rewarded with bless-ing, while another asks why the wicked prosper and the righteous suffer. Indeed, the very image of God seemed to change from one passage to another: warrior, mother, father, husband, rock, whirl-wind, rarely omniscient, often uncertain, frightening as often as comforting, mysterious more than informative. Moreover, there appeared to be many inconsistencies: conflicting versions of key events in the Gospels, such as what happened at the empty tomb, for example, and different accounts of creation that were not easy to sync. I knew what Bible answers I was supposed to find. But actually opening and reading the Bible was undermining my be-lief in it.

I remember getting into a heated argument about the opening chapters of Genesis with one of my more secular-liberal friends while playing pool in his basement. He was pointing out a seri-ous contradiction he'd noticed when reading Genesis for world history class: in one, humankind is created last, and in the other, a single human is created first. "So which is it?" he asked. As I struggled in vain to answer, his smug grin grew. My blood began to boil and I almost threw the cue ball at him. At which point we both knew I'd been bested. I knew he was right, but I was not ready to acknowledge it consciously. Doing so would have threatened my whole belief in the Word — as I knew it.

I got my first Bible when I was five. It was my prize in Vacation Bible School for being the first to recite the names of all the biblical books in order. But the first Bible I really bonded with was one I got when I was in junior high. It was called *The Way: The Living Bible Illustrated*. First published in 1972, it was the result of an innovative collaboration between a new publisher, Tyndale House, and the editors of *Campus Life* magazine, a slick, popular publication of Youth for Christ.

In fact, *The Way* was the biblical flagship of the neo-evangelical Christian youth movement. Combining innovative form and content in a way that appealed specifically to the popular youth culture of the early 1970s, it was a breakout Bible. The floppy dark green cover of *The Way* looked more like a Doobie Brothers album than the Holy Bible: big groovy capital letters filled with photos of hip stringy-haired teens smiling and hanging out. Only the subtitle, in a much smaller, standard font, let on that this was "the Bible." Inside were more images of young people, black and white, male and female, playing guitars, laughing and talking. Other pictures illustrated contemporary issues: a homeless man curled up on a sidewalk vent, a razor-wire fence, a garbage dump. At the beginning of every biblical book was a short introductory essay that spoke to concerns shared by many youth: poverty and homelessness, war and peace, love and marriage, making a living versus making a life.

Its biblical text was that of *The Living Bible,* a hugely successful modern English paraphrase of the American Standard translation, done by Kenneth N. Taylor while he was working at Moody Bible Institute, a cornerstone school and publishing house of

Cover and introduction to the Psalms from *The Way: The Living Bible Illustrated*, published by Tyndale House in 1972. Combining a trendy, youth-oriented magazine style with the modern English paraphrase of *The Living Bible*, *The Way* was a neo-evangelical breakthrough in Bible publishing.

neo-evangelicalism in Chicago that gained prominence during fundamentalism's separatist decades. During Taylor's long commutes to and from work, he wrote what he called "thought for thought" paraphrases of the New Testament Epistles. When Moody and several other publishers declined to publish them as a book, Taylor and his wife, Margaret, created their own press, Tyndale House, named after the sixteenth-century English Bible translator William Tyndale, who was martyred for translating the Bible into a common tongue. The Taylors did not share Tyndale's fate. Operating out of their dining room, they self-published *Living Letters* in 1962. A year later, the book won the enthusiastic endorsement of Billy Graham, who ordered more than half a million copies to offer to his television audiences. Taylor's *The Living Bible* (1971), encompassing the entire Christian Bible, was an even greater success. It was the *New York Times* nonfiction bestseller in both 1972 and 1973. In 1983 Taylor presented the

The deepest thoughts, the fullest emotions find their outlet in music ... when you can't come out and say what's going on inside, you find (or create) a song ... then you feel relaxed, unthreatened. As one current troubadour said, "If it's done right, a song is almost like a birth. You take many things into your head over which you have very little control, you gestate, and it comes out when ready."

This book, by far the most popular in the entire Old Testament, is a songbook. David, whose ability on the lyre (the early forerunner of the guitar) got him a job with King Saul, is credited with 73 of these psalms, many of them written during personal tragedies and victories. The others were written by Asaph, the sons of Korah, Solomon, and others, some as late as Ezra's time after the captivity. And people have been singing them ever since.

28 millionth copy to President Ronald Reagan in commemoration of the Year of the Bible. As of 1996, *The Living Bible* had sold over 40 million copies.

I loved my *The Way* Bible. I took it to youth group meetings and read it in bed every night. By "read," I mean I mostly looked at the pictures and read the introductory essays. These were the parts that appealed to me. They spoke to me in clear, engaging, contemporary terms. And they said the kinds of things I thought the Bible was supposed to be saying. Reading these extrabiblical supplements, I felt like I was reading the Bible.

Occasionally I would even dip into the biblical texts themselves, paraphrased in ways that made them much easier going than any of the English translations from Hebrew and Greek that I'd tried in the past. I realize now that they felt that way precisely because Taylor's *Living Bible* not only down-converted the traditional American Standard translation to a junior high reading level, but also took pains to disambiguate biblical ambiguities and resolve biblical contradictions that are actually, literally present in the text.

So for a time, *The Way* saved me, or at least distracted me, from the growing doubts about my childhood faith in the Bible. That is, it saved my iconic idea of the Bible from the disillusion that came from literally reading it. Indeed, this was the true innovation of *The Way*: it offered a reading experience of the Bible that didn't entail all the complexities and frustrations that came when I actually read the biblical text. It felt like what reading the Bible was supposed to feel like, even while it distracted me from the real ambiguities and uncertainties of the biblical text itself.

The Way sold an unprecedented 6.4 million copies. Although no one made a dime on it (the *Campus Life* editors took it on as a creative outreach project, and Tyndale donated all profits from sales to Christian missions), its huge success, along with that of *The Living Bible,* drew attention to the tremendous profit potential for publishers interested in reinventing the Bible in new, value-added forms. The publishers of *The Way* had discovered a market for updated, supplemented, and retranslated Bibles that soon became the cornerstone of the neo-evangelical Christian culture industry that is booming today.

So Long, Judas

In the long run, I didn't turn out to be much of a biblical consumer. Although *The Way* sustained my iconic idea of the Bible for a few more years, the cracks in it eventually began to grow, and I found my journey with the Bible on a road less traveled. One crack I remember especially well was my discovery of another piece of 1970s pop Christianity, Tim Rice and Andrew Lloyd Webber's rock opera *Jesus Christ Superstar.* In fact, I owe this discovery to my parents. In 1973, a few weeks before we moved from Oregon to Alaska, their Young Life group gave them a copy of the double album as a going-away present. They warmly accepted it, of course. But later that evening, after the kids had shared memories, prayed together, hugged their teary goodbyes, and left, Mom confided to me that they must not have realized that the record's representation of the Gospel story was considered blasphemous at some points. Not that my parents were the record-burning type. They always modeled a gracious, thoughtful open-mindedness to me. They had their opinions, but never made me feel like my soul was in jeopardy if I didn't agree. Nor were they about to discard a heartfelt gift. So they slipped it in the back of their record case and soon forgot about it.

But I didn't forget. A couple years later, when my folks got a new hi-fi stereo for the living room and I got the old one, I found the record and took it up to my room. Over the next several years, especially around Easter, I played it again and again. I was especially fascinated with the character of Judas, the one who betrayed Jesus, as performed by Murray Head. I was blown away by his intense, tormented, half-screamed expressions of righteous indignation and passionate love. Such a deeply conflicted disciple, wanting to be free from Jesus, needing to be loved by him, and not knowing how to love him back. And he was a tragic figure, too, Jesus's right-hand man who was literally set up by God to betray him.

Lying there on my red shag carpet in front of tan upholstered hi-fi speakers, I wore the record out. Sometimes I would sing along passionately in my best hard-rock voice. Other times I'd transcribe the words. Occasionally I'd even look up the biblical texts that inspired them. In the process, I learned that there were actually two different versions of what happened to Judas. In one, from the Gospel of Matthew, Judas ultimately regrets betraying Jesus, returns the blood money, and hangs himself. In the other, from the book of Acts (the second volume of the Gospel of

Luke), he never repents, but buys a field with the reward money, trips on a rock, and disembowels himself. Tim Rice and Andrew Lloyd Webber obviously went with Matthew's version. And then went further, offering a fuller interpretation of the character of Judas. Their interpretation didn't contradict the biblical text, but it allowed my imagination to find its way into the gaps in the story—what was left unsaid, between the lines. It brought the story to life in ways that raised profound questions without trying to answer them. So, not only did Judas in *Jesus Christ Superstar* open my eyes to blatant contradictions within the Bible; it also opened my heart and mind to a different way of engaging it, not as the book of answers but as a place to explore, to play, to find new angles of interpretation and imagine things differently.

I'll return to the story of my own rediscovery of the Bible later in this book. Suffice for now to say that Head's hard-rock Judas was soon sharing time on my hi-fi with many other artists who found inspiration in biblical literature, from Bob Dylan to U2 to Ani DiFranco. As time went on, these and other artists conversed in my head with the biblical scholarship I was studying in college and graduate school. I found my understanding of biblical literature and interpretation getting quite a bit more complicated, but also, and more importantly, a lot deeper. As I persevered in my studies of biblical languages and literature, the cultural history of the Bible, and the history of biblical interpretation, I began to see that the very idea of the Bible with which I was struggling was not very old. It was by no means the only way that Christian Scriptures had been understood and interpreted throughout history. I was coming to see it as a cultural construction, "the Word as we know it," with a fairly short history and a less than promising future.

Christian consumer culture and the Bible business have come a long way since *The Way*, as we'll see. The Bible business has burgeoned into one of the biggest and fastest-growing fields of publishing, selling many thousands of different Bibles in every imaginable form for many hundreds of millions of dollars a year. Within this brave new world of Christian consumerism, it's getting harder and harder to tell the difference between spreading the Word and selling it.

But the flagship consumer product, the heart of the industry, remains this cultural icon of the Bible, shaped by nineteenth-century Puritanic Biblicism, refined by early-twentieth-century fundamentalism, and repackaged, again and again, by neo-evangelicalism. That's what the Bible biz is selling in pop culture form. And that, I have come to believe, is a dead end.

The icon of the Bible as God's textbook for the world is as bankrupt as the idea that it stands for, of religious faith as absolute black-and-white certainty. Just as the cultural icon of the flag often becomes a substitute for patriotism, and just as the cultural icon of the four-wheel-drive truck often becomes a substitute for manly independence and self-confidence, so the cultural icon of the Bible often becomes a substitute for a vital life of faith, which calls not for obedient adherence to clear answers but thoughtful engagement with ultimate questions. The Bible itself invites that kind of engagement. The iconic image of it as a book of answers discourages it.

The Course of This Book

This book begins in the present, exploring the culture of biblical consumerism, in which marketing teams are the new evangelists and spreading the Word goes hand in hand with moving product. As publishers race to reinvent the Bible in an ever-widening variety of forms, all competing in the marketplace of faith to be the ultimate realization of the cultural icon of the Bible, I argue that they are stretching that idea to its breaking point. The icon of the Bible, The Book of books, is in the process of deconstruction.

And that, I believe, is a good thing. It's the end of the Word as we know it, and I feel fine. The Word as we know it is not very old, as we have already begun to see, and it's a distraction from the Scriptures themselves. Its end is an occasion to find a fresh approach to the Bible that is truer not only to its content but also to its fascinating history.

Many will be surprised to realize that there never has been a time when we could really talk about *the* Bible in the singular. There is no such *thing* as the Bible in that sense, and there never has been. The Bible has always been legion, a multiplicity of forms and contents, with no original to be found. In early Judaism and Christianity, there were many different scrolls and codices, variously collected and shared in many different versions, with no standard edition. Even in the early centuries of the print era, after Gutenberg, we find a burgeoning Bible-publishing industry with literally thousands of different editions and versions. The difference between Bible publishing then and now is a matter of degree more than kind.

As we explore the cultural history of the Bible, beginning with earliest Christianity, *before the Bible,* and continuing through the print revolution into the present day, we come to realize how differently Christian Scriptures have been produced, understood, and used in different times and places. In the process, we begin to question the received wisdom that the Bible as we know it today is the way it's always been known. The closer we look at its history of development, the more richly complex the picture becomes. Here, then, is an opportunity to *rediscover the Bible after the Bible.* The end of the Word as we know it calls for another way of knowing.

As a professor of religious studies in a secular university, I never presume that the students in my classes share a common religious or nonreligious background. A typical class includes a wide diversity of religious perspectives and perspectives on religion. A lot of them are Christian or Jewish. Most are not. I am very comfortable teaching in this kind of context, and I hope that this book will reach similarly mixed company.

At the same time, students of every background often remind me of what I knew very well back when, as a student, I fell in love with what I now teach: that the most powerful educational experiences always come very close to the bone. Our hearts race. Our faces flush. Our skin tingles. We find ourselves making connections between what matters inside the classroom and what matters outside. We find the histories we're exploring in class speaking to our own personal stories.

Often, toward the end of a course, after final papers have been handed in and things are winding down, a student will raise her or his hand and ask me how I personally make sense of what we've been studying. It usually goes something like this: "You're a Christian, right? So what does the Bible mean to you in your spiritual life?" Or more bluntly, "How can you still be a Christian?" It's usually a conservative Christian student who asks the question. But most students in the class perk up to hear how I'll respond. For some, like the questioner, the course has challenged their understanding of the Bible and its history in profound ways. They can't look at the Bible the same way as they used to. They're wondering if it's still relevant to their faith. I've obviously been through a similar process. How did I do it? For others, especially those who are not religious or who are even antireligious, it seems like I've laid out plenty of good reasons to throw out or at least play down the importance of the Bible. Yet I don't want them to. Why not? Where's the value, let alone the necessity, in continuing to read it religiously? Moving through the first two parts of this book, many readers, I expect, will have similar questions. And they matter very much to me, too. In the last chapter, I hope to clear some space to reflect on them.

That, in a nutshell, is the course of this book: from the present, to the past, to the future. It's the end of the Word as we know it. There's no going back. But there is a way forward.

My Utmost, Revisited

Shortly after I began my first job as a professor of biblical studies at Eckerd College in St. Petersburg, Florida, I received a package from my parents in my office mailbox. Inside was a brand-new copy of the devotional classic *My Utmost for His Highest*, by Oswald Chambers, a beloved Scottish preacher and founder of the Bible Training College in London. Published ten years after his untimely death in 1917 of acute appendicitis, *My Utmost* is a collection of Chambers's teachings that were transcribed and edited by his widow, Gertrude Hobbs, into 365 daily devotionals. Each begins with a biblical passage in the familiar King James Version, followed by an exhortation inspired by that passage. For as long as I could remember, a very well-worn copy of this book had lain open on Mom's nightstand, next to her Bible, and I had often seen her reading from it during her daily prayer times.

A short handwritten note from Mom bookmarked the entry for December 15, my birthday. The biblical passage at the top of the page was from Paul's second letter to his disciple Timothy, my namesake, in the New Testament. It reads, "Study to show thyself approved unto God, a workman that needeth not to be ashamed, rightly dividing the word of truth." In the brief exhortation beneath the passage, Chambers takes on the voice of Paul, encouraging his reader, as though a young disciple, to struggle to find a way to express God's truth for himself so that his words can strengthen others in their faith.

In the note, Mom wrote that she and Dad had made this biblical passage and Chambers's reflection on it their lifelong prayer for me. They had read it together and prayed for me every December 15 since my first birthday.

I'm ashamed to admit it, but at the time I didn't fully appreciate this gift. Moved as I was, and always have been, by my parents' steadfast, prayerful care for me, I was put off by the book and the biblical quotation in it. I'd never read *My Utmost,* but I had dismissed it as sentimental and moralistic. When it came in the mail, I immediately associated it with the kind of fundamentalist Biblicism that I had rejected.

Reading Chambers's exhortation now, however, I can see what my parents must always have seen: not a command to submit to authority for approval, but a call to wrestle with what presents itself as authoritative in order to find my own voice in relation to it. "If you cannot express yourself on any subject," Chambers begins, "struggle until you can." He describes this struggle, this suffering for words, as going through the "winepress of God," where inherited expressions of truth get crushed like ripe grapes. "You must struggle to get expression experimentally, then there will come a time when that expression will become the very wine of strengthening to someone else." He concludes,

> Always make a practice of provoking your own mind to think out what it accepts easily. Our position is not ours until we make it ours by suffering. The author who benefits you most is not the one who tells you something you did not know before, but the one who gives expression to the truth that has been dumbly struggling in you for utterance.

Struggling to divide the "word of truth" that I've inherited, wrestling with the theological traditions in which I'm steeped, with the Word itself, experimenting to remake those inheritances into words that I can write or say with integrity, words that might mean something to someone else, which is what my parents had prayed and wished for me. This is the struggle and experiment of my life. It is, I daresay, my calling, my vocation as a writer and teacher. It is both an intellectual, scholarly struggle and a personal, religious one.

What I had once seen in myself as an unacceptable struggle with the meaning of the Bible, and a drawn-out rebellion against the biblical faith of my parents, I now recognize as an answer to prayer. Whether or not prayer can move mountains, there's no doubt that it can be powerfully transformative for the one praying, and for those prayed for. As the very wise minister to whom I'm married reminds me, prayer is most essentially the expression of deep desire. Pray ceaselessly, Paul exhorts. Over time, you may live into the desires of your most heartfelt prayers. I believe that my folks, especially Mom, lived into their December 15 prayer for me. They created a safe and loving home space in which the striving to understand and articulate articles of faith for myself, dividing words of truth, was not only allowed but encouraged and celebrated, even when the outcome, often born of much angst and struggle, was an articulation of faith that neither of them could themselves entirely affirm. Even today, I notice a quickening flush of pride and joy on Mom's face when we argue, which we often do, about the Bible and theology. Likewise when she reads, with an occasional furrow or flinch, something I've written.

Although I've drifted quite a distance from the familiar biblical waters of the conservative evangelical tradition in which I was raised and which my parents so admirably represent, I hold much respect for that tradition and gladly acknowledge my own enduring debt to it. Its emphasis on introspection in search of personal growth has challenged me always to dig deep within myself in order to examine critically my own presuppositions and vested interests. Its emphasis on working out one's own salvation with fear and trembling has inspired in me a lifelong restlessness of mind and spirit. Above all, its biblical literalism and its supreme valuing of every iota of the Bible have instilled in me an abiding passion for biblical interpretation and a love for the smallest details of the text. All these gifts have served me well not only as a teacher and scholar of religious studies but also as a person of faith.

At the heart of the evangelical tradition, aptly captured in Chambers's exhortation, is struggle. There is no way to grow and mature in one's faith without wrestling with the ideas and traditions that one has inherited. No one else can do it for you — not parents, not ministers, not youth group leaders, not professors, not Bible publishers. The iconic idea of the Bible as a book of black-and-white answers encourages us to remain in a state of spiritual immaturity. It discourages curiosity in the terra incognita of biblical literature, handing us a Magic 8 Ball Bible to play with instead. In turning readers away from the struggle, from wrestling with the rich complexity of biblical literature and its history, in which there are no easy answers, it perpetuates an adolescent faith. It keeps us out of the deep end, where we have to "ride these monsters down," as Annie Dillard put it, trusting that it's not about the end product but the process.

I have tried to write a book about the Bible and its place in society that will mean something to a lot of people from a lot of different backgrounds, liberal and conservative, religious and nonreligious. For some, what I'm saying here will be liberating, an opportunity to overcome a dominant idea of the Bible that has felt oppressive to them for many years, perhaps a lifetime. For others, however, my argument may be unnerving. After all, I'm challenging the very foundation of the idea of religious faith as a search for clarity, suggesting that faith dwells as much in questions and mystery as it does in answers and certainty. I want to acknowledge that sense of unease, and confess that I, as a person of faith, sometimes feel it, too. But I also want to ask, as a fellow Christian, does this not follow the pattern of God's revelation that is at the core of the Gospel? Isn't this quintessentially the Christian experience? Should it surprise us that the God who took on human nature would leave us with a text with as much complexity as the human experience? Indeed, like so many encounters with Jesus in the Gospel stories, we might go to the Bible looking for answers, but we usually come away with more questions.

That said, it's not necessary to believe that the Bible is a divine creation or product of "intelligent design" in order to appreciate what I'm trying to do in this book. Like so many stories, including some in the Bible, you can find God in this one if you're looking, but you don't have to. I myself usually think of the Bible's growth and development as something akin to the science of chaos. I see it emerging in all its wonderful complexity — "coming to life," if you will — in the course of a long and often chaotic process involving multiple, often conflicting interests and influences. Perhaps that way of seeing it works better for you. Or perhaps you think both make sense. In any case, it's a wonder to behold.

For now, I'm happy to make Chambers's final exhortation my own prayer for this book: to provoke myself and others to think through what we may accept too easily when it comes to the Bible, and in the process to rediscover Scriptures in fresh new ways.

2

The Greatest Story Ever Sold

TONIGHT, WE ARE MAKING sure America understands that sometimes one small smooth stone is even more effective than a whole lot of armor." So declared Republican presidential hopeful and Southern Baptist preacher Mike Huckabee after his unexpected, if not miraculous, wins against Mitt Romney and John McCain in the Super Tuesday primaries of February 5, 2008. His rock-beats-armor metaphor was a biblical one, taken from the story of the future king, David, who toppled a purportedly invincible Philistine, Goliath, with one of "five smooth stones" that he plucked from a nearby river valley and shot from his sling. Huckabee's implication, for those in his conservative Christian base with ears to hear, was that he was more than just some comeback kid; boldly conquering the Philistine giants of the party faithful, he was claiming divine ordination.

"And we've also seen," he continued, "that the widow's mite has more effectiveness than all the gold in the world." Another biblical reference, this one to the Gospel story, found in both Mark and Luke, in which Jesus praises a poor widow who contributes all she has, two small coins, or "mites" in the King James

Version, to the temple treasury. Jesus declares that her offering is more valuable than those of the others in the congregation, who gave from their great wealth. The implication: Huckabee's supporters may not be as rich as those supporting the party giants, but God will use their humble offerings to bring blessings to his campaign well beyond their monetary value. What his backers lack in funds is more than made up for in righteousness.

Having set his face toward Washington, the Baptist minister and champion of biblical inerrancy was infusing his campaign speeches with biblical phrases and story references meant to inspire his well-versed base.

Sodom and Gomorrah Equals Love

Just how broad was Huckabee's base? How many actually had ears to hear? Probably not as many as he hoped. National Public Radio's Barbara Bradley Hagerty did a little Jay Leno–style research on the National Mall to see how many passersby recognized the candidate's smooth stone and widow's mite as biblical. One conjectured that the smooth stone might have something to do with war. Or maybe peace? None seemed to recognize it as biblical. What about the widow's mite? A mite's a bug, right? Maybe a spider?

These responses were no great surprise to American religious historian Stephen Prothero, author of *Religious Literacy*. If Huckabee's intention was to give a wink and a nod to his biblically well-versed base, Prothero told Hagerty, "It's an exceedingly small target audience, about as small as the percentage of animals climbing on Noah's ark." Nor was popular ignorance of these biblical references any surprise to organizations like the Bible Literacy Project, which lobbies for the academic study of biblical literature in public schools, arguing that it is a fundamental component of cultural literacy. How, they ask, can anyone read Shakespeare or Steinbeck, let alone understand American identity politics or even Huckabee, without some basic level of biblical literacy?

Yet few people have it. Recent polls and surveys offer these biblical revelations:

> Less than half of all adult Americans can name the first book of the Bible (Genesis, in Hebrew *Bereshit*) or the four Gospels of the New Testament (Matthew, Mark, Luke, and John).
>
> More than 80 percent of born-again or evangelical Christians believe that "God helps those who help themselves" is a Bible verse. I suspect that many would also say that "The Serenity Prayer" and the "Footprints in the Sand" parable are in there somewhere.
>
> More than half of graduating high school seniors guess that Sodom and Gomorrah were husband and wife, and one in ten adults believes that Joan of Arc was Noah's wife. (Those two must've been multiple-choice questions.)
>
> Almost two-thirds of Americans can't name at least five of the Ten Commandments. Some of these people, moreover, are outspoken promoters of them. Georgia representative Lynn Westmoreland, cosponsor of a bill to display the Ten Commandments in the chambers of the House of Representatives and Senate, could remember only three when Stephen Colbert asked him to recite them on *The Colbert Report* (Colbert, who I hear teaches Sunday school at his church, would probably have done considerably better).

Let me add another datum, albeit more or less anecdotal. Among the few hundred students I've taught in college-level introductions to biblical literature over the past couple of years, I estimate that more than half came to class on the first day with more ideas about the Bible derived from Dan Brown's 2003 novel *The Da Vinci Code* than from actual biblical texts. In the old days, biblical studies professors talked about demythologizing the Bible in order to, for example, sort out the "Jesus of history" from the "Christ of faith." Nowadays we might want to add demythologizing *Da Vinci* to the learning objectives.

There are, of course, exceptions to the generally very low levels of biblical literacy. In many churches, for example, there are core groups of people who know their Bibles inside and out. They read them daily, and many gather weekly in small groups in homes or neighborhood restaurants for Bible studies. For the most part, such meetings follow a format that has not changed much since the fundamentalist Bible-study-group movement of the nineteenth century: led by a minister or experienced lay teacher, they begin with a time to share joys and concerns, then prayer, then reading and in-depth discussion of a particular biblical passage, and then closing prayer (often followed by dessert!). Members of such groups will obviously have a greater level of biblical literacy. But we're talking about a truly exceptional population — a remnant, to use a biblical metaphor that they might appreciate. Even among the majority of Christians who identify themselves strongly with the Bible, Bible reading is a rare activity. In a 2005 nationwide study of religious values, practices, and behaviors by Baylor University's Institute for Studies of Religion, more than half of those identifying themselves as "Bible-believing" said they had not participated in any kind of Bible study or Sunday school program at all in the past month.

Biblical Consumerism

In response, many take George Gallup Jr.'s oft-quoted lament that America has become a nation of "biblical illiterates" as a rallying cry for a renewed commitment in churches and in the general public to education in biblical literature. I can sympathize. I even wrote a book about it. But I also think it's important to ask *why* biblical literacy is so low.

One explanation is that biblical literacy is simply a subset of book literacy in general, which is clearly in decline. A recent report by the National Endowment for the Arts indicates that, between 1992 and 2002, the number of adults who read at least one literary book in the course of a year had dropped by 14 percent. The number of adults who read a book of any kind also dropped, by 7 percent. Judging from data on younger readers, the future of bibliographic culture is not bright: among adults eighteen to twenty-four years old, the decline in literary reading was 55 percent greater than it was among the general adult population. The book is losing its preeminence as the dominant medium for reading and writing as newer digital media scoop more and more market share and leisure time. Insofar as the Bible is tied to the fate of book culture, we can expect biblical literacy rates to continue to drop.

The decline in overall book reading is part of the story. But other puzzling details call for further explanation. First, while biblical literacy is extremely low, popular reverence for the Bible is extremely high. Recall the polling data mentioned in the last chapter. About three-quarters of Americans believe that the Bible is the Word of God, and almost half of those say that it should be taken literally, word for word, as such. Roughly half of all Americans agree with the statement "the Bible is totally accurate in all of its teachings" (only 35 percent did in 1991). About two-thirds of Americans believe that the Bible "answers all or most of the basic questions of life" — and 28 percent of them admit that they rarely or never read it! There seems to be no correlation between reading the Bible and revering it. The Bible appears to be the most revered book never read.

Second, and even more puzzling, while biblical literacy is

about as low as it can get, Bible sales have been booming. The biggest Bible publishers in this highly competitive business guard their sales data closely, but reliable industry sources estimate that 2007 saw about 25 million Bibles sold, generating revenues of about $770 million in the United States alone. That was an increase of more than 26 percent since 2005, which saw U.S. sales of about $609 million. In fact, the Bible-publishing business has been enjoying a healthy compounded growth rate of close to 10 percent per year for several years. Even during the high point of economic crisis in late 2008, when other book sales were hurting badly, Bible sales continued to boom, with an estimated $823.5 million that year. Indeed, Bible publishing tends to thrive during times of war and financial disaster. Although it's too early to know for sure as I write, it may well turn out that the latest economic bust will be another boom time for the Bible business.

Bible publishing has come a long way since the Taylors began publishing their *Living Bible* out of their living room. This is no mom-and-pop Christian cottage industry. In fact, the two biggest and most ambitious Bible publishers are owned by larger non-Christian media conglomerates. Thomas Nelson, which publishes more than three hundred different Bibles and controls about 20 percent of the biblical market share in the United States, was purchased in 2006 by the private equity firm Inter-Media Partners VII in a deal worth $473 million. Zondervan, which lists more than five hundred different Bibles in its online catalogue and controls about 35 percent of the biblical market, was purchased in 1988 by HarperCollins, which is part of News Corporation, Rupert Murdoch's media empire.

That the two largest Bible publishers are now part of even larger media conglomerates does not imply religious commitments on the part of executives in the companies that bought them. Rupert Murdoch didn't acquire Zondervan because he wanted to spread the Word any more than he acquired My-Space because he wanted to expand his friends list. As owner of HarperCollins, he also publishes occult classics like *The Satanic Bible* and *The Necronomicon*. Getting into Bible publishing is simply good business.

So biblical literacy is low to zip, even while biblical reverence remains high and Bible sales rise. What's going on?

Could it be that biblical literacy is being replaced by biblical consumerism? In today's consumer culture, we are what we buy, wear, and carry. We identify ourselves by our patterns of consumer choices, by the market niches we buy into. It's gone beyond that post-Cartesian proof of existence, "I shop, therefore I am." Today, it's closer to "I shop for what I am." The culture industry makes and markets identities. I want to be outdoorsy, so I buy a lot of Gore-Tex, some "Life is good" shirts, and a Yakima rack for my Subaru. High school and college students identify the cultures on different campuses by brands: this school is very Hollister; that one's more American Apparel.

At the same time, we consumers are convinced that the shortest route to self-improvement is through new products. Products change lives, right? My big New Year's resolution might be to become an organized person. So the first thing I do is go to the home store and buy a bunch of plastic boxes. Never mind the empty ones in my basement that I bought a year ago.

Or say I want to strengthen my identity as a Christian and grow deeper in my faith. I want a more God-centered life. I want to be "in the Word." I feel like I should be reading the Bible a lot more than I do. After all, like most people, I believe that the Bible is God's Word, that it's totally correct in all of its teachings, and that it holds the answers to all of life's most basic questions. So what do I do? Buy a Bible. Or, more likely, buy another Bible. A marketing executive at a major evangelical publishing company told me that, according to their research, the average Christian household owns nine Bibles and purchases at least one new Bible every year.

Expectations of Biblical Proportions

But biblical consumerism only partially explains the negative correlation between (high) Bible sales and (low) Bible literacy. There must be more to it. After all, buying a Bible obviously doesn't *prevent* a person from reading it. Just as I want to do more with that bike rack than drive around town with it, and just as I want to do more with those storage bins than leave them empty on my basement floor, so too a biblical consumer wants to do more with a Bible than buy it. What do these potential Bible readers want that they're not getting? How is their desire to read the Bible frustrated so that they end up not reading it?

Nearly two decades of teaching the Bible in college classrooms and church Sunday school classes (all ages) have shown me that the most common source of frustration stems not from the Bible itself but from the expectations that come with it. The Bible does not deliver what readers have come to believe it's supposed to deliver. The experience of reading biblical literature doesn't sync with the common idea of the Bible as God's textbook on what to believe and do.

Many of my college students begin the semester feeling as though they have been discouraged from reading the Bible. Most have given up trying, not because they're uninterested in it, but because they worry that they're not getting what they're supposed to get from it. It feels like others — pastors, parents, "better" Christians, God — are reading over their shoulders, arms crossed, shaking their heads. "No, no, no. That's not it." The questions it raises for them don't seem to be welcomed by the

religious authorities they have encountered in churches, campus
ministry programs, religious talk shows, and the news.

I realized how pervasive this feeling is among students during my first year as a college teacher. I was fresh out of graduate
school and eager to begin teaching a freshman seminar course
that I had just put together. It was called Howling in the Wilderness, which was meant to give a nod both to "the voice of one
crying in the wilderness" in Isaiah and to poet Allen Ginsberg's
Beat manifesto, *Howl*. The idea was to explore biblical and biblically inspired prophetic writings, from Isaiah to Ginsberg and
beyond.

The first assignment was to read several chapters of the
prophet Isaiah. I was excited for our session, expecting students
to be fired up about what they had read. I knew that most did
not think of themselves as religious, and none of them had spent
much time reading the Bible, let alone prophetic literature. I expected they would find it both strange and fascinating.

"Did everyone read the assignment?" I asked as they were set-
tling into their seats around the seminar table. They all nodded. "Well, what did you think?" There was complete silence.
Everyone looked down, flipping randomly through her or his
Bible, carefully avoiding eye contact with me.

Finally, a friendly, ponytailed, Birkenstocked young man let
out a heavy sigh and raised his hand. Relieved, I invited him to
speak. "I couldn't get anything at all from it," he confessed. "All
I could think about when I tried to read it was whether I was
getting from it what other students were getting from it. I never
read this stuff before and don't know what it's supposed to be
about. What was I supposed to be seeing? Was I getting what
you want me to get? I ended up getting nowhere." Now everyone
was making eye contact with me. "Did anyone else feel that way?"
I asked. Nearly all of them nodded vigorously.

I was flabbergasted by this nearly unanimous confession of biblical paralysis. I had not expected students like these, who had little or no experience reading the Bible, to feel so intimidated by it, so worried about "getting it right." Over the years since, I've learned that they are not the only ones. Most students don't trust their own insights and questions when they are reading a biblical assignment. They expect that there must be a point, a right reading that they're missing, and that they don't have the authority to suggest any other interpretation.

By Whose Authority?

For many Christians, this experience of feeling flummoxed by the Bible can be even more disconcerting. It invokes not only frustration but also guilt for doubting the Bible's integrity. They feel that others have the keys to it and speak for it — the preacher, who waxes so inspirationally about it from the pulpit every Sunday, and those pillar members of the church who've been reading it for decades and who regularly meet in Bible-study groups to explicate it in depth. "I feel such a mixture of desire and fear when I try to read the Bible," someone recently told me after a class I'd taught at a local church. "I have a strong desire to get into it, explore it, begin to understand it. But there's even more fear that I'll . . . get it wrong." A university professor with a Ph.D. in organizational behavior and a successful career in academic publishing, she's not exactly the kind of person who typically shies away from reading something and telling you what she thinks about it. But the thought of reading the Bible for herself feels uniquely daunting.

It's like the proverbial Sunday school class in which the teacher asks if anyone knows what is small, furry, has a long tail, and chatters from the trees. A girl raises her hand and says, "I know the answer is Jesus, but it sure sounds like a squirrel." When people actually read biblical literature, honestly and closely, they discover a multitude of potential meanings. This makes them uneasy, because they believe that there is supposed to be one right reading for any biblical text. Like the girl in the children's sermon, they may even know what they're supposed to see. But they don't see it. They begin to distrust themselves and what they do see, to assume that there must be something wrong with their thinking. Something dangerously unorthodox.

Even veteran Bible readers sometimes feel this way about the Bible. On one occasion I was talking about this book, then a work in progress, with an older woman who is a longtime lay leader in her Bible church. She reads the Bible several times a day and hosts weekly Bible studies in her home. She admitted that she often finds herself perplexed by ambiguities and seeming contradictions in the Bible. She wouldn't bring them up in Bible-study group, because she worries that they could be a stumbling block to faith for some less-experienced members. At the same time, she expects other members, less comfortable with such ambiguities, would quickly dismiss them with standard resolutions, familiar from a century of biblical fundamentalism, that she considers too easy. "So when questions like that come up for me while I'm reading, I just step back and pray, well, Lord, I'll just look forward to you explaining that one to me!" On the one hand, this response is one of faith that the Bible does not ultimately possess such ambiguities — that it's a problem of human misperception, and must therefore be deferred to the afterlife, when she will no longer see things through a glass darkly. On the other hand, it expresses at least a little anxiety that what the Bible is supposed to be isn't what it appears to be. The expectation is that the question is answerable, but there is at least a little worry, even in this woman who is the epitome of a Bible-believer, that it's not.

Driving biblical consumerism is this disconnection between

what potential Bible readers expect from the Bible and what they experience when they crack it open. It's testimony to the power of the iconic idea of the Bible that so many readers believe that the problem must be with them — they just don't get it — rather than with their expectations for Bible reading. Successful Bible publishers know that there is a huge market of people who believe in this idea of the Bible and want to experience it for themselves. They also know that most have been frustrated in previous attempts. Is the problem that potential readers just haven't found the product that finally fulfills that desire, once and for all? Or is it that that desire cannot be fulfilled? Which would be better for the Bible business?

Biblical Values

A TWENTY-SOMETHING WOMAN sitting next to me on the plane thumbs distractedly through a fashion-and-lifestyle magazine. It's called *Becoming*. On the cover is a Jennifer Aniston look-alike in designer casuals, smiling confidently as she gives the camera one of those hair-care-commercial shoulder turns. Cover lines surround her in bright green and blue type on a purple background:

13 STORIES OF SURVIVAL

THE MUST-HAVE for Your Wardrobe

LOVE: WHAT IS IT? And How to Find It

As she flips back and forth, spending little more than a few seconds on any one page, I catch images of women in yoga-like poses, couples walking hand in hand on the beach, a bathroom scale. There are columns about how to lose weight, how to balance work and play, how to find and keep the right man. Standard *Marie Claire* or *InStyle* fare, perfect for killing time during the flight. But then I notice other, not-so-standard elements: boxed features and callouts and columns about "Bible Women" and "Bible Stuff to Know," and longer articles with titles like "Matthew," "Romans," and "Revelation."

What my row-mate is perusing is not just any magazine, or not exactly a magazine. It's a Bible magazine — a "Biblezine," one of a growing line of niche-marketed Bibles in magazine form published by Thomas Nelson. There are Biblezines for just about everyone. *Becoming* targets college-age and young professional women. *Explore* is for preteen boys, and *Refuel* is for teenage boys. *Blossom* is for preteen girls, and *Revolve* is for teenage girls. *Magnify* is for the Nickelodeon Channel generation. *Align* is for young professional men, and *Redefine* is for baby boomers.

The marketing genius behind Biblezines is Hayley Morgan (now Hayley DiMarco), whom Nelson hired away from that ultimate branding machine, Nike, in 1998 to be its young-adult brand manager. Using market research techniques that she learned at Nike, she was able to develop the Biblezine and Extreme Teen brands from nothing to $10 million in four years, at which point she left Nelson to develop her own brand of Christian content for teen girls. Since her departure, Biblezines have continued to do very well for Nelson.

The most successful Biblezines include multiple versions, with new ones coming out every season or so. Over the past several years, Nelson has produced more than a dozen versions of its best-selling *Revolve*, each with a different theme and selection of Scriptures. *Revolve Devos,* for example, is a collection of scriptural devotionals (*devos* being a clever play on "devotional" and "diva," which, by the way, is Latin for goddess). Like magazines, Biblezines tend to have short shelf lives. Planned obsolescence, biblical style.

Each Biblezine is a market-specific combination of text boxes, short articles, graphic hooks, ads for other Nelson products, and selections of biblical literature. The cover of the first installment of *Refuel,* for example, is deep burnt orange with an edgy sketch of an ancient battle scene. Cover lines promise to reveal "How

Unstoppable Warriors Got So Awesome," "70 Ways To Live Out RADICAL FAITH," "HOW TO IMPRESS THE GIRLS!" "TONS MORE RANDOM COOL STUFF LISTS," and "All New Extras: MONEY, FOOD, SPORTS." The biblical selections included focus on ancient Israel's conquest of Canaan (Joshua and Judges), the story of Ruth (which comes after Judges in the Christian Bible), and the rise and fall of the Israelite and Judean monarchies (the books of Samuel, Kings, Chronicles, Ezra, and Nehemiah). As in other Biblezines, these scriptural texts within the magazine's pages are typeset in a much more traditional, old-style bookish font, which makes them look much more Bible-ish, if also more boring.

On every page, the plain biblical text is overwhelmed by bold and colorful callouts, special columns, and other extras laid out in catchy fonts and colors. Whereas most of the biblical literature

Cover and page from the Thomas Nelson Biblezine *Refuel*, marketed to teen boys. The biblical text is literally overwhelmed by bold, colorful callout boxes and features, most of which have little or nothing to do with the biblical context. Note the "extra" about "How to Grill the Perfect Steak" next to the story of the death of King Saul in 1 Samuel 31.

is about real, bloody battles, including some of the most explicitly described violence in Scripture, these value-adding extras speak of metaphorical battles: how to "guard your heart" when dating, how to resist peer pressure to drink, use drugs, or have sex (and how to deal with embarrassment as a Christian who doesn't do those things); how to maintain eye contact with a girl when talking with her; how to do your own laundry and dishes; and how to promote a creationist viewpoint to your biology teacher and classmates.

It's hard to imagine that many teen boys are reading the biblical text in this Biblezine. In contrast to the colorful, jump-off-the-page text boxes about highly relevant topics of teenage life, the bland, colorless biblical text quickly recedes into the background. The content of those biblical books, moreover, isn't exactly easy reading. Much of it concerns territorial boundaries and monarchical chronologies. To be sure, there are some fascinating stories here, including some of the all-time greatest femmes fatales, like Jael, the non-Israelite woman who becomes an Israelite heroine after tucking the fugitive army commander Sisera into bed and then driving a peg through his head. But those stories are buried. There are no "Guard Your Heart" features anywhere near Jael.

Felt Needs

Thomas Nelson has been conducting extensive research into the "felt needs" of Bible buyers. As Wayne Hastings, vice president of the company's Bible division, says, "Buying is an emotional decision. It seems no matter how much 'logical' work we do, when it comes to the final decision, we're emotional." The aim of Nelson's Felt Needs Bible Merchandising System is to respond to "consumer definitions" of the Bible, that is, what buyers themselves feel they're looking for when they walk into a store or go online to buy a Bible. The research has identified three especially common felt needs, which often overlap: first, to find a gift Bible for someone else, usually a member of the buyer's own family (this is the most common need, shared by more than 60 percent of shoppers); second, to gain a deeper and more thorough knowledge of the Bible (whether in oneself or in the one to whom the Bible is being given); and third, "readability," that is, a felt need for special features that will increase the chances that a Bible will actually be read. Readability includes everything from an accessible translation and notes, to callouts and text boxes, to size, color, and formatting.

Biblezines speak to all three of these felt needs. The most popular ones are designed for teens and young adults but are usually purchased as gifts by older customers — parents, grandparents, and youth ministers, for example. Biblezines promise to be exceptionally readable, as easy to carry and peruse as that most readable of all popular literary forms, the magazine. As such they speak to the felt need for more and deeper biblical literacy as well.

The *Refuel* Biblezine for teen boys is a great example. Along with lots of advice on dating, sex, and manners, there's a feature on "How to Grill the Perfect Steak." Why? What does that have to do with the Bible? It's part of a total package of practical advice meant to address what many teenage boys are really looking for, what they feel they need to know: how to become a successful man. What more iconic image of American masculinity is there than the holy trinity of a guy, a steak, and a barbecue grill? In another era, it might have been about how to build a fire, dig a well, or shoot and dress out a deer. But today, it's definitely how to grill a steak. *Refuel* gets that.

When I was in ninth grade, a friend I admired for his confidence with girls gave me a magazine-sized paperback book called *Man in Demand,* a practical manual for teenage boys on how to become a good, successful Christian man in a secular world. Loaded with cartoons and special features, the book included a wide range of practical advice on everything from preventing acne, choosing a hairstyle that works well with your head shape, and avoiding wearing horizontal stripes, to asking a girl out on a date, impressing her parents with your conversation skills, and discreetly removing gristle from your teeth at the dinner table. I read every word many times. A faithful "man in demand" was exactly what I wanted to become, and I was hungry for practical advice. That was my felt need. This book didn't claim to be the Bible per se, but it did claim that its advice was biblically based, and it often spiced its pages with brief biblical quotations. And I devoted myself to it as though it were Scripture — *Man in Demand's Bible,* if you will.

I confess my religious devotion to *Man in Demand* because I don't want to pretend condescension about the felt need that Biblezines like *Refuel* speak to. I remember feeling it very powerfully. I think my ninth-grade son feels it now. And I have to admit that I myself want it for him, in some sense. I don't care if his haircut matches his head shape or his steaks are perfectly seared, and I don't want him to think that creationism is a viable alternative to evolutionary biology, or that homosexuality is sinful. But I do want him to look people in the eye, clean up after himself, and grow up to be a responsible, happy, self-confident, loving, honest man who cares about justice and the needs of other people.

Given our culture's iconic ideal of the Bible as the answer book to all of life's important questions, it's not surprising that many teens and parents would expect it to address these felt needs directly, practically, and authoritatively. *Man in Demand* spoke to this expectation by claiming to be biblically based, supplementing its advice with occasional passages from the Bible. *Refuel* takes the next big step, integrating the practical advice on becoming a man into the Bible itself. The effect is that these "supplements" become quite literally biblical.

On first glance, customer reviews seem to indicate that Nelson's Biblezines are successfully fulfilling the felt needs of Bible consumers. Gifters are happy. "I know some folks will be put off by the contemporary wrap of this easy to use tool," one mother said about *Becoming*, "but I am so glad to have it! I gave copies to my daughters and plan on giving out more, especially to those who won't open a 'real' bible." "I intend to buy the teen versions for my two nieces," said another repeat customer, "and I am sure friends will be finding copies of this Bible wrapped in birthday paper over the coming months."

Recipients of Biblezine gifts also seem satisfied. "I received this Bible as a gift because I was struggling with my daily Bible reading," one reader of *Becoming* explains, "and my friend felt I needed encouragement. I had to say from the moment I received it I haven't been able to put it down." And a parent who bought *Explore* for her twelve-year-old son for Christmas exclaimed that she and her husband have "actually 'caught' him with it under the covers when we come to tuck him in at night!"

But what are these Biblezine readers actually reading? What is so readable? Not, it appears, the biblical texts themselves. One reader of *Becoming* exclaims, "This has been my favorite magazine of all times! Love to sit by the pool and get spiritually refreshed with some fun facts and trivia!" A reader of *Refuel* especially likes that "it has a whole bunch of reviews. It reviews books, movies, and music!" Another praises *Real* because "the format appealed to my ADD daemon." The twelve-year-old boy's mother mentions only that "on every page there are 'cool' and interesting facts and other sidebars," and the reader who got *Becoming* as a gift says,

"The articles are informative and show me how to apply God's word to my daily life . . . The quizzes are fun and really just entertain you which is good." She concludes, "I can't wait for the next one to come out."

Why does she want to buy the next one? Because what Biblezine customers are finding so "readable" is not the biblical literature therein but the value-adding extras — those fun facts and trivia, informative articles and entertaining quizzes, pop culture reviews, and interesting sidebars, all presented in an attention-deficit-friendly format. At the same time, that other felt need, to read the Bible more, feels like it's being satisfied. It's similar to what the food industry does with fruit: processing apples and pears into sweeter and more colorful roll-ups, punches, sauces, and squirtable foams that I buy for my kids' lunches after passing the produce section as though it were for display only. Because the product says "fruit," I feel like I'm feeding them healthful food, and they feel that way too. Similarly, when I'm reading a Biblezine, I *feel* like I'm reading the Bible, like I'm getting my daily dose of the Bible. After all, what I'm reading is included in a Bible, of sorts. The person who gave it to me identified it as such, and so does the book's title, sort of. And honestly, these various extras seem more "biblical" than the biblical text itself. That is, they speak to me more directly, even personally, in my own terms, about things that matter most to me. That's what the Bible is supposed to do, right?

Values Added

In fact, no one needs to buy a Bible. Free ones abound. Ancient biblical texts have no copyright, and many translations, including the King James Version, are in the public domain, part of free culture. They are very cheap to produce in book form, and essentially free to publish online. Any church I know, moreover, would happily give a Bible to anyone who asks for one or even looks potentially interested. And just about every time you spend a night in a hotel, there's a Bible in your nightstand that you're free to take home, courtesy of the Gideons International. The Gideons say they place more than 63 million free Bibles and New Testaments in hotels and other human traffic lanes around the world every year. That's 120 free Bibles per minute. And they're not the only ones handing them out. Throw a rock and you're as likely as not to hit a free Bible or someone who wants to give you one.

How do you monetize Bibles when so many are freely available? The challenge is to keep reinventing the Bible in new got-to-have, value-added forms. Which is what Bible publishers are doing. In 2005 there were 6,134 different Bibles published, which was over 600 more than were published in 2004.

In some cases, adding value is simply a matter of packaging. Although the fully armored *Metal Bible* from Tyndale House boasts "the hippest exterior ever!" for example, its insides are the same as one of its publishers' standard editions, available in many other formats. Likewise, Tyndale's handbag/Bible combination (the bag has an outside pocket made to fit the Bible perfectly); also *The Waterproof Bible* (Bardin & Marsee) and *Immerse* (Thomas Nelson), popular with outdoor enthusiasts, troops overseas, and tub soakers; and Nelson's *Duct Tape Bible,* which offers that extremely well-read look. Like the fashion jeans industry, the fashion Bible industry understands that many customers prefer products that look like old favorites right off the shelf. Oh and yes, of course, Bibles are available in a number of denim washes.

In most cases, however, adding value goes well beyond innovative packaging and physical format. We've already begun to see this with Biblezines, which do much more than simply graft the Bible onto another popular media format. They literally drown out the biblical text under a cacophony of loud and colorful added content, "extra," "supplemental" material that is very clearly meant to be the center of the reader's attention. In true magazine fashion, all this added content distracts from serious, sustained reading. It's the biblical text that becomes supplemental. Yet as we've seen, readers often feel that they're finally reading the Bible. They've finally satisfied that felt need for greater readability.

At the heart of all felt needs is the longing for the iconic Bible, the literal Word of God between two covers. Bible publishers are not selling Bibles. What they're selling is that iconic idea of the Bible. Their value-added biblical content promises to provide answers to questions, solutions to problems, and speaks in no uncertain terms about God's plan for your life and how to live it. Adding value to the Bible almost always means adding "biblical" *values* that are either missing or really hard to find in the Bible itself but that provide that feeling of Bibleness so many seek.

Finding Your Niche

A niche-marketed Bible promises to speak directly and personally to its target reader. It understands his interests and questions, and claims to address them in familiar terms. The niche may be sports-related. *The Golfer's Bible,* for example, includes meditative photos of golf courses and reflections on passages by golf tour chaplains. Or it may appeal to people preoccupied with a big upcoming event. *The Bride's Bible* includes notes and articles that relate biblical passages to issues of marriage and family. Or it may address readers associated with a particular group or program. *The Life Recovery Bible,* the *Celebrate Recovery Bible,* and *Serenity* are Bibles with notes and meditations that relate biblical passages to eight- or twelve-step programs. There are also Bibles for specific ethnic groups of women and men. Popular titles for African Americans include *Aspire: The New Women of Color Study Bible: For Strength and Inspiration* from Zondervan, and the *Men of Color Study Bible* and *The Strength and Honor Bible for Young Men of Color* from World. In fact, market research indicates that African Americans own more Bibles per household than the general population and read their Bibles more often.

Another winner for publishers is to combine Scripture with one of their celebrity Christian authors. Thomas Nelson has been particularly successful in these ventures, with titles like *Holy Bible, Woman Thou Art Loosed! Edition,* featuring the renowned African American author and preacher T. D. Jakes, and Max Lucado's *The Devotional Bible: Experiencing the Heart of Jesus,* which comes in a variety of sizes and formats, all including extensive notes, short articles, and devotional excerpts from Lucado, whose inspirational books have sold well over 40 million copies. Another from Nelson, favored by many conservatives and fundamentalists, is the *MacArthur Study Bible,* replete with detailed notes from the well-known conservative intellectual preacher, author, and radio personality John MacArthur. With each of these Christian celebrity Bibles, we see a compounding of value: the Bible adds value to the author even as the author adds value to the Bible.

Clearly, many Bible niches are gendered, suggesting that the Bible speaks differently to men than to women. *Every Man's Bible,* for example, which is the foundation piece for a series of bestselling books, boasts of having more than three hundred text boxes and one-page perspective essays on a range of manly topics, "hard-hitting instructions from the Bible on work, sex, competition, time management, and much more." For the man's man who doesn't have time to mess with gray areas (no pun intended), this Bible promises "real answers, real fast . . . No more second guessing what God really means." Inserted at the beginning of each book of the Bible is a feature titled "What's the Point?" in which a short answer is given to satisfy every man's need to get to the point, fast. What's the point of Leviticus? "God pays attention to detail." Of the Song of Songs? "The love of a good woman is worth cultivating." Of Zephaniah? "Actions lead to consequences." Of the Gospel of Luke? "Jesus cares about the individual." Of Revelation? "In the end, the Great One wins."

Inserted in each biblical book are brief articles that clarify what God says in the Bible about how to be a godly man in this world — one-page moral lessons on male biblical characters titled "Someone You Should Know," for example, and half-page displays titled "Men, Women, & God." The one-pager on Samson in the book of Judges begins, "The National Football League has a message for ambitious coaches: Do you want to win? Then you first have to master yourself." It goes on to describe Samson as a man whose potential was ruined because he couldn't control his lust, greed, and anger, ultimately making him vulnerable to the seductions of a bad woman, Delilah. It concludes with "THE POINT: No man wins without controlling his own passions." Thus a very complex story with a complex character is boiled down to a lesson on how to win through self-control, especially around women like Delilah. On the next page, a "Men, Women, & God" feature called "A Treacherous Woman" continues with this theme. It warns, "We just can't believe that the gorgeous object of our affection would ever succumb to selfishness . . . Lust is a powerful force, and believe it or not, many women — and men, too — are skilled in the art of manipulation." One must wonder whether the inclusion of "and men, too" was something of an editorial afterthought. After all, the piece is clearly an exhortation to men to avoid the perils of being sexually manipulated by women, not vice versa.

Not only do these kinds of moral bios often steer readers toward long-standing gender stereotypes and anxieties about women's sexuality; they also steer readers away from the ambiguities and questions that arise when one reads the biblical texts themselves. In my experience, in fact, the Samson story (Judges 13–16) is an excellent example of the kind of biblical ambiguity that can quickly lead readers into uncharted territory. Imagine for a moment that you're in a Bible-study group discussing the story of Samson and Delilah. You're vaguely familiar with their names — especially Delilah's, from a song by Chuck Berry, maybe, or the Grateful Dead, or the Plain White T's. And wasn't Samson that strong man who wore his hair long, like an ancient Israelite version of a modern-day professional wrestler? But you've never actually read the story until now. As you find your way into the details, it's not the big-man-taken-down-by-a-beautiful-woman tale you expected to find. Things grow fascinatingly complicated, and surprising questions emerge. Wasn't Samson quite the trickster himself? And although he's humiliated and ultimately dies, doesn't he in fact *win* in the final act when he pulls the pillars down on himself and everyone else? Doesn't he play the final trick? And on the sex front, was he really any worse than King David, whose lust for Bathsheba led ultimately to his choreographing of her husband's death in battle, not to mention the deaths of untold others as collateral damage? Approached from a slightly different angle, very unlike David, but a lot like David's divinely doomed predecessor, Saul, might Samson even be something of a tragically ill-fated figure, caught up in a larger divine plan that is less than clear, especially to him?

What about Delilah? Is she not also caught in a potentially lose-lose situation depending on what she does? And don't I remember the Israelites celebrating Jael, a sexual trickster who played for their side? Is that the main difference? Very quickly, the idea that this is a moral lesson about how the wrong woman can ruin a guy's shot at winning the game begins to look absurdly simplistic.

In fact, these are all questions I have heard raised by college students and church Bible-study group members when reading this story without deferring to the special notes and comments of study Bibles and the like. And these are the kinds of biblical stories that led my grandpa, an irreverent union man who used to roll his eyes at us kids during dinnertime prayers, to begin reading the Bible for himself in the last few years of his life. "I had no idea *this* kind of thing was in there!" he joyfully exclaimed to me. Reading on his own, he had begun to see the Bible as something quite different from the book of dos and don'ts that he, like so many others, had expected to find.

No doubt many an Every Man "reads" this Bible without ever reading very much biblical text. He focuses instead on the various callouts, sidebars, and other features, whose biblical values steer clear of the thickets of questions that are so often raised by biblical literature, and therefore more clearly and directly address his felt needs. He sticks to "the point" in a way that the Bible itself does not.

Necessary Supplements

The back cover of Tyndale's best-selling *Life Application Study Bible* captures the felt need of many potential Bible buyers and repeat buyers: "How many times have you read your Bible and asked: 'How can this possibly apply to my life, my job, my friendships, my marriage, my neighborhood, my family, my country? . . . Why can't I understand what God is saying to me through His Word?'" The Bible is supposed to be God's clear and unambiguous Word, offering practical guidance and solutions to every problem. Other Bibles have not come through. This Bible understands.

In fact, about one-third of the text in the *Life Application Study Bible* is extrabiblical, "supplementary" content, including notes on verses, synopses, charts and diagrams, topical sidebars, and reflective essays. Its main competitor in the field of devotional study Bibles is Zondervan's *NIV Study Bible,* which boasts more than twenty thousand notes. Nearly half of this Bible is "supplemental." Some of the added material offers to help readers delve deeper into the biblical text itself, providing information about historical contexts, or alternative translations of the original Greek or Hebrew. More often, however, the intention is not to encourage readers to interpret for themselves but to interpret *for* them, to control meaning, dispelling doubts and questions and directing readers toward specific conclusions.

Often these values-adding editorial controls focus on texts that could have something to do with present-day hot-button issues. Take, for example, the small handful of biblical passages usually cited in discussions about homosexuality. The popular cultural assumption is that the Bible very clearly says that homosexuality is an abominable sin. Biblical literature itself, however, is not so clear. In fact, it has very little explicitly to offer by way of moral teaching or legislation on matters of sexuality, let alone homosexuality, and what it does have to say does not speak directly to the issue as it appears in contemporary society. Two passages in the legal corpus of Leviticus (18:22 and 20:13) prohibit a man from lying with another man "as he lies with a woman." This commandment appears along with prohibitions against bestiality, adultery, sex with a menstruating woman, and marrying a divorced woman, a former prostitute, or a brother's widow (a practice that is required elsewhere in Scripture). These two passages in Leviticus do not offer a blanket prohibition against all homosexuality per se. They do not address lesbianism, for example, or even sexual orientation, but only male-male intercourse. Leviticus, moreover, is not exactly a font of legal counsel for most

Christians on other moral and ethical matters: it prohibits eating shellfish and pork, wearing mixed-fiber clothing, and planting different plants in the same garden; it requires ritual sacrifices; and it condones slavery.

In the New Testament, Jesus has nothing to say about homosexuality and very, very little to say about sexuality in general. Paul's letters do disparage some specific male-male sexual practices common in the larger Greco-Roman society (e.g., pederasty, or sexual "mentoring" of young men by older men, and soliciting young male prostitutes). But Paul never condemns consensual same-sex relations between adults. That's not to say that if Paul were time-machined to the present he would be an advocate of gay marriage. It is to say that one can — and many do — interpret the Bible in ways that are supportive of homosexual unions and gay rights. The simple fact is that the Christian Scriptures are not clear on this issue. It is a matter of biblical interpretation and ethical reflection in which faithful Christians can and do disagree.

Yet the supplemental features in many Bibles, especially those marketed to teens, make much ado about the "biblical view" of homosexuality — that is, "what God says" about it in the Bible. The NIV Teen Study Bible from Zondervan, which has sold over 2.5 million copies and is the best-selling Bible among twelve- to fifteen-year-olds, is typical. On the same page as Leviticus 18, there is a "The Bible Says" feature called "Only One Right Choice," which decries the idea that homosexuality could be an "alternative lifestyle." According to the commentary, Leviticus 18 clearly states, "It's wrong to have homosexual sex," and "this isn't the only Bible passage that says homosexual sex is a sin. Read also Romans 1:26–27. If someone tells you homosexuality is an alternative lifestyle — meaning that it's OK — don't let those words fool you. It's an alternative all right. A sinful one." Then, four pages later, near Leviticus 20, there is a full-page image of a piece of lined stationery with a "Dear Sam" note from "Chris in Crystal Springs." It's meant to look like a note that's been slipped into Chris's Bible at this particular spot. Chris writes that he doesn't understand how he can follow Jesus's teaching to love everyone, including homosexuals, without accepting their "alternative lifestyle." A response from Sam on what looks like a sticky note gives the answer: love the sinner but hate the sin; understand that the Bible is very clear that homosexuality is a sin. "You can't approve of something evil that God has forbidden." In both of these "helps," the plain intention is to remove the ambiguity that exists in Scripture itself, thereby leaving no room for interpretation.

I have yet to find anyone, adult or teen, who has seen a Biblezine in her or his Bible-study meeting (many Bible-study participants, when shown a Biblezine, respond in shock and horror, "What's *that?!*"). But several report having seen people bring study Bibles such as the *NIV Teen Study Bible* or *Life Application Study Bible*. These tend to be group members who have had less experience reading the Bible, on their own or in such a group. As one woman, a veteran of many different Bible-study groups, sympathized, it can be intimidating for newcomers to participate in Bible study without a study Bible, because they're often afraid that they might say something wrong, or ask a question whose answer is obvious to others.

Values-added content purports to be supplemental, intended simply to make clear or amplify what the Bible is already saying. It speaks for the Bible, indeed for God. But why does it need to do that? The biblical text itself is right there, on the same page, albeit in a plainer, smaller, less visually attractive font. Why not simply let it speak for itself? Perhaps because it doesn't speak that way. It's not that kind of literature. The Bible is not an instruction manual. It doesn't give "real answers, real fast."

Still, Bible publishers know that simple, black-and-white answers are what the majority of biblical consumers expect from their Bibles. Remember, most Americans believe that the Bible has the answers to all of life's important questions and is infallible in its teachings.

In most Bibles, as we've seen, pages are designed so that the supplemental helps stand out visually from the main body of biblical text. They appear in larger print, using contemporary fonts and graphics (often in color), with catchy titles. They jump off the page and grab the reader's attention. They purport to supplement the biblical text, but the reverse is true. They are the center of attention and the biblical text is background. Practically speaking, they become part of the Bible, if not its central and unifying voice. It would be perfectly understandable for a thirteen-year-old with an *NIV Teen Study Bible* to say that the Bible clearly prohibits homosexuality and that it's not an alternative lifestyle. The Bible says so. Or was it Dear Sam? Whatever.

If That's What It Means, Why Doesn't It Say So?

In still other cases, translators make the biblical text itself agree with the likes of Dear Sam, adding values that are not clearly present in the text they're translating. The New Living Translation, for example, which is the text used in the *Life Application Study Bible* and many other Bibles from Tyndale, puts its interpretation right into its translation of Leviticus 18:22: "Do not practice homosexuality; it is a detestable sin." Although this version claims to be an actual translation from the Hebrew, the wording of this passage is virtually identical to that of its predecessor, *The Living Bible*, which was an interpretive paraphrase from another English version ("Homosexuality is absolutely forbidden, for it is an enormous sin"). As we've seen, the Hebrew text refers specifically to a man lying with another man as though with a woman, not to homosexuality or homosexual behavior in general. The Hebrew word translated "abomination" (*to'evah*), moreover, does not carry the Christian meaning of "sin" as moral wrongdoing. It is not about moral guilt so much as impurity. The American Standard Version, from which *The Living Bible* was paraphrased, maintains this sense: "Thou shalt not lie with mankind, as with womankind: it is abomination." The New Living Translation and *The Living Bible,* however, seem to know better. They implicitly claim that the thought, the intended meaning, behind that ancient Levitical prohibition was to forbid homosexuality (taken most broadly to refer to male-male sexual acts, female-female sexual acts, homosexual identity, and homosexual unions) as sinful. They agree with Sam, and they take his point one big step further, adding it directly into the biblical text.

Tyndale's New Living Translation is what's known as a *functional* equivalence, or "meaning driven" translation. Central to this approach is the idea that translating biblical texts from the Hebrew, Aramaic, and Greek languages in which they were originally written is, and should be, an act of interpretation, determining what they mean as clearly as possible. Contrary to the traditional *formal* equivalence approach to translation, whose goal is to translate words, phrases, and other forms of speech into their closest English counterparts, the goal of functional-equivalence translations is to give what the translator considers to be the full meaning of larger units of speech. There are more than thirty-five translations of the Bible on the market today. Although the King James Version remains the bestseller, the market for functional-equivalence translations is big and getting bigger.

Nearly all translations depend to some degree on functional equivalencies in order to put ancient Hebrew, Aramaic, and Greek figures of speech into sensible English. A good example is the common Hebrew phrase for divine wrath, imagined as God's red-hot nose. When God learns of Aaron's golden-calf project, most translations have God tell Moses something like, "Now let me alone, so that my wrath may burn hot against them" (Exodus 32:10). But "wrath" is a euphemism, of sorts. The Hebrew word is *'aph,* "nose." Here, as in many other places in the Bible, God's nose burns hot. One might take that as strictly figurative if it weren't for the next story, in which God tucks Moses into a cleft in a rock and then walks past, allowing Moses to behold the divine backside.

Given such English refigurings of God's hot Hebrew nose, it's not surprising to learn that another, more bawdy Hebraism is also usually lost in translation. In Samuel and Kings, a male is sometimes referred to as, to quote the King James Version, "one that pisseth against a wall," that is, who pees standing up. That's a very literal translation of the Hebrew phrase (*mashtin beqir*). Consider the story of the future king David, on the run in the wilderness from King Saul, seeking food for his army from a rich man named Nabal ("fool") in exchange for their protection of his estate. When Nabal refuses, most modern translations, tuned to our delicate post-Victorian ears, have David vow to leave not one single "male" alive by morning. But in the more graphic Hebrew, David declares that not one person will be pissing against the wall by morning. The threat is not only bawdy but poetic: "against the wall," *beqir,* sounds very like "morning," *boqer* (read it aloud to hear for yourself: *ad ha-boqer mashtin beqir*). David's expression gets further literary play after Nabal's wife, Abigail (soon to be one of David's wives), convinces David to relent. When she returns to Nabal, she finds that he's hosting a party and already very drunk. So she waits till morning, "when the wine had gone out of him" — which could mean after he was sober or after he had literally pissed it out — to tell him what almost happened. At that news, he sinks into a depression and dies ten days later. Clearly, the functional equivalent "male" loses a lot in translation.

In most cases, functional-equivalence translations go much, much further than losing nuance and wordplay, to the point that they are really writing something new that is more or less inspired by the text in its original language. Often, the translator will read several sentences in a row before putting into English what he or she determines the overall meaning to be. To get a clearer sense of the difference between a formal-equivalence and functional-equivalence translation, compare these three translations of the opening verse of Psalm 1. First, here is my rather wooden, strictly form-driven translation from Hebrew:

> Happy the man
> > who does not walk in the counsel of wicked ones
> In the way of sinners he does not stand
> > In the seat of scorners he does not sit

Now here is the same verse in the King James Version, the old standard of formal-equivalence translation:

> Blessed is the man
> > that walketh not in the counsel of the ungodly,
> nor standeth in the way of sinners,
> > nor sitteth in the seat of the scornful.

Seventeenth-century *-eths* aside, this is fairly close to mine, albeit aesthetically more resonant. "Ungodly" is a stretch for a word (*resha'im*) that invariably refers to those who act wrongfully or wickedly. But the metaphorical actions of walking, standing, and sitting are maintained. This translation also captures the Hebrew repetition, in the last line, of *yashav*, used in verb form for "sitteth" and in noun form for "seat." Note too the verse's finely crafted parallelism, which is a key element in the craft of Hebrew biblical poetry:

that walketh not	in the counsel	of the ungodly
nor standeth	in the way	of sinners
nor sitteth	in the seat	of the scornful

The effect of this kind of synonymous parallelism is more than simple repetition. It's not just about reiterating an important point — "avoid bad guys." This is poetry, not pool rules. Each new metaphor and term adds intensity, tension, and depth. It slows us down and creates space for imagination, contemplation, and self-reflection.

Now compare the Contemporary English Version, a functional-equivalence translation produced in 1995 by the American Bible Society under the supervision of Barclay Newman, whose background was in the mission field, where he translated the Bible into languages *and* cultures (which are the contexts of meaning) often radically different from Western ones.

> God blesses those people
> who refuse evil advice
> and won't follow sinners
> or join in sneering at God.

Here everything is transformed. Whereas the previous two form-driven translations (mine and the King James Version) remain faithful to the Hebrew text's metaphorical language, which offers a series of images that evoke feelings as much as ideas, this functional-equivalence translation removes them. Whereas the previous two translations begin correctly with an adjective, "happy" or "blessed," this translation changes the adjective into an active verb and supplies it with a subject, God, thereby removing the inherent ambiguity in the Hebrew. Whereas the first two translations refer in the end to scornful or mean-spirited people — people who might be that way to other people, to God, or even to themselves — this one gives the scorn an object, God, thereby once again reducing the possible interpretations that were allowed by the Hebrew. And whereas the first two are both faithful to the poetic parallelism of the verse, this one disregards it altogether, opting instead to have each line make a slightly different moral point.

Kenneth Taylor, the father of *The Living Bible*, said that the idea of a "thought for thought" paraphrase of the Bible came from his frustration during dinner-table devotionals with his children. His recollections reveal both the felt need that leads to such disambiguating, simplifying versions and the reality of biblical ambiguity that they try to erase. "All too often," he explained, "I would ask questions to be sure the children understood, and they would shrug their shoulders — they didn't know what the passage was talking about. So I would explain it. I would paraphrase it for them and give them the thought." Once, one of them responded, "Well Daddy, if that's what it means, why doesn't it say so?" He began to rewrite biblical passages in preparation for those Bible studies, "so that it would be clearer to the children, and actually to myself too."

Functional-equivalence proponents will argue that readers of form-driven translations risk not getting the right meaning from the text. They operate on the belief that a biblical passage like Psalm 1:1 has a singular, intended meaning. The goal, therefore, is to reduce ambiguity and preclude the possibility of seeing multiple meanings. To be sure, all translation is interpretation. As biblical scholar Tod Linafelt puts it, translation is a kind of survival. To survive means to live over, or beyond, something (*sur* = "over" + *vive* = "live"). A translation is an over-living, a living-beyond the original. A translation is something new, a new life for a text. So it is with all Bible translations. Be that as it may, functional-equivalence translations, which presume that ambiguity, multivalence, and contradiction are by definition not part of the Bible, take far more creative and interpretive license than formal ones in eradicating those features. In so doing, they too often try to make the Bible into something it's not.

Manga Bibles

As the Biblezine phenomenon demonstrates, one successful way to reinvent the Bible and create new consumer markets is to graft it onto other, less-bookish media that are selling well. Behold one of the latest trends: manga Bibles.

Mangas are Japanese graphic novels or comic-book-style serial publications (*man* = "involuntary" or "cartoon"; *ga* = "brush stroke" or "picture"). In Japan, about 40 percent of all print publications are mangas, including a very wide range of styles and subjects. Over the past two decades, their popularity has become a worldwide phenomenon. In recent years the market for English-language mangas in the United States has grown rapidly, especially among teens and young adults. Annual sales in the United States grew from about $60 million in 2002 to $220 million in 2007, with 1,468 titles published. Although sales dropped in 2008 along with most other kinds of books, the future of this market looks bright.

Bibles and mangas, a match made in heaven? Several Christian publishers seem to believe so, and are scrambling to gain the high ground in this new market niche. Tyndale House, for example, has partnered with NEXT, a nonprofit evangelical company of Japanese manga artists and media-savvy professionals committed to creating high-quality, innovative Christian mangas for teens and young adults in many languages. Tyndale purchased exclusive English-language rights for all mangas produced by

NEXT. So far it has published two biblical mangas: *Manga Messiah* and *Manga Bible*. The former is a full-color graphic-novel version of the story of Jesus, based on particular passages selected from the four Gospels of the New Testament. Not surprisingly, the editorial selections streamline the narrative to encourage readers to accept Jesus Christ as their personal lord and savior who died for their sins.

Note that this biblical manga is called *Manga Messiah*, not *Manga Bible*, and its back-cover blurb takes care to describe it as "adapted from the ancient texts" rather than as "the Bible." Tyndale and NEXT's *Manga Bible*, on the other hand, is far less of a Bible genre bender: it is basically comprised of Tyndale's complete Slimline Reference edition of its New Living Translation Bible with a modestly manga-ish cover and three thirty-two-page glossy inserts of manga illustrations of select biblical narratives.

A manga offers far more than simple illustrations of literary texts. Its visual images are by no means supplementary to the word, but interactive with it and with one another. Its layout invites the eye to move back and forth between frames on the page in nonlinear fashion. That is very different from the linear, left-to-right and top-to-bottom way we read the text of a typical Bible book. In its titles, Tyndale implicitly recognizes this difference and takes a more conservative approach to publishing manga Bibles, reserving the title of "Bible" for that which more closely resembles its traditional Bibles.

Zondervan has taken a far bolder approach, publishing what it calls its *Manga Bible* in a series of smaller volumes, each covering a selection of biblical narrative. Its target audience is clearly younger readers. The simple black-and-white scenes are loaded with cute talking animals, childlike biblical characters (Adam and Eve look to be about seven years old), and lots of lighthearted humor ("Excuse me!" interrupts a whale just after being created on day five, "Have you seen my son Nemo?").

Very little of the text that appears in Zondervan's *Manga Bible* is direct quotation from biblical literature. But much of it does reinforce popular biblical stereotypes. The story of Adam and Eve in the garden, for example, draws heavily from sexist caricatures of Eve that have been part of popular culture for centuries but are not explicitly part of the biblical narrative itself. In the biblical story, Eve partakes of the fruit of the tree of knowledge of good and evil because, the text says, she sees that it's beautiful, that it tastes good, and that it will bring her wisdom. In this manga Bible, however, the cute but not too bright Eve is confused into partaking. In the biblical text, Adam says nothing but simply eats what Eve hands him. In this account, however, Adam resists her urgings until she pouts, "You've changed." He then gives in, against his better judgment, and Eve winks at the reader and says, "Hee hee . . . girls can make guys do anything." You get the picture: God and Adam are buddies. Seeing that Adam needed love, God set him up with Eve, who is as beautiful and well-meaning as she is manipulative and morally weak. Here, then, is an adorable, cartoonish rendition of the millennia-long practice of misinterpreting this biblical story in order to blame women for everything that's wrong with the world and to keep them in their place. It looks progressive, maybe even a little edgy, but as biblical interpretation it's downright backward.

Frame from volume 1 of Zondervan's *Manga Bible*, subtitled *Names, Games, and the Long Road Trip* (covering Genesis and Exodus). Eve has just convinced Adam to eat the fruit of the tree of knowledge of good and evil. Her representation here reinforces sexist caricatures and the long-standing tradition of blaming Eve for the "Fall of Man."

I'm sometimes invited to lead discussions on the Bible and
Bible publishing in local churches. I always bring examples of
manga Bibles, Biblezines, and so on. I offer my analysis and critique. Most parishioners concur. Some, outraged by what they
see as a cheapening of Holy Scriptures, want to push the critique
a lot harder.

After one recent discussion, an older woman stayed after to
talk more about manga Bibles. She said she'd like to buy one for
her grandson and wondered which I'd recommend. I admit I was
a bit taken aback. I wondered to myself if she'd heard anything
I'd said about them except that they're popular with kids. As we
talked, it became clear that she had. She understood all that. She
didn't agree with the theology in the examples we looked at, and
she didn't buy the promotional shtick that they were simply the
Word of God in a novel form. Still, she was wondering if some
manga Bibles were better than others. In so many words, she
was expressing all three of the most commonly felt needs among
Bible shoppers: to buy a Bible as a gift that the recipient will find
"readable" and thus gain some degree of familiarity with biblical
literature. These manga Bibles spoke to those needs right over
the top of me.

What did I do? I wasn't about to deny the legitimacy of those
felt needs. As a father of a fourteen-year-old boy who rarely shows
interest in reading what I've devoted my vocation to studying,
I can sympathize. So I made a recommendation: *Manga Messiah,*
published by Tyndale for NEXT. Three reasons. First, it's a nonprofit venture. Second, the graphics and design are far superior
to competitors and more like the style of other popular Japanese
mangas (in fact, it was originally done in Japanese). Third, and
most importantly, it doesn't pretend to be the Bible, but rather
admits that it's a creative adaptation of select stories from the
New Testament. It is openly and self-consciously interpretive,

and doesn't pretend to be other than that. And by footnoting the biblical passages it is interpreting on each page, it enables readers to judge its interpretations for themselves. Which might provoke some interesting conversations.

A Different Cookie

The point here is not to condemn the particular values, moral and theological, that are being added in these Bibles. In fact, although they are fewer and far less financially successful, there are also values-added Bibles that lean hard in theologically and politically liberal or progressive directions. A good example is the recently completed *Inclusive Bible,* created by a grass-roots group of clergy and laypeople called Priests for Equality. This Bible often literally rewrites passages that are especially problematic for those who strive for gender and class equality in church and society, remaking it according to the gospel of love and justice that they proclaim to be the heart of Christian faith. In this Bible, patriarchal passages about how husbands should relate to their wives (often treating them as little more than property) become recommendations for how any person of any orientation should relate to her or his "spouse or partner" in a loving, respectful way. As for the infamous passage in First Corinthians that instructs women to remain silent in church and subordinate to their husbands, this Bible revises, "Only one spouse has permission to speak. The other is to remain silent, to keep in the background" out of respect, and to wait his or her turn (1 Corinthians 14). Although we might wish it were not so, such rewritings push well beyond anything that could be argued as the original intention of these Hebrew and Greek texts.

The point is that these values, whether conservative or liberal, are not simply "there" in the Bible itself. They are interpretational add-ins meant to make the Bible closer to what people expect from it. These value-added, values-added products are not simply Bibles but biblical interpretations.

By the time you read this, there will no doubt be new Bibles in new forms and formats that I can't even imagine as I write. Indeed, this chapter is far from a comprehensive discussion of Bibles available today. There's so much out there, an overwhelming variety of items being published as "the Bible": magazines, graphic novels, full-metal-jacketed, furry, duct-taped, waterproof, not to mention digital media, on the Internet, CDs, DVDs, iPods, e-books, et cetera. And all these combined in so many different ways with so many different words: dozens of translations, the most successful ones being highly interpretive, resiftings of the passages into chronological order, visual representations, and of course extras and "helps" of all kinds, both pictorial and textual, purportedly supplemental to the biblical words but in fact supplanting them.

"If you put chocolate coating on an Oreo, it's a different cookie, and you ought to be able to charge more," says Paul J. Caminiti, a vice president at Zondervan. "The packaging has to scream that this is something really new: First time! Fudge-dipped! Chocolate coated!" If I follow this metaphor correctly, the Bible is the Oreo, and the fudge dip is the extra stuff that the publisher adds. As we've seen, there's at least as much double-stuffing as there is fudge-dipping. In any case, as he himself says, "it's a different cookie." Is it still an Oreo?

4

Twilight of the Idol

The Evangelical Dilemma

Evangelicalism faces a fundamental dilemma: popularization versus preservation; getting the Word out by whatever means necessary versus protecting and preserving the sanctity of the tradition. On the one hand, to what extent should the Bible be adapted and altered, in form or content, in order to make it more available and accessible? On the other hand, to what extent should its holiness or sanctity be preserved and maintained, at the expense of easy availability and popularity?

Taking as its motto the apostle Paul's declaration, "I have become all things to all people, so that I might by any means save some," American evangelicalism since the 1950s has leaned harder and harder in the direction of popularization and away from preservation. These days we're accustomed to thinking of evangelicalism as conservative in every way. But when it comes to this dilemma, it tends to be the most liberal of Christianities in its willingness to adapt its Scriptures and traditions to new contexts in order to make them more appealing to popular audiences. Recall that it was the neo-evangelical movement Youth for Christ that was the first to adopt entertainment-industry strategies in rallies during the mid-twentieth century. A couple decades later, evangelicals were the first to bring rock music into even bigger rallies, and later into church worship services. Evangelicals have been among the quickest to use new media, be it radio in the 1940s, television in the 1960s, or the Internet today. And let's not forget Oreo-and-milk Communion services, birthday cakes for Jesus on Christmas, and clown ministry (I once saw a clowning troupe do a version of the Passion play). A hallmark of evangelicalism in America is its disposition to adapt traditional Christian practices and canons to popular interests and consumer demands in order to make them more readily available and attractive. As we saw in the introduction, evangelicalism's openness to cultural adaptation is what has distinguished it most sharply from the more culturally conservative, often sectarian orientation of its sterner parent movement, fundamentalism, which continues to disapprove.

Marshall McLuhan famously declared that the "medium is the message," that there is no separating content from form or meaning from technology, and that the electronic age is bringing an end to the age of print. Evangelicalism often seems to be pronouncing a counterdeclaration to the McLuhanian one. The medium is by no means the message. The message is entirely independent of the medium. Indeed, as the Word of God, it transcends whatever form we use to mediate it.

The collaboration between the editors of *Campus Life* magazine and Tyndale House that culminated in *The Way* Bible staked its faith on popularizing the message by whatever media means necessary. The magazine editors, whose offices were next door to Tyndale's, were especially ambitious in reaching to fit in with the popular youth culture of the '60s and early '70s. It was a time of cultural revolution, and any Bible trying to speak to that ethos would inevitably be pushing against traditional boundaries. They designed the layout, wrote all the introductory essays, and provided the images, but nothing went forward until it was approved by Tyndale House. In most cases, the two editorial teams were simpatico. Occasionally, however, Tyndale would ask for something a bit less edgy.

Given that this collaboration was between a Bible publisher and a magazine publisher, it was no accident that The Way turned out to be something of a hybrid of the two print formats. Its floppy cover, trendy fonts, varied layouts, contemporary photomontages, and upbeat, engaging introductory essays gave it a magazine feel. At the same time, it's clear that Tyndale was concerned to preserve a sense of the publication as "the Bible" as well. This concern is most clear on the pages of the biblical text itself, which offer a strong visual contrast to the introductory parts. The biblical text is very plain, laid out in the traditional two-column style, with traditional fonts and no pictures.

In the hybrid mix of Bible and magazine that is The Way, and in the creative tension between the Bible publisher and magazine publisher that brought it to market, we may recognize the desire to hang on to both horns of the evangelical dilemma, popularization and preservation.

Selling Out

Not that The Way and its parent version, The Living Bible, were without critics. The neo-evangelical movement of the mid-twentieth century had brought fundamentalist Christianity back into the mainstream of American culture, but it had not brought all fundamentalists with it. Many more sectarian-leaning Christians remained critical of the new movement for its desire to reengage popular youth culture by adapting the Bible and Christian values to mainstream-entertainment media forms. And so, although many influential evangelical leaders like Billy Graham and organizations like Youth for Christ supported *The Way*, many other fundamentalists did not. Implicitly agreeing with McLuhan that medium and message are inseparable, they condemned its paraphrasing, incorporation of contemporary photos, trendy fonts, magazine-like page layouts, and social-minded essays, as at best a dilution of the Word and at worst a seductive diversion from it.

Still, no one could have accused *The Way*'s creators of being motivated by personal gain. They didn't make a dime on the project, and none of their names appear anywhere in it. Conservative critics were right, however, that it was a dilution and distortion of the Word — as they knew it, anyway. The fact that only the smaller, plain-font subtitle on the cover announced it as a Bible, and even then as *The Living Bible Illustrated*, suggests that even its publishers were a little uneasy on this front. It was indeed challenging commonly held standards for what is and isn't the Bible.

In the decades since *The Way*, tensions have continued between evangelical and fundamentalist Christians concerning the extent to which Christianity and its Scriptures should be adapted to the mainstream. Indeed, these disagreements have intensified, as popular culture has really become synonymous with consumer culture. To make something popular requires making it appealing to consumers. Is there any aspect of popular culture that can't be purchased or made into an object of consumer desire? If there is, it won't remain so for long. In this cultural climate, the mission to popularize Christianity, especially the Bible, means promoting it within consumer culture, generating consumer desire for it. In today's world, the mission of popularizing the Bible, of making it widely available, accessible, and attractive, is increasingly a marketing program. To popularize is to monetize. To spread the Word means to sell more of it.

The vast majority of people in Christian Bible publishing are wholehearted evangelicals who sincerely believe they are called to the work they do. The mission of evangelism isn't masking a "real" motive of profit. And although most inevitably fall out of the dilemma on the side of popularization, many within the industry express concern about going too far. "There is a line, because it's God's word," remarked Brian Scharp, vice president of Bible marketing at Zondervan, in a recent *Los Angeles Times* interview. He was referring to a 3-D pop-up Bible that the publisher had passed on. Still, he continued, "It's hard to draw the line in any one place and say, 'We're never going to cross that.'"

To which fundamentalist-leaning Christians respond, "It's a slippery slope!" If the Pauline mantra for neo-evangelicals who favor popularization is, "I have become all things to all people, so that I might by any means save some," the one for these more conservative Christians is, "Do not be conformed to this world." As the leader of one Bible-study group explained to me, "Our goal is to live lives that are faithful to the instructions and principles of Scripture (and in contrast to our secular society)."

Indeed, most of these critics are quick to condemn the industry for already having slid far too far down that slope. Wondering how low it can go, one customer reviewer of Biblezines exclaimed, "What's next? The swimsuit edition?" Beholding *Becoming* for the first time in a Christian bookstore, another woman reported that she and her husband were "deeply saddened and disturbed to find that God's Holy Word had been placed within the pages of such immature chatter." She continues,

> Our society has become so dependent upon the visually stimulating that now even Christians aren't satisfied with the pure Words of the Bible without being entertained and pampered while reading it. It's not our place to attempt to "bring God down to the

level of the world." . . . When we try to paste beads, feathers . . . or fashion models on the sufficient Word of God, then we make a mockery of His power and the purity of His Word.

For critics like these, the Bible industry is not only selling itself out. It is selling the Bible out as well.

Although she and others sympathetic to her conservative critique wouldn't put it in these religiously neutral terms, her essential point is that Bible publishers are selling off what I would call the Bible's *sacred capital*. Let me unpack this statement.

Sacred, from the Latin *sacer,* means "set apart." The sacred is that which is set apart from the ordinary, everyday, "profane" world of human existence. At the same time, it is what makes that everyday world meaningful. In Christian tradition, as in many other religions, that which is sacred is believed to be set apart, in some sense, by and for God.

Capital is accumulated value. It doesn't have to be financial value, that is, economic capital. There are many kinds of social and cultural capital: memberships within certain organizations and social networks, both formal and informal, for example, as well as degrees and certifications from schools and other institutions. Some of these, like a clubhouse membership or a private-school education, may easily translate into economic capital. Others, like friendships with powerful and influential people, may not. In any case, part of what makes these forms of capital valuable is that they are perceived to be rare, not too readily available. Like the dollar, their value depends to a degree on controlling how freely available they are.

Like other kinds of capital, sacred capital may be accumulated, preserved, and spent down. In Christian tradition, taking care of what is valued as sacred, preserving and protecting sacred capital, is understood as stewardship. Stewardship is the opposite of sacred spending and consuming. It is the preservation side of the dilemma referred to earlier.

So let me say it again: Bible publishers are selling down the sacred capital of the Bible, inundating the market with a bewildering and unprecedented array of new editions and versions in an ever-growing variety of translations, layouts, and material forms. To the point that you could be forgiven if, standing in the Bible section of your local bookstore, you were to cry out in despair, "Where is the Bible?" As publishers lean ever harder away from preservation and toward popularization, the Bible is losing its set-apartness. It is being washed away in a market flood of biblical proportions.

Contrast this situation with how the more narrowly defined sacred capital of scriptures in other religious traditions is accumulated and preserved. A good example from Judaism is the Sefer Torah, a Torah scroll that is meticulously hand-copied according to strict scribal regulations on particular kinds of parchment made from kosher animals. Lovingly housed in the *aron kodesh,* or holy ark, in the synagogue or temple, veiled by an embroidered curtain, and adorned with a crown, breastplate, and bells, it is taken out and carried through the congregation to be reverently touched and kissed by members before it is read by a cantor who uses a little hand-shaped pointer called a *yad* ("hand") so that her or his finger doesn't touch its parchment. Through these various highly regulated methods of production, care, and use, the Sefer Torah accumulates sacred capital as the center of Jewish religious belief and practice.

Similarly, in Eastern Orthodox churches, the four Gospels of the New Testament are set apart in a separate book, the Gospel Book. Made and decorated according to elaborate specifications, it is believed to be an icon of Christ and is treated with great reverence during the Divine Liturgy as well as in other liturgies.

During the prayer of consecration for a new bishop, for example, the Gospel Book is opened and placed, face-down, on the back of his neck. When he dies, he will be buried with it resting on his chest.

In both of these examples, we can see how a scripture's sacred capital resides in a particular, highly regulated and carefully preserved combination of *word, thing,* and *idea.* Sacred capital resides not only in the words on the page, the literary content, but also in the thing itself, made a certain way with certain materials, and in the idea of it, the shared perception of it. The various ritual practices and beliefs that surround it are forms of stewardship that build and maintain that trinity of word-thing-idea. If one element of that triad loses meaning, the whole thing suffers a loss of sacred capital. Within such a closely regulated religious context of belief and practice, it would be difficult to convert sacred capital into economic capital.

In the biblical consumerism of American popular culture, by contrast, sacred capital resides in an idea that is being attached to a wider and wider variety of words and things, with no regulations other than the free market and the consciences of Bible publishers and consumers.

This situation is analogous to the phenomenon of "brand dilution." The cultural icon of the Bible is similar to a brand. It enjoys wide cultural appreciation akin to brand recognition. Brand recognition is a measure of the value that potential consumers perceive in a brand — how much trust they have in its value. When a brand has high value or "brand equity," a company may want to extend it into other areas and products. It may want to use a strong brand as a vehicle for new or modified products or services. For example, Nike or Puma moves into clothing. Or Honda moves into chain saws. Or Sony moves into moviemaking. That's brand extension. But how far can you extend a brand? How many different products can you attach to a brand before it begins to lose its meaning? That's brand dilution.

One major difference between the Bible and a brand is that the Bible is not owned or controlled by a company or institution. It can't be trademarked or copyrighted (although proprietary translations can be). No one can restrict its extensions in the consumer world. The only check on what new and modified products get attached to it is the market. Its "brand extension," if you will, is a matter of consumer vote. And so the extension continues ad infinitum, to the point of absolute brand dilution. Biblical liquidation.

Type's Setting

The larger setting in which all this is happening is the twilight of the bibliographic regime of print culture and the dawning of the digital revolution. Traditional books like the one you're reading (if, in fact, you're reading this book on pages bound between two covers) are losing ground as the dominant medium for reading and writing. In the context of the digital revolution, cultural understandings of literary media are undergoing radical transformations.

The digital revolution began with the convergence of three inventions in the 1980s. First, personal computers with common software platforms made sharing documents, software, and other content easy. Second, digitization brought together widely varied analog media (texts, sounds, still images, videos) into a common, easily interchangeable electronic format based on a binary code, allowing for the creation of new works that incorporate older media within them. Third, new communication technologies developed networks that connected computers to one another, to larger remote servers, and, most importantly, to the potentially limitless network of the World Wide Web, which runs on the Internet. Taken together, the convergence of these three inventions is radically transforming the ways we communicate and interact on every level, from the local to the global.

This media revolution means something much more significant for reading and writing than putting the text of books into digital form and reading it on a backlit screen. It's not a simple conversion or supplement to print. What McLuhan wrote about the Gutenberg revolution is equally apt with regard to the digital revolution: it is no more an addition to print culture than the motorcar was an addition to the horse. Books within print culture fostered what Walter J. Ong described as a sense of fixity, closure, and self-containment. Once it appeared in a book, it had been finalized. In the emerging networked, digital media culture, by contrast, everything is editable, movable, cut-copy-and-pastable. There's no reaching a state of completion. Moreover, the line between inside and outside becomes fuzzy, if it doesn't disappear altogether. Texts are constantly being connected, disconnected, and reconnected to other texts. The word "hypertextual" aptly captures this new media experience: "hyper" means excessive, overflowing. Hypertext Markup Language, or HTML, is the language of interactive connectivity that allows Web designers to embed links and other objects into the main text. Thereby a text can become linked to other texts, and so on. The World Wide Web is fundamentally hypertextual, expanding and overflowing from link to link indefinitely. Reading and writing in this new media environment is open, interactive, and fluid in ways book culture could never be. Value is created not simply by individual authors but collaboratively by communities of reading writers and writing readers.

Suffice it to say that the end of print culture and the rise of a digital, networked media culture means the end of the book as we know it. And the end of the book as we know it cannot be divorced from the end of the Word, The Book of books, as we know it.

Distress Crop

There was a grand old grapefruit tree in the far corner of our backyard in St. Petersburg, Florida. Decades earlier, the land now covered in a patchwork of colorful little stucco houses had been a citrus orchard, and I'm sure that our old tree had been there since then. Its dark, thick limbs reached almost to the middle of the yard, and our kids played on it almost as much as they did on the swing set.

A couple years after we moved in, our beloved tree appeared to be getting sick. Its bark began to peel away. The leaves on many of its branches yellowed and fell. It produced fewer and fewer fruit each year. Still, it looked like its decline would be slow and gradual, and that it would continue to provide enough grapefruit to meet our daily allowance of vitamin C and keep us in happy-hour cocktails for a long time to come.

Then, one year, it produced an unexpectedly huge load of fruit, several times even its healthiest yield. Clumps of grapefruits weighed down its tired old branches like giant clusters of yellow grapes. Our family couldn't eat, juice, and give away enough to keep up.

A year later, it was dead.

I learned from my dad, a retired forester, that our tree's huge, premortem crop was called a "distress crop." When a fruit tree is under severe stress, whether in the later stages of disease or facing a fatal climate change, it puts out a distress crop before dying. Sick unto death, it redirects its resources from growth and foliage production to seed production, even to the point of depleting its own root system of necessary nutrients.

I suggest that something similar is going on with the Bible business. Its boom is not a sign of the survival of the old-growth book trade or the Bible as we know it, flying in the face of the fatal climate changes all around. It may look like a bumper crop of Bibles, but it's not. It's a distress crop.

To a point, fundamentalist-leaning critics and I agree about what the Bible business is doing to the Bible. By reinventing it in an ever-widening variety of things and words, all marketed as the one and only Word of God, these publishers are devaluing the very thing they're selling. I disagree, however, about what exactly is being sold. As I argued in the last chapter, what the Bible business is trading on is not the Bible itself, but rather the cultural icon of the Bible. In fact, as we've seen, Bible publishers are distracting readers from authentic engagement with the Bible itself. It's not about selling the Bible for all it's worth but about selling the icon for all it's worth.

Which is why I feel fine. I have no interest in rescuing the Word as we know it from the Bible business. I welcome publishers' unwitting deconstruction of it.

In fact, I am an active contributor in that process. In 2009 I published a book called *Biblical Literacy* that was a cross between a Bible and a book about the Bible. About half of it is comprised of selections of the Bible's "greatest cultural hits," those stories from the Hebrew Bible and New Testament that enjoy heavy rotation in mainstream culture outside the church — the stories that everyone, religious or not, should know. The other half is my own writing — introductory essays, brief lead-ins to the selections, callouts, and other "extras." But these various "supplementary" bits and pieces don't serve to shore up the iconic idea of the Bible or preserve its sacred capital. Rather, they draw attention to those elements that call that idea into question. Is this book a Bible — *the* Bible? Sort of, but not really, I hope.

I welcome Bible projects that contribute even more ambitiously to its deconstruction. The best recent example is the *Bible Illuminated,* a large-format, glossy art-magazine Bible published in two volumes (Old and New Testaments) by a media-savvy Swedish company called Illuminated World. Started by advertising genius Dag Söderberg and a group of religiously diverse colleagues interested in exploring new formats that would attract a new generation of readers to the Bible and other ancient religious texts, the *Bible Illuminated* is as far from Biblezines as Stockholm is from Nashville. The mission of this project is "to present traditional things in a non-traditional way" in order to "drive an emotional reaction and get people to think, discuss, and share," and thereby to "trigger bigger moral questions."

Bible Illuminated was first published in Sweden in 2007. It was hugely successful, expanding the country's Bible market by 50 percent without cannibalizing traditional Bible sales. The first volume in English, titled *The Book, New Testament,* appeared in 2008, and the second, *The Book, Old Testament,* is planned for 2011. The text is the American Bible Society's Good News Translation, printed four columns per page, without notes or commentary, and without verse numbers. Interspersed throughout its pages are visually rich, provocative photographic images.

The relations between the images and their biblical contexts are suggestive but not at all obvious. Sometimes, a nearby biblical passage, highlighted in a yellow box in the main text, will appear on the same page as the image, almost as a caption. Under an image from the 1970s of Arnold Schwarzenegger flexing his bicep, for example, is a caption from Paul's first letter to the Corinthians: "You should not fool yourself. If any of you think that you are wise by this world's standards, you should become a fool, in order to be really wise." On another is a low-angle shot of a young boy pointing a handgun directly at the camera, accompanied by this saying of Jesus from the Gospel of Matthew: "Do not think that I have come to bring peace to the world. No,

I did not come to bring peace, but a sword." In its creative, provocative, often intensely ambiguous interplay of word and image, the *Bible Illuminated* undermines readerly expectations of the Bible. It "illuminates" in a way that turns the icon of the Bible inside out, provoking new questions about the Bible and, in the process, defamiliarizing readers with what has become all too familiar.

Behold Your God

The life of faith can often feel like wandering in the wilderness, as it was for the Hebrew people after the exodus. Where are we? Where are we going? Where is God in all this? Are we going to be abandoned out here? In response to the anxieties of the Hebrews, weary of insecure, day-to-day uncertainty, Aaron fashioned a golden calf. "Behold your god," he declared, offering them something solid in place of Moses's God, whose presence with them was not often easy to discern or even trust. The idea of the Bible as a divine guidebook, a map for getting through the terra incognita of life, is our golden calf. It's a substitute for the wilderness wandering that the life of faith necessarily entails. And the Bible business is selling it for all it's worth. "Behold your god"; that is, God's Word made flesh, bound between two covers, incarnation by publication. No more guessing. No more wondering. No more wandering.

We sometimes hear people accuse fundamentalist Christians of "bibliolatry," worshiping the Bible as an idol in place of God. Be that as it may, it's not what I'm talking about. An idol is an iconic image that stands in for something else — usually something that's harder to pin down, to be clear about, to control. God, for example. When I say we've made an idol of the Bible, I don't mean that we've idolized the Bible itself, as a stand-in for God; I mean that our iconic idea of the Bible as God's Word incarnate is an idol that stands in for the Bible itself, which is no such concrete, black-and-white thing.

Like Aaron, Bible publishers are responding to a felt need. In an effort to give the people what they want, they produce Bibles that better approximate the iconic idea. Which is part of the reason biblical literacy is declining even while Bible sales are rising: people are reading all the value-adding extras more than they're reading the biblical literature itself. After all, those extras seem more biblical.

I see no ill intentions among Bible-publishing companies, any more than I do in Aaron. I've found no fat cats in smoke-filled rooms conspiring to exploit the cultural icon of the Bible for all it's worth. Some within the industry are more than a little uneasy about going too far in proliferating the Bible in too many different forms and formats. But most clearly think it's a win-win situation. Selling more Bibles means putting the Bible in more hands means spreading the Word. They don't see themselves in the endgame of the evangelical dilemma of preservation versus popularization. They don't believe that the medium is the message. True to their neo-evangelical heritage, they believe that the message, the Word, transcends whatever new media is used to spread it.

Some may say I'm naive. Maybe, on some more or less conscious level, many Bible publishers have come to agree with McLuhan. Maybe they got his message, took it to heart, but then tucked it discreetly away in the back of their Bibles (or maybe in Numbers, where few would look). Maybe they are far from denial about the twilight of print culture, or about the inextricability of medium and message, and in fact are intentionally selling off the Bible's sacred capital before there isn't any left. Maybe, but I doubt it. In any case, the fruit of their labors is proving McLuhan right.

5

What Would Jesus Read?

F ACED WITH THE SCENARIO I've presented in the last two chapters, one's first response might be to call for a back-to-basics campaign. Things have gotten out of hand, clearly. We need to get back to the original, fully concentrated Bible. Back to "that old-time religion" some of us used to sing about in Bible camp. "It was good for the Hebrew children . . . It was good for Christ's disciples . . . It's good enough for me." After all, behind these many newfangled Bibles with all their varied translations, supplements, and forms, there must be a pure source, an origin from which they all descended, the Adam of all Bibles.

It's a reasonable assumption. But it's nonetheless wrong. There is no single, unadulterated Bible, no pristine original, at the base of this crazy biblical family tree. In fact, the very idea of the Bible as a fixed canon of scriptures bound into a single book, not to mention believed by many to be the literal, divinely authored Word of God, would have been completely unfamiliar, indeed inconceivable, not only to Jesus and his disciples but also to the first few centuries of Christians.

To begin to realize just how foreign such an idea would have been, let's try to reconstruct the scriptural culture of the early

Christians, asking not only how they interpreted their Scriptures, but also how and where they were actually read, how they were copied, published, and cared for, and what they looked and felt like.

Jesus Sings

We begin with a story that many early Christians knew and shared about Jesus's own relationship to Scripture:

> And he came to Nazareth, where he had been brought up, and entered the synagogue, in keeping with his custom on the day of Sabbath, and stood up to read. The scroll of the prophet Isaiah was handed to him and, after unrolling the scroll, he found the place where it was written,
>
> > The spirit of the Lord is upon me,
> > > because of the fact that he has anointed me
> > > > to preach good news to the poor;
> > he has sent me out to herald relief to the captives
> > > and recovery of sight to the blind,
> > > > to send out those who are broken in relief,
> > > > to herald the acceptable year of the Lord.
>
> And after rolling up the scroll and returning it to the attendant, he sat down. All eyes in the synagogue were intent on him. Then he began to speak to them: "Today this scripture has been fulfilled in your hearing" (Luke 4:16–21; my translation).

This is how the Gospel of Luke marks the beginning of Jesus's public ministry, with his reading and interpretation from the prophet Isaiah in his hometown synagogue. In fact, this is the first time in this Gospel that we see Jesus interacting with other people as an adult.

The people gathered are initially impressed by his reading from Isaiah and his proclamation that the time of liberation described therein is at hand, "fulfilled in your hearing." They ask each other, "Isn't this Joseph's son?" Apparently they've heard about great things he's done in the surrounding area: teaching in other synagogues, and perhaps performing healings. But Jesus's next words preempt any hopes they might have had for similarly mighty works back home, and soon the good feeling of the homecoming turns sour.

"You will probably tell me the proverb, 'Physician, attend to yourself. What we have heard happened in Capernaum make happen here too, in your own homeland.'" Without giving them even a moment to respond, he recites another parable as his answer to the first: "Truly I say to you, no prophet is acceptable in his own homeland." Then he tells two stories from Scripture about other prophets, Elijah and Elisha, who performed their miracles not at home in Israel but elsewhere. These words infuriate the crowd, now turned mob. They take him outside and try to throw him headlong off a cliff. He escapes their clutches and slips away unharmed.

This is a very familiar story to most Christians. Apart from the birth and infancy narratives, regularly remembered in Christmas pageants, it's probably the most well-known story in the Gospel of Luke. For many of us, it's so familiar that we tell it and hear it as though we were actually there. It's like a family story about a notable ancestor. We've heard it so many times that we begin to insert ourselves as eyewitnesses. We're not so different from those medieval patrons of paintings depicting Jesus reading from an illuminated Bible book to a crowd of themselves gathered under the arch of a huge cathedral. Unwittingly, we take the content of what Jesus says and how the people react out of its ancient context and put it into our own world, as though Jesus is standing at a church pulpit on Sunday morning reading from a big, black, leather-bound King James Version Bible.

But have you ever stopped to think about *what* Jesus was actually reading? I don't mean just what words, but what the thing was that he held in his hands and read from. What did it look like? Feel like? And *how* did he read it? Handle it? How did he sound when he read it? What was the scriptural culture in which he moved and breathed and had his being?

"The scroll of the prophet Isaiah was handed to him . . ." The Greek word for "scroll" is *biblíon*. That's what Jesus would have had handed to him. Later, during the transition from scrolls to books, *biblíon* came to be used for both media. Later still, as books became the dominant medium for literature, it came to mean "book," and most of Christendom forgot that the Scriptures now bound in books began as scrolls.

Most English translations have perpetuated the anachronistic image of Jesus opening and reading from a book. The King James Version of 1611 had "the book of the prophet Esaias" delivered to Jesus. So did the American Standard Version, the New American Standard Version, and the Revised Standard Version, among many others. So it's not surprising that so many illustrations of this story throughout much of Christian history, including the popular icon of Christ the Teacher, picture Jesus holding a Bible book.

In fact, it's highly unlikely that Jesus ever saw, let alone read, a book in his life. He almost certainly never saw a version of Isaiah, or any other Jewish Scripture, in book form. What Jesus would have been handed was a scroll. In early first-century Jewish Palestine, as throughout the Greco-Roman world, the scroll was the exclusive medium for literature.

Most scrolls were made from papyrus, a tall reed that grew in marshy regions along the Nile and in the plantations of paper makers. In his *Natural History,* the first-century naturalist Pliny

This sixth- or seventh-century icon of Christ Pantocrator ("ruler of all") from Saint Catherine's Monastery in Sinai, Egypt, where tradition holds that God appeared to Moses from the burning bush, is an early example of what became a common image of Jesus Christ holding a Bible book. The historical Jesus, however, never saw, let alone held, any such thing. *By permission of Saint Catherine's Monastery, Sinai, Egypt*

the Elder described how papyrus scrolls were made during his time. Paper makers cut thin strips of the plant's pith, laid them out in two crosswise layers, and pressed them flat. The pith's natural juices served as glue to fuse the layers together. Once the material dried, they sanded both sides with pumice, polished them with shell, and cut them into sheets. The recto side, on which the grain ran horizontally, was best for writing. These sheets, which commonly measured about ten inches high by about seven inches wide, were then glued together along their edges and rolled with the recto on the inside. The typical roll included about twenty sheets and was about eleven feet long. These rolls were cut to shorter lengths or glued together into longer ones in order to accommodate different text lengths.

Although papyrus was the most common material for scrolls, Jesus would probably have been reading one made from parchment, which would eventually become the normative form for scrolls of Jewish Scripture. To make parchment scrolls, animal skins (usually calves, sheep, or goats) were soaked in lime solution, washed, and dried on stretchers. Then the outside was shaved and the inside was rubbed smooth with a stone or bone. Although the hair side (verso) was more absorbent of ink, the flesh side (recto) was smoother and thus the preferred side for writing. After being whitened with chalk, the skins were cut into sheets, sewn together, and rolled into scrolls with the recto on the inside. Each sheet was made from one whole side of an animal's hide, cut lengthwise along the spine and middle. So, for example, a scroll made from eight parchment sheets would have required four whole animals.

Most scrolls in the ancient world were between twenty and thirty feet long. Much longer and they were hard to handle. In fact, texts were written to accommodate this general standard of length, once again illustrating the inseparability of medium and message.

In our story, Jesus was handed the scroll of the prophet Isaiah. What would that have looked and felt like? Probably a lot like the scroll of Isaiah that was discovered among the Dead Sea Scrolls at Qumran, known as 1QIsa-a (Cave 1, Qumran, Isaiah, copy "a"). This "Great Isaiah Scroll" dates to the first century BCE and could well have still been in use by the community at Qumran, not far from Jerusalem, during Jesus's time. It's a parchment scroll, made from seventeen sheets of sheepskin that were sewn together with linen thread. That's eight and a half sheep! It's a little over ten inches high and about twenty-four feet long. The text of Isaiah is divided into fifty-four columns, each about four inches wide, separated by narrow margins. The work appears to have been done by a single scribe using a thin piece of reed with a chisel-shaped point dipped in an ink solution made from lamp-oil soot. In some spots you can see vertical lines that were drawn to keep the margins straight and consistent, and horizontal lines

Columns 32 and 33 of the Great Isaiah Scroll (1QIsa-a), discovered in the first cave at Qumran in 1948. The scroll measures about ten inches high and twenty-four feet long and was made from seventeen sheets of sheepskin. Dating to the first century BCE, the scroll might still have been in use during the time of Jesus. *Photograph © John C. Trever, Ph.D.; digital image by James E. Trever* that served as writing guides. Although the Hebrew text is set very closely together, with little space between words, it has been laid out in paragraphs, so a reader can find a particular passage more easily.

Where would Jesus have read? In a Jewish synagogue among fellow Jews. Jesus and all his disciples were born and raised Jewish in Jewish Palestine. They remained so throughout their lives. Jesus's teaching is not comprehensible except as interpretation of Jewish tradition, especially Jewish Scripture.

We know very little for sure about the architecture of synagogues or what happened in them during the early first century CE. Most information about them comes from the second century, well after the destruction of the Temple (70 CE), a time when their organization and liturgy were being standardized. In fact, this story in Luke, probably written in the 80s CE, is the earliest known description of a Shabbat synagogue service. Nonetheless, most agree that the synagogue was the center of Jewish life in Palestine and throughout the Roman Empire.

Although there was probably variety from community to community, there was likely a typical order of events. At the center of the service was the reading and interpretation of Scripture, especially (if not exclusively) the Torah. Communal study of Scripture gave shape to the religious community.

What might his hometown synagogue have looked like? There's no way to know in any detail. Many synagogues during Jesus's time were probably simple gathering places set aside in people's houses for communal Scripture reading, study, and prayer on Shabbat. Perhaps some had benches for people to sit on. Perhaps there was a particular spot from which a leader would read and instruct. There must have been a means of storing the scrolls, probably a portable round wooden chest, or *capsa*. As was typical for nonreligious scroll collections in the Greco-Roman world, the scrolls probably had identification tabs on their ends. Such a crude library would have included some or all of the Torah scrolls as well as some of the Prophets and other writings, such as the Psalms. It might have included more than one copy of a text. It probably would not have included all the texts now in the canon of Jewish Scriptures, and it might well have included some texts that were not part of that canon. Some, at least, would have been written in biblical Hebrew. Others might have been in Aramaic, the lingua franca of Jewish people in Palestine and Mesopotamia during that time — the language spoken by Jesus and everyone he knew. There were, moreover, different versions of Jewish Scriptures circulating in both languages. In addition to various Hebrew versions from which our modern-day Bibles descend, others came from what is now known as the Samaritan Pentateuch, a version of the Torah identified later with the Jewish sect of Samaritans (a few hundred of them live in Israel to this day). Aramaic versions (Targums) retold Scripture in expanded forms, often revising and elaborating on their source material extensively.

Outside Palestine, in the Jewish Diaspora, where Greek was the Jewish vernacular, Jews used the Septuagint, or "Seventy," a name for the collective Scriptures that refers to the legend that seventy-two Jewish scholars, working independently, produced the identical Greek translation of the Torah for Ptolemy II in the mid-third century BCE. That legend is betrayed by the fact that there were different versions of these scrolls in circulation. More likely there were multiple Greek translations from different Hebrew versions over the course of centuries (translations of the Torah among the earliest).

The Nazareth synagogue library might also have included what scholars today call *testimonia*, which were short anthologies of snippets taken from other scriptures. In some cases, these anthologies were organized around a particular theme. A good example is 4Q Testimonia, also found among the Dead Sea Scrolls. Dating to the first century BCE, this single page of parchment includes three Hebrew biblical quotations (two of them from something close to the proto-Samaritan version Torah, mentioned earlier, but none of them exactly like any known version) and a fourth quotation from a text known as the Psalms of Joshua, also discovered at Qumran. Taken together, the excerpts center on messianic expectations and an imminent time of disaster. Needless to say, there was no closed canon among Jewish communities, nor were there established standard versions of any particular Jewish scriptural texts.

How would Jesus have read an Isaiah scroll such as the one described here? The story says he stood to read. This is not an impromptu move, made as the spirit leads, but a formal, ritual act, as is the attendant's presentation of the scroll. Of course, like many ritual acts, this one is also practical: it's much easier for a reader to project and be heard clearly by a congregation when she or he is standing.

Think about the scroll itself. Unrolled, it's about twenty-four feet long. There's a lectern on which to set it and hold it open with both hands. "He found the place where it was written . . ." That place is toward the end of Isaiah, about twenty-two feet through the scroll, well into the seventh sheep. But he doesn't have to roll his way through the whole thing to find that place. Imagine how long that would take! Remember, searching for a particular passage in a big scroll is not like flipping through a book. We can presume, then, that the scroll was already rolled to roughly that particular place when the attendant handed it to him. That was probably where the previous reader left off.

So let's imagine that he's finally found the right spot in Isaiah. He's holding the two rolls several inches apart so that he has a clear view of the passage framed between them on the lectern. He opens his mouth and begins to read. How would that have sounded? Like music. Jesus would have chanted the passage in an elevated, melodic style. He would have sung it into speech.

The Jewish Talmud quotes Rabbi Johanan sharply criticizing "anyone who reads the scripture without tunefulness." Although this text comes from a later period, scholars agree that first-century Judaism had already developed a formal, rhythmic, melodic style of chanting Scripture during public readings.

In early Judaism, as in other ancient religious traditions, the written word and its oral chanting were interdependent. Scriptures were written and copied with the assumption that they would be chanted, and that their meaning would be made clear through such melodic ritual performance. They needed to be intoned, especially given that most texts were written without accents or punctuation. In Greek texts, there were no spaces between words. Chanting a text was an interpretive act, insofar as it provided the pauses, flows, cadences, accents, and so on that gave it meaning when it was heard. To an extent, the words on the page determined how they should be properly chanted; chanting was in service of clarifying the meaning of a text. That goes without saying. Yet the one chanting would also *make* certain meanings, and not others, by the way she or he chose to give it voice. Chanting Scripture was a public performance that both drew out and generated meaning.

In fact, cantillated, musical reading was the primary mode of reading throughout the Greco-Roman world. Literacy rates were low (probably around 10 percent), and very few people owned their own collections of texts. But that did not mean that this was not a literary culture. What it meant was that literature needed to be shared publicly, through oral performances and discussions called *recitatios*. When a poet had written a volume of poetry, for example, she or he would have read it aloud to a group of friends, patrons, or even the general public. And the mode of reading would have been prosodic, tuneful chanting.

"Today this scripture has been fulfilled in your hearing," Jesus proclaimed. "Fulfilled," or, more literally, "filled out," completed, made meaningful, in the moment of its hearing. What does this suggest about where the "sacred capital" of Scripture resided in Jesus's own Jewish scriptural culture, in which there was no set canon or standard version of any particular text? Where was sacred capital invested? As this story suggests, and as historical research affirms, it resided in the live *event* of sharing Scripture, of the community's hearing. This hearing, moreover, involved more than the simple reading of Scripture alone; equally important was interpretation, making meaning of it in the present moment.

Christianity Before the Bible

Ironically, the writer of this story and the early Christians who shared it were not present with Jesus to *hear* him proclaim this Scripture's fulfillment. They were out of hearing range by a good half century. The Gospel of Luke was probably written in the early- or mid-80s CE. Like the other Gospels, it was originally anonymous. Its attribution to Luke, mentioned as a companion of Paul in his letter to the Colossians, was made more than a century later. But whoever the author was, we can be sure she or he did not hear Jesus read from the Isaiah scroll, in his hometown synagogue or anywhere else. The Gospel's opening address admits as much:

> Since many have undertaken to set down an orderly account of the events that have been fulfilled among us, just as they were handed on to us by those who from the beginning were eyewitnesses and

servants of the word, I too decided, after investigating everything
carefully from the very first, to write an orderly account for you,
most excellent Theophilus . . . (Luke 1:1–4)

The writer never saw or heard Jesus. She or he was not one of the
"eyewitnesses" who handed the stories down to later generations
of Christians.

Note, moreover, that the writer is fully aware that there were
"many" other gospels in circulation. And this one was by no
means a simple reiteration of any of them. On the contrary, the
writer readily acknowledges that this is one interpretation among
many others, based on research in various sources of information,
both written and oral.

Although we don't know who wrote it, we know to whom it
was originally addressed: "most excellent Theophilus" (Luke 1:4).
This may refer to an individual named Theophilus, who may or
may not have been Jewish. Many Jewish people in the Greco-
Roman world had Greek names. In fact, a Jew named Theophilus
served as high priest of the Jerusalem Temple from 37–41 CE. Or
perhaps this name, which is a Greek compound of *theos,* "God,"
and *philos,* "love," meant that this Gospel was written to anyone
who loves God and might be interested in the story of Jesus and
the early Jesus movement that was beginning to spread and grow.
Or maybe it was a pseudonym for a patron who helped publish
and promote the work. In any case, the reason we now have it in
the New Testament canon is that it eventually reached well beyond its originally intended audience into other early Christian
communities.

So, with the story of Jesus's homecoming reading of Isaiah, we
are looking at a story that is as much about the scriptural culture
of early Christians as it is about the scriptural culture of Jesus.
The world of Jesus and the world of his followers over half a cen-

tury later are tangled together in this story. What we see here is how early Christians from the late first century remembered how Jesus understood and used Jewish Scriptures.

It's more than appropriate, therefore, to ask not only how Jesus would have read the Isaiah scroll in his hometown synagogue, but also how this story might have been experienced in an early Christian community around the end of the first century or beginning of the second. What was their scriptural culture? What and how did early Christians read about Jesus reading?

Imagine a setting similar to that of a synagogue. It might well be a Shabbat service. Earlier, a passage from Jewish Scripture, the community's canonical core, was read and interpreted. Now, a woman stands to read another text, a gospel, in the form of a small book, or *codex*, a new medium that's increasingly popular among Christians. She places it on the lectern and opens it, running her fingers across the thin vertical grains of dried papyrus. The text is in Greek capital letters, strung together without punctuation or spaces. Practice has made her familiar with it, and she finds the place where Jesus enters his hometown synagogue on Shabbat, according to his custom. She begins to read. Like Jesus in the story, she chants. She sings it into speech, bringing to life Jesus's melodic proclamation of Isaiah's proclamation. Fulfilled, filled out, made newly meaningful, "in your hearing."

That's a fiction, of course. But it's historical fiction.

The Gospel of Luke was originally written in Koine ("common") Greek, which had been the lingua franca in the Greco-Roman world since Alexander the Great, and remained so throughout the Roman Empire until Latin took hold in the West during the third century. Outside Palestine, in the Diaspora, members of the early Jesus movement, like other Jewish communities, would have used Koine Greek, and their versions of Jewish Scriptures would have been Greek Septuagint texts. Although the early communities who read and shared this Gospel probably would have included Gentiles as well as Jews, the Gospel of Luke takes for granted that its hearers were familiar with Jewish customs and Scriptures, especially the Torah, the Prophets, and the Psalms. In all these respects, early Christian communities would not have looked very different, if at all, from other Diaspora Jewish communities. The Jesus movement was simply another form of Jewish diversity, another school of Jewish interpretation trying to make sense of the past, present, and future in light of Scripture and tradition.

Indeed, Jewish identity is very important and highly valued in the Gospel of Luke. The text takes pains in its early chapters to establish Jesus's authority in terms of his Jewish identity as an interpreter of Scriptures. It tells the story of how, at only twelve, he garnered an audience of rabbis in the Temple who, after three days of discussion, "were astonished at his understanding and answers." And right before the story of his synagogue homecoming, he had spent forty days in the wilderness, during which he refuted each of the devil's temptations with a quotation from the book of Deuteronomy in the Torah. In Luke, Jesus's primary idiom is Scripture.

Here again, as with Jewish synagogue communities, we are talking about an oral scriptural culture. Recall that literacy in the Greco-Roman population was probably around 10 percent, never higher than 20 percent. Some believe that it might have been lower still within some early Christian communities. Yet reading and interpreting Jewish Scripture was central (gospels and other early Christian texts would not have had the same authoritative status), and knowledge of scriptural content was a hallmark of Christian identity. Scripture was chanted and discussed aloud, in community.

The centrality of Jewish Scriptures among Christians did

not fade as Christianity and Judaism gradually became divorced from one another. The artwork in the underground Christian funerary complexes of the Roman catacombs suggests that, even as late as the third century, Jewish Scriptures remained the foundational Scriptures for Christians. All the biblical illustrations from that period are drawn from Jewish Scriptures (Abraham's near sacrifice of Isaac, Daniel in the lion's den, and Jonah in the whale, for example).

It's possible that some very early Christian communities had buildings dedicated exclusively to their gatherings for worship and study, but no solid archaeological evidence survives. More likely, early Christians met in "house churches," spaces set aside in people's homes. Two of Paul's letters, written in the middle of the first century, mention Prisca and Aquila, a couple who helped spread the Jesus movement to Gentiles, "and the church in their house" (Romans 16:5 and 1 Corinthians 16:19). This referred not to an architecturally modified space in their house but to the group of believers who met there. It's very possible that the house of Jesus's friends Mary and Martha, central in the Gospel of Luke as well as John, was also among the earliest house churches. And, as these two examples suggest, there's every reason to believe that early house churches would have been hosted and led by women as well as men.

In early Christian house churches, as in synagogues, the public reading *and interpretation* of Scripture was a central religious activity for the community. Interpretation was not simply a matter of trying to ascertain passively the meaning of a text. It was active and creative. Clear evidence of this fact is found in the early Christian literature that we find in the New Testament itself. Paul's tremendous influence on the shape, scope, and theology of the early Jesus movement was based on his scriptural interpretations. And these interpretations were often quite creative, very like the Jewish rabbinical tradition of *midrash,* a Hebrew word meaning textual interpretation (from the verb *darash,* "pursue" or "seek").

Consider, for example, Paul's use of passages from Torah to argue that one is justified before God by faith rather than by works in his letter to the Galatians. Central to his argument is a passage from Deuteronomy 21 that concerns, in its original context, what to do with the body of someone who has been executed by hanging from a tree. It is commanded there that the body not be left on the tree overnight but buried on the day of execution, because "anyone hung on a tree is under God's curse. You must not defile the land that the LORD your God is giving you for possession." The text thus seems to be concerned to avoid defiling holy land with an untended, accursed corpse. Paul takes this passage out of that context and reads it as a reference to Christ's crucifixion, since Christ, too, was hanged from a tree of sorts (albeit not overnight). Thus, Paul says, Christ has become accursed under the law for the sake of saving others who are otherwise accursed, including Gentiles who stake their faith in him. Far from a simple explication of Torah, early Christian interpretations such as this one constructed ingenious new meanings in new contexts. Indeed, this is how both the Jewish Scriptures and the New Testament developed over the centuries, as layers of interpretation built on previous layers. The Bible is interpretation all the way down.

"Today this scripture has been fulfilled in your hearing." To be sure, the earliest Christian hearers of the Gospel of Luke were already well beyond the hearing range of Jesus's reading and interpretation. By the time the words "in your hearing" were canted by a reader in their own community, that shared event with Jesus is already history. Yet the event of their own fresh hearing of the Scripture becomes a new moment of fulfillment, a new horizon of meaning. Here again, sacred capital resides not exclusively in the text — either that of Isaiah or that of the Gospel of Luke. The sacredness of the text is as much about who's reading it and what they do with it as about what it is and does.

No Original

What Scriptures might early house churches have had in their collections? The answer would have varied greatly from one to the next, depending on practical matters concerning what texts in what languages were available for copying. It also would have depended on the theological orientations of particular communities. Which Scriptures best spoke to the interests and practices of which communities? For indeed there was a great diversity of Christianities during the first three centuries, and the differences among them were reflected in the differences in their libraries. In both forms of Christianity and forms of Scripture, there was variety from the get-go.

The core of most early Christian collections would have been scrolls of Jewish Scripture, including Torah — though perhaps not all five scrolls — some of the Prophets, and other writings such as Psalms or Daniel. Outside Palestine, these were usually written in Greek, as they were in many synagogues in the Jewish Diaspora. They probably also had brief *testimonia* much like the Jewish *testimonia* described earlier, drawing together series of brief quotations from Jewish Scriptures believed to pertain to their emerging Christology of Jesus (imagine a page of search engine results or a string of related "snippets" on Google Books). In fact, some argue that early Christian writers like Paul and the authors of the Gospels used such documents when quoting Scripture. Perhaps this is why the Gospel of Mark, for example, begins by quoting a pair of passages from Isaiah and Malachi as though they were a single passage from Isaiah.

House-church communities also would have had other early Christian texts that were gaining importance and authority as interpretations of the community's faith in light of Jewish Scripture. Likely they would have had copies of letters attributed to Paul, Clement, Peter, James, Ignatius of Antioch, or Barnabas, or perhaps excerpts of such letters. They might have had apocalyptic texts, such as the Apocalypse of John, which is now part of the New Testament canon, or the Apocalypse of Peter, which is not. Perhaps they had the Gospel of Thomas or some similar early collection of sayings of Jesus. They probably would have had at least one gospel, including perhaps the Gospel of Luke and its second volume, the Acts of the Apostles, which tells of the early Jesus movement's growth after Jesus's death and resurrection, including its expansion among Gentiles and Jews outside Palestine. Still other Aramaic-speaking Christian communities would have preferred an Aramaic gospel text, such as the Gospel of the Nazareans, which has survived only as translated quotations in other non-Aramaic texts. By the late second century or so, moreover, some communities in the West were using Latin translations, and some in the East were reading Scriptures in Syriac, an eastern dialect of Aramaic. And by the third century, Egyptian communities were using translations in Coptic, which is essentially the Egyptian language written in an adapted Greek alphabet. A community might also have had a harmony of the four Gospels and other sources, such as the popular *Diatessaron* done by Tatian, a Christian with Gnostic tendencies who died around 185 CE. Sounds a little like what some Bible publishers are doing today, doesn't it?

Who knows what other texts these early Christian communities might have had? Some texts have survived in what eventually became the New Testament canon. Others, including the now famous Coptic translation of the Gospel of Thomas, a collection of 114 sayings of Jesus that may in fact predate the New Testament Gospels, have been discovered only recently. Still others we only know by references or brief quotations in other texts that are bent on refuting their value, and that obviously succeeded in doing so. But many, many others are lost without a trace. Indeed, the texts that we now have from this period are but the tip of an iceberg of early Christian writings that were important to a tremendous variety of Christianities.

Nor do we have originals of any of these texts, including those now in the Christian canon. There are many variants among the more than fifty-three hundred early New Testament manuscripts and manuscript fragments that survived in the Greek language alone (not to mention early Latin, Syriac, and Coptic translations). The oldest of them (from the second, third, and fourth centuries) are the most divergent. Granted, many of the variants among different manuscripts are not terribly significant. But a good number are. Some of these differences were no doubt the result of accidents, but some clearly were not. Early manuscripts of the Gospel of Mark, for example, offer four different endings. In the Greco-Roman world of the first and second centuries, long before copyright laws, works of literature quickly lost touch with their authors. They were copied, edited, supplemented, and distributed through decentralized, informal networks in ways that the writers could not anticipate or control.

Before the discovery of the Dead Sea Scrolls, which include many Hebrew biblical manuscripts dating between 250 BCE and 68 CE, most scholars believed that there was not much variation among different copies of the Jewish Scriptures by the time of Jesus and Paul — that the text was pretty much fixed by then. The earliest known copies of Jewish Scriptures in Hebrew dated to the tenth and eleventh centuries CE, and among them the differences were mostly small and insignificant. Taking them as witnesses to the earlier texts from which they were copied, it seemed logical to conclude that these many homogeneous texts must have derived from a common original via a highly accurate scribal tradition. But evidence from the Dead Sea Scrolls seems to contradict this conclusion. Among the hundreds of biblical manuscripts discovered there, many of which are more than a thousand years older than anything scholars had ever seen before, we find not uniformity but diversity, including many significant differences. The logical assumption now is that Jewish Scriptures became more uniform and free of variants over time, as scribes gradually established a more or less standard edition.

There is reason to believe that the copies of Jewish Scriptures used by early Christians were no less varied than they were among Jewish communities. We already mentioned how the Gospel of Mark begins with a quotation that conflates lines from Isaiah and Malachi, attributing them to Isaiah alone. Perhaps that was how the writer's copy of Isaiah looked. Or perhaps the writer drew the quote from a *testimonia* document of scriptural passages believed to contain messianic references. Or perhaps the writer simply drew the quote from memory and wasn't that worried about being altogether accurate. In any case, the Gospels of Matthew and Luke, both of which appear to have used Mark as one of their literary sources, implicitly correct Mark's merging of the two prophetic passages by quoting the passage from Isaiah alone (Matthew 3:3 and Luke 3:4).

As another example, consider the passage from Isaiah that Jesus reads in the Gospel of Luke. It appears to be a quotation from a Greek edition of Isaiah, but it differs significantly from any version of the Septuagint that has survived. The line "he has sent me out to herald relief to the captives" normally appears two chapters earlier in the Septuagint version of Isaiah. Moreover, the phrase "to heal the brokenhearted," which appears in the Septuagint version of Isaiah 61, does not appear in most surviving copies of Luke (some copies do include it as if to correct the original omission). What to make of these differences? Either the Gospel writer felt at liberty to move things around in the process of quoting Isaiah, or was working from a different version of Isaiah, one that has been lost. In either case, we must conclude that the text of Isaiah was far from fixed and changeless among different Christian communities in the late first century.

We're used to picturing the genealogy of a text like a family tree: one original at the base ascending like a single trunk, with copies branching off it, and copies of copies branching off them. And so on throughout the generations. We imagine an original from which all the generations of diversity spring as scribes make revisions and introduce copying errors. But the reverse seems to be the case when it comes to the origins of the Bible: the further you go back in its literary history, the less uniformity there is. Scriptural traditions are rooted, quite literally, in diversity.

No Canon

Nor was there anything like a closed canon of Scriptures among early Christians. Not in the first century, not even in the third or early fourth century. In the second letter to Timothy, we read, "All scripture is inspired by God and is useful for teaching, for reproof, for correction, and for training in righteousness." Does this refer to Paul's own letters as they now appear in the New Testament? Certainly not. No one in the first century could even have imagined such a thing as a New Testament canon, let alone the Bible as we think of it these days. Does it refer to the Gospels? No. The earliest of those wouldn't even be written until long after Paul died. Same with the other writings that eventually made it into the New Testament. No, this passage refers to Jewish Scriptures, probably the Torah and the Prophets. It was not talking about the Bible. There was no such thing.

Likewise when John of Patmos, in an ancient attempt at divine copyright protection written at the end of the book of Revelation (aka the Apocalypse of John), promises plagues of apocalyptic proportions for anyone who dares change a thing in "this book":

> I warn everyone who hears the words of the prophecy of this book [*biblion*]: if anyone adds to them, God will add to that person the plagues described in this book; if anyone takes away from the words of the book of this prophecy, God will take away that person's share in the tree of life and in the holy city, which are described in this book. (Revelation 22:18–19)

This passage is often used to argue that the Bible claims its own authority, that its perfect inerrancy is built in, and that messing with even one jot or tittle of it is grounds for damnation. But just because this writing, originally a scroll (*biblion*, like the scroll of Isaiah that Jesus read), eventually ended up as the last book of the New Testament and thus the Christian Bible doesn't mean that its warning here refers to the whole Bible. "This scroll" (a more accurate and less misleading translation) circulated independently for hundreds of years before it was bound together in a big book along with what eventually became the Christian canon of Scripture. Indeed, its inclusion in the canon was a matter of dispute among many Christian leaders well into the fourth century. And its author could never have even imagined such a thing as the Bible. Not even in his wildest dreams. And some of his dreams were wild indeed, including one in which an angel hands him a little scroll, not to read but to eat. No, this warning refers not to the Bible but to this particular text.

Adding insult to injury, there are significant variants among the earliest surviving manuscripts of Revelation. Although most manuscripts say that the infamous "mark of the beast" is 666, for example, the earliest known copy, which dates to the late third or early fourth century, has 616. Another has 665.

Early Christian Network Society

Imagine: small house-church communities made up of very different populations scattered throughout Palestine and the entire Greco-Roman world; many Jewish, many Gentile, some literate, most illiterate; various groups translating, copying, and disseminating scrolls and codices of Jewish Scriptures, *testimonia,* and early Christian writings, sharing with one another through loose networks and informal patterns of exchange; communities that were more or less marginal to state power and regulation. Different communities inevitably had different collections of texts, different libraries of Scripture. These libraries were never closed or fixed, but were interconnected with the libraries of other communities, so that texts flowed and morphed within larger, noncentralized social networks. Not unlike the emerging digital network culture of today.

It was not until 367 CE, in an Easter letter from Athanasius, Bishop of Alexandria, that we find a list of the twenty-seven writings of the New Testament as they now appear in the Christian canon. Of course, the fact that he wrote this letter did not mean that the canon was effectively closed. Indeed, he admits that he's compelled to write the letter because others are promoting different canons that include additional texts. He thinks those texts are fakes and that their promoters are deceiving and misleading Christian communities. We don't have the other side's point of view in this debate, but we can imagine they beg to differ. In any case, it's clear that the reason Athanasius wrote out his closed canon was that the Scriptures he rejected were being embraced as canonical by other Christian leaders and communities. His letter is proof that, as of 367, the canon was still open.

A few decades before Athanasius wrote his letter, another influential bishop, Eusebius of Caesarea, took a descriptive rather than prescriptive approach to the question of canon. In his *Ecclesiastical History* (325 CE), he made a catalogue of early Christian writings, grouping them according to three categories. First are the "undisputed" writings (*homolegomenon,* "same voice," i.e., unanimous), which, he says, all Christians recognize as authoritative and authentic. Among these are the Gospels of Matthew, Mark, Luke, and John, the Acts of the Apostles (the second volume of Luke), the letters of Paul, the first letter of Peter, and the first letter of John. He also includes the Apocalypse of John (Revelation), "if it seems right" to do so, suggesting that this text's status was less secure among some Christians. Note, moreover, that his list of "undisputed" writings does not include five other writings that eventually became part of the New Testament canon: the second letter of Peter, the second and third letters of John, and the epistles of James, Jude, and Hebrews.

Eusebius's second category is for writings that are "disputed" (*antilegomenon,* "contradicted"), accepted by some but not others. Interestingly, he includes the Apocalypse of John here as well as in the previous category. He also includes the second and third letters of John, the second letter of Peter, the letter of James, and the letter of Jude, all of which eventually became part of the New Testament canon (he doesn't mention Hebrews). Others in this category, however, did not ultimately make the canonical cut: the Shepherd of Hermas, the Apocalypse of Peter, the letter of Barnabas, the Didache (Teachings of the Apostles), the Gospel of the Hebrews, which he acknowledges to be popular among Hebrew-speaking Christians, and the Acts of Paul, which included the very popular short story about Thecla, a woman who abandoned her family and fiancé to follow Paul.

Eusebius's third and final category is for writings that should be rejected as "fictions of heretics." These writings claim to go back to the disciples and earliest Christian leaders, but he considers them to be fakes, insofar as their literary style and theological ideas diverge from those early texts that he considers normative. He offers only a few examples: the Gospel of Peter, the Gospel of Thomas, the Gospel of Matthias, and the Acts of Andrew and John. Apparently there were many others, too many for him to list conveniently. And again, we can be sure that his assessment of them as heretical was itself disputed by those who embraced them in their communities. Otherwise, why mention them at all?

History is usually written by the powerful. Canons too. Eusebius and Athanasius were certainly among the most influential Christian leaders of the fourth century, as Christianity came to be identified with Roman state power under Emperor Constantine and, in the process, developed parallel structures of government and control. They were no doubt instrumental in establishing a narrower theological orthodoxy in what was by then a Christian empire, and in ruling out those Christian texts that did not fit well within that orthodoxy. Yet even during their time, after Christianity had become the religion of the state, three hundred years since Jesus's time, scriptural network cultures continued to thrive, thereby resisting centralized, top-down attempts to close the canon definitively. Roman Christianity had a loose canon at best.

6

The Story of the Good Book

Remembering What's Lost

A massive obelisk towers above the Piazza Santa Maria Maggiore on the Esquiline Hill in Rome. On its tiptop, overlooking the ancient ruins of the Forum and the Colosseum a mile away, stands a most imposing bronze statue of the Blessed Virgin Mary. When I first beheld her, having just huffed up the hill from the Forum, I thought she was an emperor or crusader saint. Broad-shouldered and muscular, she carries the baby Jesus like a rugby ball in her left arm while extending her right hand toward her audience below. Erected in the sixteenth century, it is an imposing image of the church as masculine, patriarchal power.

A stone's throw down the hill from Mary Maggiore is the modest church of Santa Pudenziana, now the Filipino center of the Roman Diocese. One of the oldest churches in Rome, its construction began in the fourth century. Its floor is several feet below the city's modern-day street level, so you have to walk downstairs to the main door. Buried beneath it is another, earlier level of occupation: an ancient Roman complex believed to be the remains of a first- or early-second-century Christian house church. Excavations during the late nineteenth century revealed a series of rooms connected by narrow hallways along with the remains of a thermal bath system. Many of these areas were badly damaged or filled in when the church's foundations were built centuries later. The excavation area has now been deemed structurally unsound and is closed indefinitely.

The docent was kind enough to take me to a poorly lit back area where there were two small holes in the floor that offered partial views of the ancient space. She slid back the wrought-iron grate covering one of them, and I peered down with a flashlight. I saw a small room with a floor of round, flat stones. On one wall was a narrow archway leading I know not where. I looked into the other hole and saw even less, a stone shaft leading down into seemingly bottomless blackness.

What extremely partial windows onto the past! They reveal very little, almost nothing. I tried in vain to imagine life down there, before churches, before cathedrals, before the Holy Roman Empire, before a follower of Jesus could even have imagined such a melding of religious faith and state power so boldly proclaimed by the obelisk of Santa Maria Maggiore.

I did visit other, somewhat more whole, remains of what might have been early house churches in Rome. Beneath the nearby twelfth-century Basilica San Clemente, for example, is an older basilica whose construction dates back to the fourth century. Beneath it are two large complexes of rooms and hallways divided by a narrow alley. In the first century, they probably comprised two separate houses. Legend holds that one of them was the house church of Saint Clement, an influential early church leader and author of a letter that was widely influential among early Christians. One problem with this claim: the only religious space found thus far among the earliest remains is a small, second-century temple dedicated to the service of the Persian god Mithras. Built to resemble a cave, it is a windowless space with a low, arched ceiling and raised benches along the walls where initiates shared ritual meals during services. On the east end is a stone podium on which is carved a depiction of the young, energetic Mithras slaughtering a bull whose tail looks like a shock of wheat, representing springtime fertility. A religion based on rites of initiation, Mithraism was popular in Rome, especially among the military, until the fourth century, when the newly Christianized empire eradicated it.

On the nearby Aventine Hill is the church of Santa Prisca, built over what was long believed to be the first-century house church of Prisca and Aquila, the couple mentioned in Paul's letters and in the book of Acts. In 1934 Augustinian Fathers from the adjacent monastery began excavations in search of remains. What they found was another late-second-century Mithraeum, very similar to the one under San Clemente. Again, no signs of that early Christian community, only of another religious import, which thrived alongside Christianity for centuries.

These and other ancient remains shed no more light on earliest Christianity than do the iron-grated holes in the floor of Santa Pudenziana. More than anything else, they convey the attendance of an indeterminate past. They testify to what has been irrevocably lost. They bear witness to the presence of an absence that shapes us in ways we can never articulate. Being accountable to them means never forgetting what's been forgotten. It also means resisting the temptation to project the present into the silent gaps of the past, pretending that the way we are is the way they were.

Scrolling Down to the Book

In the house churches of the early decades of Christianity, most of the copies of Jewish Scriptures and early Christian writings would have been scrolls and, increasingly by the second century, codices. As we have seen, scrolls were the dominant medium for literature throughout the Greco-Roman world at that time. Codices were used primarily as notebooks for lists and writing practice. They were usually made with one or more wooden pages that were hollowed out and filled with an effaceable surface like wax. Later, as they came to be used for literary works, they were made by stacking sheets of papyrus or parchment together, folding them down the middle, and stitching them together along the fold. So one sheet made two leaves with four pages, and a quire of four sheets would make sixteen pages. These quires could then be stacked together and bound into larger books.

The media revolution of the book was a slow and mostly quiet one. It took a good three centuries. During most of that time, scrolls and codices coexisted. The earliest reference to the use of a codex for literature comes from a Roman poet named Martial who, writing in the 80s CE, recommends that his poems be kept in a small codex with parchment pages. Interestingly, archaeological evidence suggests that early Christian communities may have been among the earliest adopters of the new medium. Most, though not all, surviving Christian manuscripts dating as far back as the second century are papyrus codices. The oldest, which dates to the first half of the second century, is a tiny fragment of a codex of the Gospel of John. Intact, it measured about eight inches square and contained about 130 pages.

The prevalence of the codex among early Christian manuscripts of the second and third centuries stands out sharply against the larger Greco-Roman cultural context of the same period. There, the vast majority of literature continued to be published in scroll form. So striking is the contrast between Christianity's apparent preference for the codex and its larger literary-culture's preference for the scroll during this time that some historians believe that the codex was essentially a Christian innovation.

Why this Christian propensity for the codex? Some reasons were probably practical. Codices were somewhat cheaper to produce, since they allowed for text to be written on both sides of each sheet. Still, other inefficiencies in early Christian manuscript production suggest that such savings were not the primary motivation. More importantly, a single codex could hold more writing than a reasonably sized scroll. One of the oldest Christian codices, dating to around 200 CE, includes all of Paul's letters in its 208 pages. A scroll with all of Paul's letters would have been absurdly long and unwieldy.

Perhaps the predominance of the codex in early Christian scriptural culture is rooted in the very origins and early spread of the movement itself. It has been suggested that Paul and his disciples used small codices in order to publish and disseminate his letters in highly portable and handy form (a single sheet folded over two or four times to make eight or sixteen pages). It has also been hypothesized that Jesus's disciples, as well as the followers of other rabbis during his time, used simple codices like handy notebooks in order to write down the sayings of their teacher.

Whatever led to the unique rise of the codex among early Christians, the new medium was profoundly influential on the scriptural culture that developed around and by means of it. Above all, it facilitated new practices of reading. A scroll prescribes a linear reading experience. You start in one place and continue to scroll along in one direction. You don't easily jump back and forth in the text. Cross-referencing is not practical. Nor is reading short passages from different parts of the text (*testimonia* may have originally emerged as a remedy to this problem). Codices, by contrast, readily accommodate random access. A reader can easily jump backward or forward in the text, or between two different texts in the same codex, without losing her place. She can even bookmark related passages to read together, one after another. In this way, the codex encourages readers and hearers to discover intertextual connections. This particular feature of the codex probably appealed especially to early Christian communities interested in relating different passages to one another by means of cross-referencing.

Still, early Christian codices were not like modern books, especially in their storage capacities. The longest were not more than two hundred pages, and most were considerably smaller than that. Given that they were intended for public reading, moreover, their handwritten scripts were quite large. The technology of the codex did not reach the point of being able to hold anything close to an entire canon of Jewish and Christian Scriptures until the fourth century. Nor was there any such thing as a closed canon of those Scriptures until that time. The closing of the canon and the binding of it into a single big book seems to have gone hand in hand.

It is no coincidence that this establishment of the Bible as a single closed canon of Scriptures for all Roman Christians, and the concomitant establishment of a narrower Christian orthodoxy, took place in the century after Constantine's conversion, as Christianity ascended to state power. As the imperial religion, its increasingly hierarchical structures not only enabled but encouraged greater regulation and uniformity.

The main point I want to make here is that neither Jesus nor his followers nor Paul nor any of the authors of any of the texts now in the New Testament, let alone any Christians who lived during the first three hundred years of Christianity, could possibly have imagined the Bible, a single book containing a closed canon of Jewish and Christian Scriptures. It was both physically and socially impossible. Not only were there just too many different varieties of Christianity with too many different important writings with too many variants in too many different languages; there was simply no medium to bear anything close to that large of a library. It took the twin emergences of a top-down imperial Christianity and a big enough book to make the Bible possible.

Scattered Throughout the Whole World

By the fourth century, the technology of the codex had reached the point that it was possible, if still not very practical, to hold a body of literature as large as the Christian canon of Scriptures in a single volume. What would such a book have looked like? The earliest known Christian Bible, Codex Sinaiticus, dates to the mid-300s. Reconstructed from loose pages found in a waste bin in the library of Saint Catherine's Monastery on Mount Sinai in 1844, it would have been about twenty inches high and seventeen inches wide and would have contained about 700 pages of parchment. That's a lot of animal hide. Analysis of the handwriting indicates that three or four different scribes wrote the text. Needless to say, not only was this Bible book large and cumbersome; it was very expensive to produce. Even this complete Bible book, moreover, is not identical in contents to the canon as we now have it: its Old Testament includes some Apocryphal Jewish texts but is missing others that eventually were included, and its collection of Christian Scriptures includes two texts that eventually did not make the canonical cut: the Letter to Barnabas and an abbreviated version of an early Christian text known as the Shepherd of Hermas.

The invention of the big codex did not lead to the immediate publication of the Christian Bible as a big book. In fact, most Bible manuscripts dating to the fourth and fifth centuries were not whole Bibles but collections of certain biblical texts — the Psalms, for example, or the four Gospels. As is well known thanks to novelist Dan Brown, Constantine commissioned Eusebius in

322 to produce fifty copies of the "sacred Scriptures . . . written on prepared parchment in a legible manner, and in a convenient, portable form, by professional transcribers thoroughly practiced in their art." None of those copies survive, but it is likely that they were Gospel Books, not whole Bibles or even whole New Testaments. It would have been impossible at that time to produce a conveniently portable codex of anything more. Moreover, as Eusebius himself made clear in his catalogue of "undisputed," "disputed," and "heretical" Christian writings (discussed earlier), the canon of the New Testament was not yet fixed.

Nor did the media invention of the big book and the concomitant rise of Christianity to imperial power mean that biblical texts were suddenly standardized and made uniform from one copy to the next. Biblical manuscripts of the late fourth century were widely and significantly different from one another. It was this fact that led Pope Damasus, who avidly sought to make Rome the center of Christendom, to commission Jerome, at that time an up-and-coming theologian and grammarian, now remembered as the patron saint of Bible translators and librarians, to study all the various versions of Scriptures and establish a single authoritative Latin edition from them. In his preface to his edition of the Gospels, Jerome clearly recognized the challenge.

> You ask me to . . . sit in judgment on the copies of the Scriptures which are now scattered throughout the whole world . . . The labour is one of love, but at the same time both perilous and presumptuous; for in judging others I must be content to be judged by all; and how can I dare to change the language of the world in its hoary old age, and carry it back to the early days of its infancy?

The task was especially daunting given that there were so many significantly different Old Latin translations being used in Rome.

So many, in fact, that Jerome complained, "There are almost as many forms of texts as there are copies!"

By the time of his death in 420, Jerome (probably working with a team of translators and scribes) had produced an entire Bible written in the Latin of his time. His primary sources were the Greek and Hebrew texts that he had been able to collect, but he also consulted Old Latin versions. The result was the basis of what eventually became the standard Vulgate ("common" or "popular") Bible for all of Western Christendom.

Still, it would be wrong to suppose that, as soon as Jerome finished his edition, Western Christianity had finally found its single, established, authoritative version of the Bible (even if it wasn't original but based on comparing various earlier versions). Not at all. For one, whole Bibles, including all of the Old and New Testament texts in a single bound volume, were still relatively rare. The oldest surviving whole Vulgate Bible, known as the Codex Amiatinus, dates to the beginning of the eighth century. The sheer size of this volume gives some clue as to why, practically speaking, such whole Bibles were rare: it is twenty inches high, a little over thirteen inches wide, seven inches thick, has over two thousand pages, and weighs about seventy-five pounds.

For more than a century after Jerome, the Old Latin codices of Christian Scripture, which he had complained were unreliable, remained dominant. Only very slowly, by around the seventh or eighth century, did his Vulgate gain clear preeminence. Evidence for this gradual takeover by the Vulgate is found in surviving manuscripts. There are about 370 biblical manuscripts or fragments in Latin that date to earlier than 800. Only about a third of those dating to the fifth century are from the Vulgate. By the sixth century, however, there are twice as many Vulgate manuscripts as Old Latin ones. By the eighth century, there are twelve times as many.

Jerome's Vulgate itself was never fixed and changeless. At some point after his death, several additions were made to it. Passages from his other writings were copied into it as introductory prologues to various books. Even more significantly, Jerome's canon was altered. He had excluded Apocryphal books such as Baruch and Tobit, because, although they appeared in the Greek manuscripts of the Septuagint (used by Greek-literate Jews as well as Christians), they did not appear in his Hebrew manuscripts, which he believed were more original. Yet all the Vulgate Bibles that have survived include them. Jerome had not translated them, and so these Apocryphal parts of the Vulgate Bible must have come from the Old Latin versions. Ironic, since these unreliable versions were the very problem that the Vulgate was intended to remedy.

Beyond these additions to Jerome's authorized Vulgate Bible, there are many variants among the early copies of the Vulgate that have survived. Some are minor, but others are quite significant. Some of the oldest known manuscripts of this Bible include the letter to the Laodiceans, an epistle that must have been regarded as canonical by some authorities and not by others during the early centuries of Roman Christianity. Another very early Vulgate Bible has the four Gospels edited together into a single, harmonized narrative. Even with the Vulgate, then, there was a significant degree of instability. It would be more accurate to talk about the Vulgates than the Vulgate.

After Gutenberg

We might have expected the invention of the printing press and the rise of print culture, with the Bible at its center, to give the Bible the fixity and permanence that had been sought since Jerome a thousand years earlier. Mechanical printing, after all, made it possible to produce thousands of copies of one book, each identical to the next. But for that fixity to be achieved, there would need to have been a single, original book to mass-produce. When it came to Christian Scriptures, there was no such thing.

Gutenberg's first Bible, published in 1456 with a print run of about 185, was a Vulgate Bible based on one of several widely available manuscript versions. This "Gutenberg Bible" has become an icon of the print culture that he inaugurated. As printing businesses began popping up throughout Europe, however, it quickly became clear that there were many more sales to be made by publishing translations of the Bible into common-day languages. Within two decades of Gutenberg's first Bible, there were nine German Bibles in print. By the mid-sixteenth century, as Protestantism gained momentum, many different Bibles would appear in many other modern languages as well, and these would be made from different "original" manuscripts in Latin, Greek, and Hebrew.

Indeed, the Protestant Reformation was as much a media revolution as it was a theological revolution. It was in many respects a biblical-literacy movement, aimed at making the Bible as readily available and accessible as possible in order to make real the ideal of a "priesthood of all believers." At the same time, print culture was quickly transforming Bibles and other books from collectable manuscripts into tradable commodities. They were no longer held strictly within the domain of wealthy and powerful patrons who commissioned expensive hand copies of whole Vulgate Bibles, Gospel Books, and Psalmodies for churches, monasteries, and the homes of the literate elites. They were mass-produced consumer items. So emerged the business, both theological and capitalist, of publishing Bibles for the masses.

Not only did the print revolution enable the proliferation of many new Bible translations; it also helped foster a more acute awareness of the problems of biblical translation, since it soon became clear that there was no single original from which to translate. Especially influential in this regard was the great Catholic theologian and linguist, Erasmus. In 1516 he published *Novum Instrumentum,* which was the first print edition of the New Testament in Greek. The book had two columns per page: the beautifully designed Greek text on the inside column and Erasmus's Latin translation of that text on the outside column. His translation frequently diverged significantly from the Vulgate, thus implicitly challenging its authority and reliability. That challenge was softened by the book's original title: *Novum Instrumentum,* "new instrument," indicating that the text was meant to be a research tool for scholars rather than a rival edition of the New Testament. Two years later, however, he republished it under the title *Novum Testamentum.* The clear message was that the Vulgate was not the definitive embodiment of Christian Scriptures, but one among other fallible witnesses to them.

Then, in 1522, a team of Spanish scholars directed and funded by Cardinal Jiménez de Cisneros of Spain completed the six-volume, polyglot (multilingual) edition of the Bible known as the Complutensian Polyglot Bible (after its city of publication, Complutum, the Latin name of Alcalá de Henares, Spain). It remains as one of the towering monuments to print culture. I have had the rare opportunity to examine an original copy for myself, and I can attest: not only is it one of the grandest and most ambitious achievements of sixteenth-century biblical scholarship; it is also a work of great bookish beauty. Its Old Testament, published in four volumes, incorporates seven different columns of text written in four different languages using five different type fonts. On the inside top left is the Greek Septuagint with an interlinear, word-by-word Latin translation. Next to that is the Latin Vulgate version of the Old Testament. Next to that is the Hebrew. And next to that, on the far right, is a narrow column of

EYAΓΓE-
ΛΙΟΝ ΚΑΤΑ
ΛΟΥΚΑΝ

EVANGE-
LIVM SECVNDVM
LVCAM

ΠΕΙΔΗΠΕΡ πολλοὶ ἐπε-
χείρησαν ἀνατάξασθαι διήγη-
σιν περὶ τῶν πεπληροφορημέ-
νων ἐν ἡμῖν πραγμάτων, κα-
θὼς παρέδοσαν ἡμῖν οἱ ἀπ'
ἀρχῆς αὐτόπται καὶ ὑπηρέ-
ται γενόμενοι τοῦ λόγου, ἔδοξε κἀμοὶ παρηκολου-
θηκότι ἄνωθεν πᾶσιν ἀκριβῶς καθεξῆς σοι γρά-
ψαι ἱεράτιστε θεόφιλε, ἵνα ἐπιγνῶς περὶ ὧν κα-
τηχήθης λόγων τὴν ἀσφάλειαν. ἐγένετο ἐν
ταῖς ἡμέραις ἡρώδου τοῦ βασιλέως τῆς ἰουδαίας,
ἱερεύς τις ὀνόματι ζαχαρίας, ἐξ ἐφημερίας ἀβιά.
καὶ ἡ γυνὴ αὐτοῦ ἐκ τῶν θυγατέρων ἀαρών, καὶ τὸ
ὄνομα αὐτῆς ἐλισάβετ. ἦσαν δὲ δίκαιοι ἀμφότεροι ἐνώπιον τοῦ θεοῦ, πορευόμενοι ἐν πάσαις
ταῖς ἐντολαῖς καὶ δικαιώμασι τοῦ κυρίου ἄμεμ-
πτοι. καὶ οὐκ ἦν αὐτοῖς τέκνον, καθ' ὅτι ἡ ἐλισάβετ ἦν στεῖρα καὶ ἀμφότεροι προβεβηκότες ἐν
ταῖς ἡμέραις αὐτῶν ἦσαν. ἐγένετο δέ, ἐν τῷ ἱε-
ρατεύειν αὐτὸν ἐν τῇ τάξει τῆς ἐφημερίας αὐτοῦ
ἔναντι τοῦ θεοῦ, κατὰ τὸ ἔθος τῆς ἱερατείας, ἔλα-
χε τοῦ θυμιᾶσαι, εἰσελθὼν εἰς τὸν ναὸν τοῦ κυρίου, καὶ πᾶν τὸ πλῆθος τοῦ λαοῦ ἦν προσευχό-
μενον ἔξω τῇ ὥρᾳ τοῦ θυμιάματος. ὤφθη δὲ αὐ-
τῷ ἄγγελος κυρίου, ἑστὼς ἐκ δεξιῶν τοῦ θυσιαστη-
ρίου τοῦ θυμιάματος. καὶ ἐταράχθη ζαχαρίας
ἰδών, καὶ φόβος ἐπέπεσεν ἐπ' αὐτόν. εἶπε δὲ
πρὸς αὐτὸν ὁ ἄγγελος. μὴ φοβοῦ ζαχαρία, διότι
εἰσηκούσθη ἡ δέησίς σου, καὶ ἡ γυνή σου ἐλισάβετ
γεννήσει υἱόν σοι, καὶ καλέσεις τὸ ὄνομα αὐτοῦ ἰω-
άννην, καὶ ἔσται χαρά σοι, καὶ ἀγαλλίασις, καὶ
πολλοὶ ἐπὶ τῇ γεννήσει αὐτοῦ χαρήσονται. ἔσται
γὰρ μέγας ἐνώπιον κυρίου καὶ οἶνον καὶ σίκερα
οὐ μὴ πίῃ. καὶ πνεύματος ἁγίου πλησθήσεται
ἔτι ἐκ κοιλίας μητρὸς αὐτοῦ, καὶ πολλοὺς τῶν
υἱῶν ἰσραὴλ ἐπιστρέψει ἐπὶ κύριον τὸν θεὸν αὐτῶν. καὶ αὐτὸς προελεύσεται ἐνώπιον αὐτοῦ ἐν
πνεύματι καὶ δυνάμει ἠλίου, ἐπιστρέψαι καρ-
δίας πατέρων ἐπὶ τέκνα, καὶ ἀπειθεῖς ἐν φρονή-
σει δικαίων, ἑτοιμάσαι κυρίῳ λαὸν κατεσκευ-
ασμένον. καὶ εἶπε ζαχαρίας πρὸς τὸν ἄγγελον.
κατὰ τί γνώσομαι τοῦτο; ἐγὼ γάρ εἰμι πρεσ-
βύτης, καὶ ἡ γυνή μου προβεβηκυῖα ἐν ταῖς ἡμέραις αὐτῆς. καὶ ἀποκριθεὶς ὁ ἄγγελος, εἶπεν αὐ-
τῷ ἐγώ εἰμι γαβριήλ, ὁ παρεστηκὼς ἐνώπιον τοῦ
θεοῦ. καὶ ἀπεστάλην λαλῆσαι πρὸς σε, καὶ εὐαγ-
γελίσασθαί σοι ταῦτα. καὶ ἰδοὺ ἔσῃ σιωπῶν, καὶ
μὴ

QVONIAM complures
aggreſsi ſunt côtexere nar
rationem earum quę inter
nos certiſsimæ fidei ſunt,
rerum, ſicuti tradiderunt
nobis hi qui ab initio ſuis
oculis uiderant, ac pars aliqua fuerant eorû
quæ narrabât: uiſum eſt & mihi, ut cunctis
ab initio exacta diligentia peruestigatis, de
inceps tibi ſcriberê, optime Theophile, quo
agnoſcas eorum de quibus edoctus fueras,
certitudinem. Erat in diebus Herodis
regis Iudææ, ſacerdos quidam nomine Zacharias, de uice Abia, & uxor illius de filia-
bus Aaron, & nomen eius Elizabet. Erant
autem iuſti ambo coram deo, uerſantes in
omnibus præceptis & iuſtificationibus domini irreprehêſibiles: nec erat illis proles, co
quod eſſet Elizabet ſterilis, & ambo prouectæ iam eſſent ętatis. Factum eſt aût, quum
is ſacerdotio fungeretur in ordine uicis ſuæ
corâ deo, ſecundû conſuetudinê functionis
ſacerdotalis, ſors illi obuenit, ut odores incê
deret, ingreſſus in templû domini, & omnis
multitudo populi precabaꝷ foris tẽpore thy
miamatis. Apparuit aût illi angelus domini
ſtãs à dextris altaris, in quo thymiamata ſo-
lent adoleri. Et Zacharias turbatus eſt eo uí
ſo, ac timor irruit ſuper eum. Ait aût ad illû
angelus, Ne timeas Zacharia, quoniã exau-
dita eſt deprecatio tua: uxorꝗ tua Elizabet
pariet tibi filiû, & uocabis nomê eius Ioãnê:
& erit gaudiû tibi & exultatio, & multi ſup
eius natiuitate gaudebunt. Erit eñ magnus
corâ domino, & uinû ſiceraꝗ non bibet. Et
ſpiritu ſacto replebiꝷ iam inde ab utero ma
tris ſuæ, multosꝗ filiorû Iſrael conuertet ad
dñm deum ipſorû. Et ipſe precedet ante illû
cû ſpiritu & uirtute Heliæ, ut conuertat cor
da patrû in filios, & inobediêtes ad prudêtiã
iuſtorû, ut paret dño plebê perfectã. Et dixit
Zacharias ad angelû, Quo argumêto iſtuc
cognoſcã? ego eñ ſum ſenex, & uxor mea
prouectæ ætatis eſt. Ac reſpondens angelus
dixit ei, Ego ſum Gabriel, qui aſtiti in côſpe
ctu dei, miſſusꝗ ſum ut loquar ad te, & hæc
tibi læta nûciê. Et ecce futurû eſt, ut ſis tacitꝰ
nec

First page of the Gospel of Luke in Erasmus's *Novum Testamentum* (1535 edition). The left column is the Greek text, and the right column is Erasmus's own translation into Latin, implicitly challenging the authority of the Latin Vulgate version. *Courtesy of the Special Collections Research Center, Kelvin Smith Library, Case Western Reserve University* verbal roots corresponding to the Hebrew text. On the bottom left is an Aramaic paraphrase of the Torah, known as Targum Onkelos. Next to that is its Latin translation. And on the far right is a narrow column of Aramaic roots from the Targum. The New Testament, published as the fifth volume, is simpler but no less visually striking. It has parallel columns of Greek and Latin Vulgate, with the words in each version keyed to the other for easier comparison and cross-referencing. At the end of the volume is a Greek dictionary. The sixth volume includes a Hebrew and Aramaic dictionary and grammar guide for use with the Old Testament.

The sizes and appearances of the different fonts were designed to signal the status of each text relative to the others. Because Greek was the original language of the writings of the New Testament, for example, the Greek font for that text is larger, rounder, and more ornate than the one used for the Greek text of the Septuagint, since it is a translation. Likewise, the Latin font of the interlinear translation of the Septuagint (a translation of a translation) is smaller and plainer than that of the Vulgate translation. And the Hebrew font of the Old Testament is larger than that of the Aramaic paraphrase of the Targum.

Several other polyglot Bibles, produced by teams of scholars in other parts of Europe, followed over the next century and a half. The largest, known as the Paris Polyglot (completed in 1645), boasted ten volumes and included seven different versions of biblical literature (or parts of it) in six different languages: Hebrew, Aramaic, Greek, Latin, Old Syriac, and Arabic. The most highly regarded and influential, however, was the six-volume London Polyglot (1657), also known as Walton's Polyglot after its lead scholar, Brian Walton. Compiled, edited, and annotated by an all-star team of biblical scholars and linguists, its Old Testament includes nine different versions: the Hebrew, the Greek

Septuagint, the Latin Vulgate, the Aramaic Targum, the Samaritan Pentateuch, the Old Syriac version known as the Peshita, an Arabic version, and an Ethiopic version of the Psalms and Song of Songs, as well as two other versions of the Targum and a Persian translation. Its New Testament includes the Greek and Latin Vulgate versions along with many variants found in other ancient Greek, Syriac, Latin, Ethiopic, and Arabic manuscripts, along with a Persian version of the four Gospels.

On one of my visits to the archives of the American Bible Society in New York, I was allowed to browse the early rare manuscripts of its Scripture Collection. The curator and resident scholar is Dr. Liana Lupas, a Romanian American woman who is as warm and collegial as she is formal and erudite. The collection is her domain, and she knows it like the back of her hand. We started with the obvious: early English Bibles. She smiled slightly and pulled down a few extremely rare volumes from a nearby shelf. No doubt she expected me to start with those. But when I asked about the early polyglots, her face lit up. She quickly escorted me to the dimly lit back of the room. They were all there. She pulled out first editions of Erasmus's *Novum Instrumentum,* the Complutensian Polyglot, and the London Polyglot from the shelves and laid them open on the floor for me to explore. Kneeling before them, she gave me extensive guided tours of each volume, revealing as much about their beauty and craft as their literary contents. There are no better illustrations of the term "magnum opus." These were mammoth scholarly projects that demanded aesthetic as well as intellectual passion and rigor. They were all-encompassing works, demanding one's whole heart, mind, and strength.

On the front page of *Novum Instrumentum,* Dr. Lupas pointed out a beautifully handwritten Latin inscription. Although written by a later owner of the book, I think it captures the spirit of Erasmus and other early Bible editors and translators of the age. It reads, "*Ubi non est deus, ibi non lux: ubi non est lux, ibi non est ver-itas: ubi non est veritas, ibi sum variae opiniones, ubi sum variae opiniones, ibi est error.*" I'm sure Dr. Lupas, a classics scholar, could trans-late it more faithfully than I, but I think this is its gist in Eng-lish: "Where there is no God, there is no light: where there is no light, there is no truth: where there is no truth, there are various opinions: where there are various opinions, there is error." Truth is enlightenment, and enlightenment is of God. Shedding light on what passes as truth is not only permitted; it is necessary, the highest calling.

It was in this spirit of enlightenment that what began with Erasmus had, in a little more than a century, given rise to mas-sive, multiversion, multilanguage critical editions of biblical liter-ature like the London Polyglot. These works were revolutionizing biblical criticism and translation, empowering scholars every-where to study and compare all the available biblical manuscripts and variants for themselves, to assess the value of various ancient and modern translations, and to produce new ones. Translating from Hebrew and Greek manuscripts, they could claim that their translations were superior to the Vulgate, which had been cor-rupted over the centuries. They were doing essentially what Je-rome had done, but translating into present-day vulgates. In the process, they were drawing greater and greater attention to the

Opposite: Brian Walton's six-volume masterpiece, the London Polyglot Bible (1657), includes thirteen different columns in eight different languages for every biblical verse of the Torah. Pictured here is the left-hand page of the full spread for the first four-teen verses of Genesis. It includes, from left to right, starting at the top: (1) the He-brew, with an interlinear Latin translation; (2) the Latin Vulgate; (3) the Greek Sep-tuagint, with variants from other versions of the Septuagint noted at the bottom; (4) a Latin translation of the Septuagint; (5) the Syriac version; and (6) a Latin trans-lation of the Syriac. On the facing page (not pictured) are seven more versions of the same biblical verses: (7) the Aramaic Targum; (8) a Latin translation of the Targum; (9) the Samaritan Hebrew version; (10) the Samaritan Aramaic version (11) a Latin translation of the Samaritan Hebrew; (12) the Arabic version; and (13) a Latin trans-lation of the Arabic. *Courtesy of the Special Collections Research Center, Kelvin Smith Library, Case Western Reserve University*

GENESIS.   Cap. i.

TEXTVS HEBRAICVS,

ספר בראשית א

Cum Versione interlineari Sanctis Pagnini, ad Hebraicam phrasin exstruxit per Ben. Ariam Montanum, & alios.

[Hebrew text with interlinear Latin, verses 1–14]

Vulgata LATINA

Versio, juxta exemplaria emendata Sixti V. & Clem. VIII.

CAP. I.

IN Principio creavit Deus coelum & terram. Terra autem erat inanis & vacua, & tenebræ erant super faciem abyssi: & Spiritus Dei ferebatur super aquas. Dixitque Deus: Fiat lux. Et facta est lux. Et vidit Deus lucem quod esset bona: & divisit lucem à tenebris. Appellavitque lucem Diem, & tenebras Noctem: factumque est vespere & mane, dies unus. Dixit quoque Deus: Fiat firmamentum in medio aquarum: & dividat aquas ab aquis. Et fecit Deus firmamentum, divisitque aquas quæ erant sub firmamento, ab his quæ erant super firmamentum. Et factum est ita. Vocavitque Deus firmamentum, Coelum: & factum est vespere & mane, dies secundus. Dixit verò Deus: Congregentur aquæ, quæ sub cælo sunt, in locum unum: & appareat arida. Et factum est ita. Et vocavit Deus aridam, Terram; congregationesque aquarum appellavit Maria. Et vidit Deus quod esset bonum. Et ait: Germinet terra herbam virentem & facientem semen, & lignum pomiferum faciens fructum juxta genus suum, cujus semen in semetipso sit super terram. Et factum est ita. Et protulit terra herbam virentem, & facientem semen juxta genus suum, lignumque faciens fructum, & habens unumquodque sementem secundùm speciem suam. Et vidit Deus quod esset bonum. Et factum est vespere & mane, dies tertius. Dixit autem Deus: Fiant luminaria in firmamento cæli, & dividant diem ac noctem, & sint in signa, & tempora, & dies, & annos:

VERSIO GRÆCA LXX. INTERP.

Juxta exemplar Vaticani, Romæ impressi: subscriptis autem lineis lecturæ in vetusti MS. Angl. et Alexandria alteo cum Versi. V. et Ed. Rom.

CAP. I.

[Greek Septuagint text, verses 1–14]

Versio SYRIACA cum Interpretatione LATINA.

[Syriac text, verses 1–14]

In Nomine Domini Omnipotentis et tremendi impressionem libri legis Μωσῆ Prophetæ. Ac primò librum Creationis.

CAP. I.

IN principio creavit Deus esse coeli & esse terræ. Terra autem erat deserta & inculta, tenebræque super faciem abyssi: & spiritus Dei incubabat superficiei aquarum. Dixitque Deus, Fiat lux: talisque est lux. Viditque Deus lucem quod bona esset. Et divisit Deus inter lucem & tenebras. Appellavitque Deus lucem, diem: & tenebras appellavit noctem: sanque vespera, sanque mane dies unus, in ordine. Dixit Deus, Sit firmamentum in media aquarum, & fiat, divisitque inter aquas & aquas. Fecitque Deus firmamentum, & divisit aquas quæ sub firmamento, & aquas quæ supra firmamentum: fuitque ita. Appellavitque Deus firmamentum cælum: & fuit vespere, & fuit mane dies secundus. dixit Deus, Congregentur aquæ quæ sub coelo sunt in locum unum, & appareat arida: & fuit ita. Et appellavit Deus aridam, terram: congregationem verò aquarum appellavit maria: viditque Deus quod bonum esset. Et dixit Deus, Producat terra germen, herbâ sata ferendo feratur juxta genus & arborem fructuum ferentium fructus juxta genus suum, cujus planta sit in semetipsâ super terram, & sua ita. Et produxit terra germen herbâ sata ferendo feritur juxta genus suum & arbore proferentium fructum cujus plantæ sit in semetipsâ juxta genus suum. Viditque Deus quod esset bonum. Et fuit vespera, fuitque mane dies tertius. Dixitque Deus, Sint luminaria in firmamento coeli ad distinguendum inter diem & noctem: & sint in signa, & tempora, in dies, & annos:

fact that there was no single original. In the centuries since, that problem has been exacerbated by the discovery of many, many more early manuscripts, which have turned the quest for originals into an endless, if not impossible, task.

Like Jerome, moreover, many of these scholars raised questions about the boundaries of the canon itself. Remember that Jerome had excluded the Apocryphal books from his Vulgate Bible because they did not appear in his Hebrew manuscripts, but only in the Greek Septuagint. After his death, others added them back in. Now many Protestants, also working from Hebrew versions in their translations of Jewish Scriptures, were pushing these Apocryphal books back out. Many seventeenth-century editions of English Bibles, for example, didn't include the Apocrypha. The practice was common enough by 1615 that Archbishop Abbot prohibited stationers from publishing a Bible without it under penalty of a year in prison. Indeed, some more radical reformers were going so far as to question the canonical status of other, more central biblical books. Martin Luther himself said that he hated the book of Esther, that James was "an epistle of straw," and that he saw no evidence of the Holy Spirit's inspiration in Revelation. Although he did not dismiss them from the canon, later editions of his German Bible did exclude the Apocrypha.

In response to growing criticisms of the Vulgate as inaccurate and corrupt, the Roman Catholic Church under Pope Sixtus V (the same pope who erected the obelisk of Santa Maria Maggiore) commissioned a group of biblical scholars to produce a new standard edition of it based on careful comparison of many early manuscripts, the Codex Amiatinus prominent among them. First published in 1590 and then revised and republished in 1592, the "Sixtine Vulgate" became *the* Bible of Roman Catholicism for the next three and a half centuries. Of course, Roman Catholicism was by then one of many Christianities in the West, so its official Bible was but one of a great many others now being, to borrow Jerome's image, "scattered throughout the whole world."

The print revolution lent a sense of fixity, closure, and immutability to the idea of the book. As Walter J. Ong famously observed, the printed book "encloses thought in thousands of copies of a work of exactly the same visual and physical consistency." And what was true of books in general was especially true of The Book of books, that is, the Bible. Yet the reality of the Bible in the age of Gutenberg has been quite the opposite: it has led to the proliferation of more Bibles in more forms and translations than ever.

Multiplying the Leaves

Many new translations of the Bible included extensive notes and commentaries intended to lead readers toward certain interpretations and away from others. These in turn led competitors to produce Bibles with alternative perspectives. Different Bibles were arguing with each other.

The very popular Geneva Bible (1560), for example, produced by English Puritan reformers who had fled to Switzerland to escape the persecutions of Queen Mary, often spun its translations and notes in a strongly antimonarchical direction, implying affinities between England's rulers and those of Israel's enemies like Babylon and Egypt. In its marginal notes on the story of the Exodus, for example, it takes pains to point out that the Hebrew midwives were being obedient to God by disobeying Pharaoh's order to kill all newborn Hebrew baby boys, although they should have done so openly: "Their disobedience herein was lawful, but their dissembling was evil." Commenting on Pharaoh's subsequent command that any Hebrew boys be tossed into the river as soon as they're born, another marginal note adds, "When tyrants can not prevail by craft, they brast [burst] forthe into open rage." In fact, this sense of identification with the Israelites as God's people oppressed by an ungodly monarch is clear from the moment one opens the book. On its title page is an illustration of the Israelites about to cross the Red Sea, with Egyptian cavalry (dressed very much like contemporary English military) hot on their heels. Around the engraving are the words of two biblical passages, each offering the promise of divine liberation from ungodly, oppressive powers: "Feare ye not, stand stil, and beholde the salvation of the Lord which he will shewe to you this day. The Lord shal fight for you: therefore holde you your peace" (Exodus 14:13–14), and "Great are the troubles of the righteous: but the Lord delivereth them out of all" (Psalms 34:19).

Other notes identified the enemy of God's people as the Roman Catholic Church. A note in the book of Revelation, for example, explicitly identifies the beast that will rise from the bottomless pit as the pope. Later editions of the Geneva Bible added even more vehemently anti-Catholic commentary. The 1598 edition includes notes to Revelation that call Pope Gregory VII "a most monstrous Necromancer" and "a slave of the devil." Talk about a values-added Bible! Creating the Bible in one's own image appears to be as old as the Bible-publishing business itself.

The Geneva Bible was by far the most popular English Bible for more than a century, during which time about two hundred different editions of it were published. It was, moreover, what the Pilgrims and Puritans brought with them to America, and it was the Bible that Puritan-educated leaders like Benjamin Franklin and John Adams read. It was also the Bible of Shakespeare and John Bunyan, and no doubt helped inspire the anti-Royalists in the English Civil War. Still, some of its notes, especially those that supported disobedience against unjust laws and monarchs, concerned those in positions of power. King James I, for example. Although a Protestant, he complained that notes such as those found in Exodus were "very partiall, untrue, seditious, and savouring too much of daungerous and trayterous conceites."

Indeed, the King James Version, so often touted as the purest and holiest of all English Bibles, was born of the royal desire for a counterrevolutionary, unannotated alternative to the Geneva Bible. The work of fifty-four translators commissioned by King James and published in 1611, this "Authorized Version" was the officially sanctioned Bible of England. Given this vested interest, it's not surprising that the government imposed strict copyright laws controlling who could publish it and how. Only certain publishers were licensed to print it, and there were requirements and restrictions on its appearance. Most significantly, no notes or illustrations were permitted.

Yet, as you might have guessed by now, unlicensed but ambitious printers soon found profitable ways around these copyright laws. Some purchased Bibles printed by licensed printers, took them apart, inserted illustrations and other value-adding content, and then rebound and resold them at higher costs. Early examples from the 1630s include the Gospel harmonies handmade by the well-known Anglican minister Nicholas Ferrar. These Bibles were actually made by cutting up pages of a printed Authorized Bible and pasting them, along with illustrations, onto blank pages in a new book. Still other printers sold as "commentaries" or "annotations" books that happened to include all or nearly all of the text of the King James Bible. Some included only scant notes, which were placed in such a way that they could then be easily cut out by binders before binding. Other printers added maps and illustrations that allowed them to categorize their Bibles as educational material, thereby avoiding copyright restrictions.

Still others imported English Bibles that were printed in other countries, often underselling the licensed printers. Not surprisingly, some protested that these imports suffered from a lack of quality control and were full of misprints. In an imported Bible from 1682, for example, a passage from Deuteronomy about divorce addresses a situation in which a husband "ate," rather than "hate," his wife. But such protests were undermined by errors in licensed Bibles. The most well known was the so-called Wicked Bible, published in 1631 by the King's Printer, Robert Barker. It omitted a rather significant "not" in the Seventh Commandment: "Thou shalt commit adultery"!

We get a fascinating window onto this fiercely competitive early Bible market in an anonymous four-page tract called *Scintilla; or A Light Broken into Darke Warehouses,* published in 1641 by Michael Sparke, a Puritan bookseller, frequent copyright infringer, and strong critic of the aforementioned Robert Barker. In an attempt to break Barker's monopoly on the Bible trade, Sparke had been importing and selling Bibles from Holland. Barker caught wind of it, got a warrant to search the seaports, confiscated all the Bibles he could find, and sold them himself. In the tract, Sparke gives account, in real numbers, of how the "Monopolists" in their "darke warehouses" have been profiting unfairly by jacking up the prices of Bibles and other books. "But a touch of this," he concludes, "for it is too tart, and I verily beleeve picks the Subjects pockets, that eats brown bread to fill the sleeping Stationers belly with Venison and Sacke." Yet Sparke's own motives for trying to expose them are mixed to say the least. On the one hand, obviously, as a capitalist, he wants to compete in an open and fair market. On the other hand, as a Christian, he wants the Bible to be affordable, and therefore more widely available. The monopoly is making Bibles more expensive than they need to be, and thus holding back the Word. Then as now, the Bible business was both evangelistic and capitalistic, an uneasy mix of spreading the Word and selling it.

As this mixed business, whether authorized or not, continued to grow, so did the number and variety of value-added Bibles on the market. By 1800, at least one thousand different editions of the Bible in English had been published, displaying a stunning array of form and content. Here are just a few examples:

The Souldiers Pocket Bible (1643), a sixteen-page collection of brief passages, mostly from the Old Testament, used by Oliver Cromwell's Parliamentary soldiers in the English Civil War. Its subtitle is surprisingly long, given the size of the Bible itself, promising to provide "most (if not all) those places contained in holy Scripture, which doe shew the qualifications of his inner man, that is a fit Souldier to fight the Lords Battels, both before the fight, in the fight, and after the fight; Which Scriptures are reduced to severall heads, and fitly applyed to the Souldiers severall occasions, and so may supply the want of the whole Bible, which a Souldier cannot conveniently carry about him: And may bee also usefull for any Christian to meditate upon, now in this miserable time of Warre." It was revised and reprinted as *The Christian Soldier's Penny Bible* in 1693 and then again for American soldiers during the Civil War (as many as fifty thousand copies).

Seventeenth-century *dos-à-dos*, or "back-to-back" Bibles, in which a New Testament and a book of Psalms were bound back to back but with their spines reversed so they would open in opposite directions, allowing a reader to flip one book over to read the other.

The very tiny *Whole Book of Psalms in Meter According to the Art of Shortwriting* (1659), by Jeremiah Rich, one of the fathers of modern shorthand. As much a promotion of Rich's method as a Bible for reading, it's about one inch wide and two inches long. Rich created his own plates in order to print it. In 1687 another shorthand expert, William Addy, published a complete Bible in shorthand. It has 396 pages and measures about three inches wide and a little over four inches long.

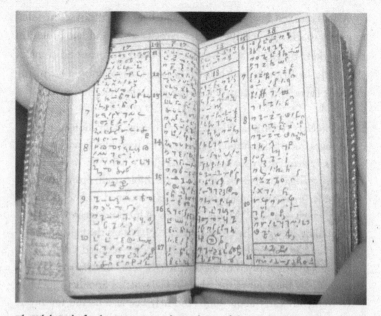

The Whole Book of Psalms in Meter According to the Art of Short-writing (1659), by Jeremiah Rich, one of the fathers of modern shorthand. *Courtesy of the Scripture Collection, Library of the American Bible Society*

Solomons Proverbs (1666), a complete reshuffling of all the verses from the biblical books of Proverbs and Ecclesiastes by Anabaptist theologian and politician Henry Danvers. He organized them under an alphabetical list of subjects ("Adversity," "Adultery," and so on).

A multivolume Bible, "Paraphras'd: With Arguments to each Chapter, And Annotations thereupon," by popular author and churchman Symon Patrick (d. 1707). Here the biblical text is integrated with Patrick's own extended paraphrases, the only difference being that the biblical text is in italics. Thus it is almost impossible to read the biblical text on its own, separate from Patrick's interpretive expansions.

The New Testament in Greek and English (1729), by William Mace, who created his own, otherwise unknown Greek edition, "corrected from the Authority of the most Authentic Manuscripts."

Mr. Whiston's Primitive New Testament (1745), a new translation by the well-known author and translator of the Jewish historian Josephus, William Whiston. Although apparently never completed, this New Testament was intended to include several noncanonical early Christian and Jewish scriptures, such as the Shepherd of Hermas, the Epistles of Ignatius and Polycarp, and a homily on Hades by Josephus.

The Family Testament, and Scholar's Assistant (1767; first edition 1766), whose long subtitle explains that it is "calculated not only to promote the reading of the Holy Scriptures in families and schools, but also to remove that great uneasiness observable in children upon the appearance of hard words in their lessons, and by a method entirely new . . ." Significantly, this new method is not about understanding difficult meanings but pronouncing difficult spellings. Following a general introduction to spelling and reading, it offers "directions for reading with elegance and propriety." Then, at the top of each chapter, it gives the accents and syllable breaks for unfamiliar words. It's less concerned with reading comprehension than with sounding learned, not so much being biblically literate than appearing so.

Scottish preacher John Brown's very popular *Self-Interpreting Bible* (first published in 1778 with several subsequent editions) was promoted as an Everyman's Bible, offering the clear meaning of every passage "in a manner that might best comport with the ability and leisure of the poorer and labouring part of mankind, and especially to render the oracles of God their own interpreter."

Matthew Talbot's completely rearranged Bible (1800), which takes all the verses of the Old and New Testaments out of their original contexts and puts them into thirty subjects, or "books" (e.g., "Deity," "Christ," "Holy Days"), which are then subdivided into 285 chapters and 4,144 sections, "whereby the dispersed rays of truth are concentrated, and every Scriptural subject defined and fully exhibited."

So much for *sola scriptura*.

In many respects, the Bible society movement, in the form of the American Bible Society and its sister organization, the British and Foreign Bible Society, began in reaction to this expanding market of value-added Bibles. Both were nonprofit and both were committed to the widest possible circulation of the Bible in the Authorized Version "without note or comment" — "cheapening and multiplying the leaves of the Tree of Knowledge and of Life" in order to get the Bible into as many hands as possible, believing that doing so was the answer to all the world's problems.

Throughout the nineteenth century, the ABS resisted adding content to its Bibles or printing them in innovative formats. Reading through the minutes from its annual meetings during its early decades, I found instances in which members made creative proposals for adding value to their Bibles and thereby making them more popular. One suggested that the ABS print the Bible as a series of newspaper issues. Another suggested that index tabs be inserted at the beginning of each biblical book for quicker searching. But these and other more or less flashy innovations were consistently rejected. In the age-old evangelical dilemma of preservation versus popularization, the ABS leaned hard toward preservation.

Yet the ABS's own Scripture Collection, which is the largest in the United States, makes very clear that other publishers continued to profit by doing exactly what the ABS resisted, thereby "multiplying the leaves" in a very different sense. In many nineteenth-century Bibles, the biblical text is almost entirely overwhelmed by the various value-adding "extras" — annotations, commentaries, and "practical notes" — provided by this or that well-known scholar or churchman. In most of these Bibles, the extras make up well over half of the text on any given page.

Others introduce novel, "got to have" formats — a finely made red velvet Bible with gold trim (1850), for example, and numerous ultra-tiny "thumb Bibles," many of which include only a few pages summarizing biblical stories. One exception is David Bryce's miniature edition (1896). "Printed upon the very thinnest Oxford India paper ever made," it measures only eighteen by fifteen millimeters and includes the entire Bible on its 520 total pages. It came in a tiny metal box with a tiny magnifying glass. Of course, even with the glass, it is pretty much unreadable.

In certain extraordinary circumstances even the ABS was willing to experiment with novel formats, if not notes or comments. It published a red leather pocket-sized Bible with a leather clasp for Civil War soldiers, and small canvas editions of the New Testament for soldiers in both world wars. During World War II it and the British and Foreign Bible Society also pub-

David Bryce's thumb-sized edition of the whole King James Version Bible, printed on 520 pages (1896). It came in a small metal box with a tiny magnifying glass. *Courtesy of the Special Collections Research Center, Kelvin Smith Library, Case Western Reserve University*

lished what I believe to be the first waterproof Bible, "for Life Boats and Rafts," small packets of pamphlet-sized biblical books wrapped and sealed in aluminum and paper.

Still other Bibles offered novel versions of the biblical text itself. In 1848 Andrew Comstock published a phonetic *Δe Nw Tes-*

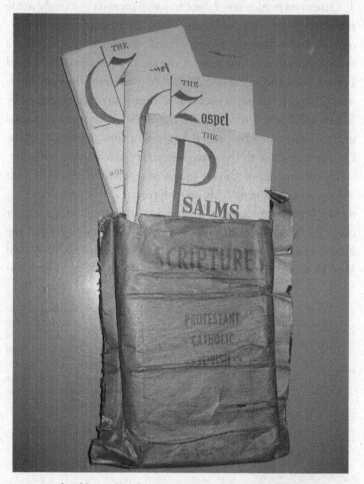

A waterproof "Lifeboat Bible" from World War II. This interfaith edition includes fascicles of Gospels and the Psalms wrapped in foil and paper. *Courtesy of the Scripture Collection, Library of the American Bible Society*

tament ov ør Lwrd and Sevyur JDizus Krist in his own "purfekt alfa-bet," which claimed to have a single printed character for every articulate sound, accent, and inflection. In 1876 Julia E. Smith published, at her own expense, the first translation of the He-brew Scriptures and Greek New Testament by a woman. In her preface, she writes, "It may be thought by the public in general, that I have great confidence in myself, in not conferring with the learned in so great a work, but as there is but one book in the He-brew tongue, and I have defined it word for word, I do not see how anybody can know more about it than I do." Others pro-duced far less "word for word" editions, such as *Stories from the Bible Put into Basic English* (1933), by C. K. Ogden, the inventor of "Basic English," a simplified language comprised of 850 core vocabulary words. Parodied as "Newspeak" in George Orwell's novel *1984*, Basic English was a foreshadow of the grade-school-level vocabu-laries used in so many more recent Bible paraphrases.

One of the most commercially successful Bibles was the am-bitious *Illuminated Bible*, a large-format family Bible published in 1846 by Harper & Brothers, which spent more than six years and $20,000 on its development. Bound in gold-embossed leather, it included over sixteen hundred lavish illustrations, most of them original, along with extensive cross-references, notes, a chrono-logical index, a concordance, and tables of weights, measures, and biblical proper names. It also included spaces to inscribe details of births, deaths, and marriages. In a very real sense, this Bible was meant to be more than simply a part of the family. The fam-ily, indeed the world, was encompassed within it.

Many nineteenth-century portraits idealize the image of the family gathered around the father or grandfather for a brief ser-vice of Bible reading and prayer. Others picture a mother reading to her adoring child, almost as though nursing. As cultural his-torian Colleen McDannell comments, "Just as breast milk gave nurture and pleasure to children, so the mother's use of the Bible fed, comforted, and delighted her progeny." In these images as in those with the patriarch at the center, parents are idealized as the pastors of their familial congregations of children, and Bible reading is their primary pastoral activity.

Supported by such images, the family Bible became the centerpiece of a form of popular American religiosity in the nineteenth century that McDannell aptly calls "material Christianity." Emerging in the Victorian era in the aftermath of the revivalism of the Second Great Awakening, material Christianity focused on physical objects to awaken powerful religious emotions, fostering devotion to certain Victorian ideals for the Christian home and family, in which the father was breadwinner and public authority figure while the mother was homemaker and domestic spiritual nurturer. At the same time, the industrial revolution was accelerating print culture, making large, ornate family Bibles more plentiful and readily affordable for a growing number of households. These factors combined to make the family Bible both the physical and iconic centerpiece of domestic Christian piety in the mid- and late nineteenth century.

Lost in Translations

At the same time as the family Bible was in ascendance, the very idea of a single, universal *translation* of the Bible for the English-speaking world was beginning to disintegrate.

Although there had been other translations available, the King James Version reigned more or less supreme from the late seventeenth century through most of the nineteenth century. That changed with the publication of the Revised Version Bible in 1881 (New Testament only) and 1885 (whole Bible). Since 1611, there had been significant discoveries of ancient biblical manuscripts, such as the Codex Sinaiticus. At the same time, scholarship in the ancient biblical languages had made great advances. Done

by an ecumenical committee of British and American translators, the Revised Bible aimed not only to update the archaic language of the Authorized Version but also to correct it in light of
these discoveries and advances. Theirs was a dream of ecumenical unity among all of English-speaking Christendom. And that
dream, they believed, would be realized through this ecumeni-
cally produced and therefore truly "common Bible."

But the dream quickly turned into a nightmare of greater conflict and division, especially in the United States. By calling into
question the authority of the Authorized Version, the Revised
Version Bible introduced (or rather reintroduced) what American religious historian Peter J. Thuesen describes as a new "Bible
market" in which there was no longer a single, correct choice, not
only for what edition of Bible to buy and use, but also for what
translation. This raised disconcerting questions that went to the
heart of biblical authority. Is any translation trustworthy? Is the
task of the translator objective or subjective? Do different translations reflect different values and vested interests? Is the Bible,
in English or in its original languages, subject to correction and
revision? What meanings might be lost in translation? Is there
one Bible or are there many? Driven by an ecumenical desire to
produce a translation of the Bible that all could embrace, the Revised Version had inadvertently reopened a can of worms that
had been effectively closed since the King James Version had
come to dominate the English-speaking world.

Most fundamentalists initially approved of the Revised Bible.
The project was, after all, consistent with its commitment to the
doctrine of inerrancy, which claims that, as the literal Word of
God, the Bible is without error or contradiction in its original
"autographs," that is, its original manuscript form. Since we no
longer have those original autographs, it is the task of the scholar
to investigate all later manuscript evidence in order to determine
the most reliably original text. Which had been the explicit goal

of the Revised Version committee. In time, however, several influential fundamentalists grew to distrust that committee's motives, seeing that some of its members were proponents of biblical higher criticism, discussed earlier, and those doubters returned to the King James Version. Eventually, they and many others came to embrace *The Scofield Reference Bible,* a King James study Bible published in 1909 by the influential theological and biblical inerrantist C. I. Scofield.

A half century later, another distinguished committee of biblical scholars under the umbrella of the ecumenical National Council of Churches of Christ produced a revision of the Revised Bible, called the Revised Standard Version (New Testament only in 1946; complete Bible in 1952). It, too, drew criticism from fundamentalists and soon came to be seen as the flagship of modern liberalism. One particular bone of contention was its translation of Isaiah 7:14, "Behold, a young woman [Hebrew *'almah*] will conceive and bear a son, and shall call his name Immanuel." Other versions had invariably translated *'almah* "virgin" to conform with the Gospel of Matthew, which quotes this verse in reference to the Virgin Birth of Jesus. In fact, the Revised Standard Version translation is correct. The Hebrew for "virgin" is *betulah,* not *'almah.* But Matthew is quoting from the Greek Septuagint, which uses *parthenos,* which does indeed mean "virgin." Such details were clearly too complicated for many critics, who were scandalized by what appeared to be a denial of the Virgin Birth. Martin Luther Hux, a Baptist minister from North Carolina, went so far as to burn that page, declaring the Revised Standard Version "a master stroke of Satan." For many, this translation soon came to represent all that was wrong with modern liberal Christianity and ecumenism.

Needless to say, the Revised Standard Version brought Christians no closer to the dream of a common Bible than had the Revised Bible. In fact, it inaugurated a proliferation of new and competing translations. In 1959 the inerrantist Lockman Foundation enlisted a large committee to revise the American Standard Version. Twelve years later, it published the New American Standard Bible (New Testament 1963; whole Bible 1971). This form-driven, often very wooden translation quickly gained popularity over the Revised Standard Version in conservative evangelical and fundamentalist circles. It was the best-selling Bible in America in 1977, and continues to be popular among inerrantists to this day. The following year, 1978, saw the publication of the New International Version (New Testament only in 1973), which has dominated the Bible market ever since. Like the New American Standard Bible's translators, its large committee of biblical scholars and ministers were explicitly committed to biblical inerrancy and aimed to revise what many conservatives saw as problems with the Revised Standard Version (both, by the way, restored the virgin to Isaiah 7:14). But the more neo-evangelical-leaning New International Version was dramatically different in that it moved away from word-for-word translation and toward the new functional-equivalence, or meaning-driven, approach. In the wake of its success, as well as that of the loose paraphrasing style of the best-selling *The Living Bible,* the majority of new commercial translations have moved even further in that direction. And so the dream of a common Bible has been replaced by the reality of a Bible that is legion.

Not a Rock but a River

As overwhelmingly vast as it is, the Scripture Collection at the American Bible Society in New York would be much vaster had the society continued to collect every edition of the Bible in English up to the present. But during my visit, the collection's curator, Dr. Lupas, explained to me that the ABS had to stop striving for total inclusiveness in the early 1970s. "At that point," she explained, "it simply became unmanageable." Indeed. Around that time, as we have seen, the number and variety of Bibles began to grow exponentially.

Still, the difference between the early centuries of English Bible publishing and today is one of degree, not kind. All the seeds of the current distress crop were there: a wide variety of physical forms and formats, often promoting novelty over read-ability; voluminous value-adding "extras" attached to celebrity ministers and authors, often overpowering, even burying, the biblical text in a mass of "supplemental" notes and comments; new and alternative translations and paraphrases; and massive abridgments, reshufflings, and rearrangements. Thus we discover a puzzling paradox in our brief history of the Bible in print cul-ture: the Bible's iconicity — the image and idea of it as The Book of books and singular, literal Word of God — has grown in tan-dem with its multiplication of forms. The image of oneness and the reality of manyness have developed hand in hand, each si-multaneously encouraging and challenging the other.

Waiting to meet another ABS staff member in the bookstore downstairs, I overheard a conversation between two dark-suited, middle-aged ministers and a young African American woman standing next to a shelf full of edgy, newfangled, youth-oriented Bibles. "These things have charred the Bible," one man said, while the other two shook their heads in agreement. Then the woman made an interesting comment. "For me, it's about the *continualness* of the Bible. My Bible is always out, on my bed stand at night, on my desk at work. It's always there, so I can always be *in* it, in the Word; it's not for certain times or places. The Bible is always there, and has always been there." I found her words insightful on more than one level. First, it reveals something about how a lot of people feel about Bible reading, or being "in the Word." It's not a book to read and then say you've read. It's about a contin-ual process of reading and rereading — not cover to cover, but all around, over and over, here and there. It's an ongoing relationship. To her, I gather, the newfangled Bibles on the nearby shelf seemed to be marketed as Bibles for certain occasions and contexts, passing novelties to enjoy for a time. But I think her concern for the continualness of the Bible resonates on another level as well. It expresses a deep desire, shared by many, for *permanence* and *stability*, for *the* Bible as something that is the same everywhere and doesn't change over time.

But if there's one thing that this "story of the Book" makes clear, it is that the only constant in the history of the Bible is change. The history of the Bible is one of perpetual revolution. In that light, we might begin to think about the Bible not so much as a fixed thing but as a dynamic, vital tradition. In light of its history, the Bible looks less like a rock than a river, continually flowing and changing, widening and narrowing, as it moves downstream.

For some, thinking about the Bible as a river and not a rock is liberating. That rock has been a millstone around the neck and a tombstone that won't be rolled away. But for others, seeing it this way can be disorienting. That rock has promised solid foundation in a stormy world. Cling to it or be swept away. I remember a very bright first-year student who came to my office after the first session of my historical introduction to the Bible course. "I really liked your opening lecture, but I need to drop the course." Before I could ask why, she continued. "I know I need to look at this stuff, but I can't go there now. The Bible is my rock, even though I know eventually I'll need to face the fact that it really can't be that rock. But right now there's just too much chaos in my life." Even when we know that the Bible is not the rock we want or need it to be, it's hard to let go. Sometimes faith is not about leaping. Sometimes it's simply a matter of letting go and going with the flow, trusting that although there's no going back, there is a way forward.

7

Library of Questions

GRANT THAT THE CULTURAL icon of the Bible as the literal Word of God and closed book of answers is a dead end. Grant that it's a bad idea anyway. So where do we go from here? It's the end of the Word as we know it. Which begs the question, what's another way of knowing, one that is true not only to the Bible's history but also to its contents?

It might be nice if we could start by giving it a new name. "The Bible" literally means "the Book." In fact, that proper name above all names came into modern English via mistranslation. The original Greek word for Christian Scriptures was *ta biblía*, which is the plural form of *biblíon*, "scroll" or "book." *Ta biblía* therefore meant "the scrolls" or "the books." It did not refer to a single, unified text in scroll or book form, but to a *collection* of biblical literature. In the Latin of the Middle Ages, however, *biblia* came to be treated not as a neuter plural, "books," but as a feminine singular, "book." Thus "the books" became known as "the book." From there it migrated into the other Romance languages as the name of a singular book rather than as a body of literature. And it is from that mistranslation that we inherit our name for it, the Bible.

It's probably impractical to launch a campaign to correct the error and begin referring to the Bible by its more original name, "the Bibles." Still, it is important to remember that the Bible is not a single book, "the Book," but rather a collection of books — or, more accurately, a collection of *writings*, since none of them were originally published as books.

The Bible, as we have seen, is not a book, and its fate is not tied to the fate of the book in our twilighting print culture. It's a collection of texts written by many different people, mostly anonymous, in many different translations, and in many different historical and social contexts. These texts were edited, revised, and translated by many others. They were copied and circulated widely in scroll and codex forms for a very long time as independent texts and in smaller collections. They were not the same from copy to copy. There was no beginning and no end to them, no first and last page. They did not have one author or one voice. They were not read in a linear way, but were read around in. And they grew through interpretation, as newer texts that created new meanings from older texts became part of collections. Eventually, when the medium of the book was finally capable of holding such a large collection, they were bound together as a closed canon in a single volume. Even then, moreover, there was never one single, official version of the whole. There were various collections, translated in various ways from a variety of earlier manuscripts, none of them original, each written in different ancient languages. The Bible, then, refers not to a single collection but rather to a kind of collection, a family of Scriptures, of which there are many significantly different versions and editions.

Centuries before "the books" became "the Book," Jerome, patron saint of translators and father of the Vulgate Bible, had used a different Latin word for the Christian Scriptures: *bibliotheca*, that is, "library." What would it mean to think of the Bible not as a book but a library? A library is a collection of writings. A library may include a variety of genres of literature from a range of periods in history. It does not presume that all in its collection is of one authorial voice. A library's collection is a matter of intentional selection and exclusion. It chooses to include certain texts and certain editions of texts and not others. Its collection has an organization and order to it. And yet, although its collections are placed in a certain order, perhaps catalogued from A to Z, a guest in a library is not required or even advised to read everything in that order. So, too, the Bible. It's not a single book with a single voice running from Genesis to Revelation. It's a library of writings, representing many different voices and times and perspectives. Like a library, the Bible invites readers to enter and read around within it. You don't need to start or end in any particular place.

And like a library, the Bible can be a place of serendipity and surprise, in which accidents and tangents often turn out to be more important than your best-laid plans. You're wandering through its collection in search of one thing but you stumble on something else, something you didn't know was even there. And that something turns out to be more interesting or more revealing than what you thought you were looking for. It raises a question you'd never asked, or opens a new direction for reflection, or inspires a new insight. The biblical library is a space that hosts accidental revelation.

I suggest that we make Jerome the patron saint of this chapter, as we reimagine the Bible after the Bible — not as a book, but as a library.

The late philosopher Jacques Derrida had a wonderful phrase: "impoverishment by univocality." Meaning that when we try to make a text univocal, "one-voiced," of one voice with itself, we deprive it of its richness. To interpret with the goal of "getting to the point" about what a text really means is an act of impoverishment.

When it comes to the Bible, many feel that there is a single right meaning — the one its divine author intended. "Well, what does the Bible say?" "The Bible is very clear about that." This is part of the iconicity of the Bible in contemporary society, the idea of it as the one and only divinely authored and guaranteed book of answers, with one answer per question. No more, no less.

For many potential Bible readers, this expectation that the Bible is univocal is paralyzing. You notice what seem to be contradictions or tensions between different voices in the text. You can't find an obvious way to reconcile them. You figure that it must be your problem. You don't know how to read it correctly, or you're missing something. You're not holy enough to read the Holy Bible. It might even be sacrilege for you to try. If the Bible is God's perfect infallible Word, then any misunderstanding or ambiguity must be the result of our own depravity. That is, our sinful nature as fallen creatures is what separates us from God, and therefore from God's Word. So you either give up or let someone holier than thou tell you "what it really says." I think that's tragic. You're letting someone else impoverish it for you, when in fact you have just brushed up against the rich polyvocality of biblical literature.

The Bible is anything but univocal about anything. It is a cacophony of voices and perspectives, often in conflict with one another. Let's explore a few examples of biblical polyvocality in a little more detail, starting in the beginning.

Sometimes diversity can be discovered not only within particular biblical passages but within a single word, even a single letter. So it is with the very first letter of the very first word of Genesis. In Hebrew, that word is *bere'shit* (pronounced *be-ray-sheet*, with the accent on the last syllable), which is also what the book itself is called in Jewish tradition.

Bere'shit can be translated two very different but equally correct ways, and each way leads to a very different meaning for the beginning of the creation story. It all depends on how we take the first letter, called *bet*, in relation to the word it modifies, *re'shit*. Christian tradition, following the lead of early Greek translators, has generally taken *re'shit* as a noun, from *ro'osh*, "beginning" (from whence we get Rosh Hashanah, "beginning" or "head" of *hashanah*, "the year"). Taken that way, the *bet* is translated as a preposition, "in." Thus, "*In the beginning,* God created . . ."

But the word *re'shit* may also be translated as a verb form, meaning "began." This is how Jewish tradition has tended to take it in this verse. Taken that way, the *bet* is translated as "when" rather than "in." So, if we take *re'shit* as a verb rather than as a noun, we get "when began" rather than "in the beginning," and the opening sentence of the Bible reads, "*When* God *began* to create . . ."

Now, compare the two resulting translations, both of which I've made from the same Hebrew text:

> *In the beginning,* God created the heavens and the earth, and the earth was without form and void. And darkness was upon the face of the deep. And the spirit of God brooded upon the face of the waters. And God said, "There is light." And there was light. (Genesis 1:1–3; my translation)

> *When* God *began* to create the heavens and the earth — the earth being formless and void, and darkness upon the face of the deep, and the spirit of God upon the face of the waters — God said, "There is light." And there was light. (Genesis 1:1–3; my translation)

What's the difference? In the first, we have creation *ex nihilo*, out of nothing. God creates the heavens and the earth, and the earth that God creates is initially a formless, chaotic void. Then God proceeds to create light and darkness, land and water, and so on. In the second, by contrast, we have creation *in media res,* in the midst of things. At the moment we pick up the story, when God began to create, the formless void of the earth is already there. Creation is not out of nothing but out of chaos. That's a big difference. And it cannot be resolved. Both readings are perfectly correct and mutually irreconcilable. Undecidability inheres to the first letter, the first word, and the first act of creation.

As we continue through the opening chapters of Genesis, the polyvocality builds. For what follows are two different accounts of divine creation, one after the other. In the first, God creates the world in six days, beginning on the grandest cosmic scale by separating light from dark and finishing on the sixth day with the creation of humankind, male and female, made in God's image. Then God rests on the seventh day, the first Shabbat. Note that here, humans are created in the plural, as the culmination of creation, God's pièce de résistance. Everything else, including all animal and vegetable life, was created before them and is already teeming by the time they arrive on the scene and are told to "be fruitful and multiply."

The second story begins halfway through the fourth verse of the second chapter (2:4b). Here, the order of creation is entirely different. God's first act of creation, before there are any plants or animals, is to form a single human, not yet male or female, by shaping it from the dust of the earth and then bringing it to life by breathing into its nostrils. Thus *ha'adam,* the human, is formed from *ha'adamah,* the earth, and becomes a living soul by divine *ruah,* which means "breath" but also "wind" and "spirit." A beautiful image of the ecological spirituality of humanity: a God-breathed and breathing lump of clay, *ha'adam* from *ha'adamah,* human from humus. The human is an incarnation of divine tran-

scendence and earthy immanence, as intimate with the ground as
with the divine.

But this second creation story is literally incompatible with
the first. Here a single human is created before any other living
thing. God creates animals later, by the same means, as potential
companions for the human. When that doesn't work out, God
puts the human to sleep, takes a side from it, and forms that side
into a woman. So one could argue that woman was created first,
and the man was the leftover. In any case, this order of creation
cannot be made to match the order in the story that immediately
precedes it, in which God creates humans in the plural, male and
female, after God creates all plants and animals.

When we look more closely at these two stories in Hebrew, it's
clear that they were drawn from two different literary sources.
They employ different names for God. They use different narrative styles and vocabularies. They have different theological interests: the first is more cosmological, concerned with the divine
order of creation as a whole, while the second is more anthropological, focusing on human relationships with God and one another. Based on these and other details, most scholars conclude
that the first story comes from the sixth century, during the Babylonian exile or shortly thereafter, and that the second probably
dates a few centuries earlier. Yet, in the final form of Genesis,
these two very different creation stories have been stitched together into a single narrative. As we continue reading, we find
many more seams, spots where different pieces of narrative from
different sources have become part of a larger literary work.

Nor are these two stories at the beginning of Genesis the only
two biblical accounts of creation. There are several others in
other biblical writings. In the divine speech from the whirlwind
in the book of Job (chapter 38), for example, the first act of creation is described as a struggle between God and the primordial

forces of chaos, called Yam ("sea"), a monstrous personification of the formless, watery deep there before the world began. Here God takes control of Yam, sets boundaries for it, and sinks deep foundations for the earth like some huge primeval offshore drilling station.

In Psalm 74, we find yet another version of creation. This one, too, envisions creation from chaos, a conflict in which God takes control and then creates cosmic order out of it. But here the conflict is much more violent, depicting a scene of creation in which God must utterly destroy the monstrous forces of chaos before establishing cosmic order:

> You yourself drove back Yam with your strength.
> You broke the heads of the sea monsters in the waters
> You yourself crushed the heads of Leviathan.
> You gave it as food for the seafaring people.
> You yourself cut openings for springs and torrents.
> You made great rivers run dry.
> Yours is the day, and yours is the night.
> You yourself established light and the sun.
> You yourself fixed all the boundaries of the earth.
> Summer and winter you yourself made. (my translation)

As in Job, we see God driving back Yam, the sea personified. Here, however, the sea itself is home to teeming hosts of anticosmic forces, the sea monsters and Leviathan. These primordial-chaos monsters are not part of the order of creation. God fights and destroys them in order to create a safe, secure, inhabitable ecology for God's people.

It's interesting that the larger context of this psalm is a crisis. The psalmist is crying out to God for rescue from what appears to be the resurgence of chaos monsters, this time taking the form of the Babylonians who have destroyed the Jerusalem Temple.

Here, cosmic chaos and social chaos are integrally related. The psalmist recalls God's original act of creation against chaos in hopes that God will once again put down the monsters and re-establish order. Just as you did not allow monsters to destroy your creation in the beginning, the psalmist is saying, so you must not allow this newly awakened monster, Babylon, to destroy your people, your city, and your Temple, which together represent the social, political, and religious center of that creation.

There are still other biblical versions of creation. Some imagine that God was not alone in carrying it out. In Proverbs 8, for example, Wisdom (*hokmah*), personified as a female companion to God, declares that she was with God "from the beginning, from the origin of the earth, there was still no deep when I was brought forth, no springs rich with water, before the mountains were sunk." When God "assigned the sea its limits" and "fixed the foundations of the earth," she declares, "I was at his side as confidant. I was a source of delight every day, playing before him all the time" (my translation). We may find echoes of this poetics of creation in the opening lines of the Gospel of John:

> In the beginning was the Word, and the Word was with God, and
> the Word was God. He was in the beginning with God. All things
> came into being through him, and without him not one thing
> came into being. What has come into being in him was life, and
> the life was the light of all people. (John 1:1–4)

The Greek word traditionally translated here as "Word" is *logos*, which can also mean not only "reason" or "logic" but "wisdom." Reread this passage with "Wisdom" in place of "Word," and it's easy to see the resonances between the image of creative Wisdom in Proverbs and this *logos* who was with God and was God in the beginning, and who has now become flesh and dwelt among us.

I've heard Christians of creationist and "young earth" persuasions declare that their faith rests squarely on the historical and scientific accuracy of "the biblical account of creation": if the biblical account is wrong, if modern evolutionary theory and cosmology are right, then the Bible is a lie and Christianity is a fraud. They are setting themselves up for a fall. The Bible's own creationism is rich in different, mutually incompatible ways of imagining cosmic and human beginnings. There is no single biblical account of creation. There are many, and they don't agree.

Mark Twain's Drugstore

Our second example of biblical polyvocality is harder to stomach for many, especially those with a more "liberal" theological orientation, who tend to believe that the true message of the Bible is love and peace.

In an essay fragment called "Bible Teaching and Religious Practice," Mark Twain suggested that the Bible is like a drugstore. In it you can find both poison and cure. The Bible was used as the basis for the Salem witch trials, and it was used to condemn them. It was used to justify slavery, and it was used to abolish it. Twain was well aware that churches during his time were splitting over the issue of slavery, each side basing its positions in the Bible. He understood, moreover, that the problem wasn't simply that slavers were bad biblical readers, distorting the text. The problem was that the poisonous texts are there. Institutions of slavery are presumed and supported in some biblical texts. Even the Ten Commandments take slave ownership for granted. Why else would they prohibit coveting a neighbor's slaves? Indeed, just a few verses after the Ten Commandments are given in the book of Exodus, we find detailed regulations for trading slaves, not to mention other possessions, including daughters. It also sets liberal limits on how much physical abuse a slave owner may deliver. "When a slave-owner strikes a male or female slave with a rod and the slave dies immediately," for example, "the owner shall be punished. But if the slave survives for a day or two, there is no punishment; for the slave is the owner's property." The passage is disconcerting enough in and of itself, but especially so given that it appears only a few pages after the story of the release of the Israelites from slavery in Egypt.

Some might hasten to say that these slave texts are all in the Old Testament and therefore are part of life "under the law" from which Jesus Christ liberates humankind. They might well note that in the New Testament letter to the Galatians, the apostle Paul declares that "there is no longer slave or free . . . for you are all one in Christ Jesus." Yet in another letter, he by no means condemns his Christian friend Philemon for owning slaves; he simply requests that one particular former slave, Onesimus, who probably had run away from his master, be accepted back with a new status as fellow Christian.

One of the most poisonous biblical interpretations in recent decades is found in the Christian white-supremacist idea of the Phineas Priesthood. Its biblical basis is a story in Numbers 25 about divinely sanctioned violence in the name of ethnic purity. In that story, the Israelites are suffering from a deadly plague, which Moses explains as God's punishment against them for marrying non-Israelites. While listening to Moses denounce intermarriage, a priest named Phineas notices an Israelite man with a Midianite woman. He leaves the congregation, follows the couple into their tent, and impales them both on the same spear. In response to this zealous double murder, God lifts the plague against the Israelites and blesses Phineas, promising him an "everlasting priesthood." Inspired by this story, white supremacist Richard Kelly Hoskins wrote *Vigilantes of Christendom:*

The Story of the Phineas Priesthood, which presents a postbiblical lineage of "Phineas Priests" who have been willing to carry out similar acts of violent racial and moral purification, and which calls forth a new generation of white Christian zealots to similar action. In the years since its publication, Hoskins's book has gained wide circulation among white supremacist die-hards and potential recruits, in and out of prison. Today, many notoriously militant racist groups lay claim to this dubious biblical heritage, declaring themselves Phineas Priests. Indeed, within these groups, the idea of the Phineas Priesthood has become a powerful means of ordaining acts of racist terror as part of a larger, divinely sanctioned racial holy war.

Countering such atrocious uses of biblical literature is not so simple as calling them misrepresentations of the Bible. We must face the fact that stories like that of Phineas are there, generating suspicion of ethnic otherness and motivating violence against others in our midst.

But they do not stand uncontested. Over against the oppressive passages cited above are many passages that proclaim God above all to be a God of the oppressed, of liberation, who takes sides with those most vulnerable to exploitation and violence. The Torah repeatedly reminds Israel of its former enslavement and oppression: "remember that you were a slave in the land of Egypt," and, "you know the heart of an alien, for you were aliens in the land of Egypt." We often find passages in the Torah and the Prophets that open up hospitable spaces for the voices of the marginalized.

> You shall not abuse any widow or orphan. If you do abuse them, when they cry out to me, I will surely heed their cry ... If you lend money to my people, to the poor among you, you shall not deal with them as a creditor; you shall not exact interest from them.

If you take your neighbor's cloak in pawn, you shall restore it before the sun goes down; for it may be your neighbor's only clothing to use as cover; in what else shall that person sleep? And if
your neighbor cries out to me, I will listen, for I am compassion-
ate. (Exodus 22:22–27)

Jesus echoes this spirit of the Torah when he declares, in Matthew 25, that any injustice against the most vulnerable and needy
among us is an injustice against him. "Truly I tell you, just as you
did not do it to one of the least of these, you did not do it to me."

And Paul declares in Galatians that all the structures of identity (ethnicity, class, and sex, for example) that keep people in
their places have been abolished in Christ: "There is no longer
Jew or Greek, there is no longer slave or free, there is no longer
male and female; for all of you are one in Christ Jesus." That's
potentially radical stuff.

Related to this biblical tension between condoning and con-
demning slavery is a deep ambivalence about the meaning of
"justice," *mishpat* in Hebrew. On the one hand, *mishpat* means law
and order. It's what keeps people and things in their proper place
within the social hierarchy of power. On the other hand, *mishpat* also often refers to a new, potentially revolutionary order in
which structures of oppression and domination are overthrown.
It is a liberationist and socially transformative idea of justice,
close to what we today would call "social justice." This is the justice envisioned by the lowly teenage Mary, mother of Jesus, in her
song of praise for what God is doing:

> He has brought down the powerful from their thrones,
>   and lifted up the lowly;
> he has filled the hungry with good things,
>   and sent the rich away empty. (Luke 1:52–53)

This is a vision of justice in which the structures of social power are turned inside out and upside down. For Mary, and for the Gospel of Luke, that is the meaning of Christmas.

Likewise when, at a crescendo in his "I Have a Dream" speech, Martin Luther King Jr. echoes the biblical prophet Amos, declaring that we must not be satisfied until "justice rolls down like waters, and righteousness like a mighty stream," we rightly hear a call for emancipation, a tearing down of the structures of racism that divide and conquer. Yet the prophet Amos himself was also and equally concerned about what he considered abuses of law and order — the other meaning of *mishpat*. He wanted to see priests and kings act justly; that is, according to the law. He was not interested in overturning hierarchies, but maintaining them in proper order.

In a poem called "Power," Adrienne Rich wrote of Marie Curie, two-time Nobel laureate who discovered radium and died from radiation sickness, "denying her wounds came from the same source as her power." For many, the Bible is a source of power and liberation. For many others, it is a source of wounds and oppression. When we read it honestly, as I think Twain did, it's hard to deny that it is a source of both, and that the two are often inextricably intermixed. The poisonous texts stand against the curative. The voices are in tension. They contradict. Sometimes, the poison is deceptively easy to take. And keep taking.

I daresay this, too, is a rich biblical polyvocality. We impoverish the Bible when we deny the poison's presence. As we saw earlier, the vast majority of values-added Bibles are conservative and moralistic, aimed at reinforcing the fundamentalist iconic image of the Bible that has so dominated American culture since the nineteenth century. But we should have as much trouble with a *God Is Love Bible* that remakes the Bible into something that's all sweetness and light, turning our attention away from these other, often violent and vengeful passages, as much as we may believe that God really is love. The deep biblical contradictions between liberation and oppression, love and hate, cure and poison, are also deep within us. Biblical interpretation is not a passive matter. It requires our own active negotiation. When we pretend that, deep down, all the voices are really saying the same thing and ought to be able to get along, we forfeit our responsibility as inheritors of this richly, sometimes disturbingly, contradictive literature.

Letting Suffering Speak

Speaking of pain. Why is there undeserved suffering in the world? This is not a problem for nontheological people, who can justifiably respond, why wouldn't there be? But for those who set their faith in God as a God of justice and love, it is the most profound of all problems.

Here we are in the territory traditionally called *theodicy*, which concerns the justice of God. Imagine the problem as a triangle: on one corner you have the belief that God is just; on the next you have the belief that God is all-powerful; on the third, you have the observation that people suffer unjustly.

It's a logical problem. You can't hold the three corners of the triangle together. So any solution to the problem of theodicy inevitably lops off one of them. A traditional Christian response has been to decide that God is not all-powerful: God gave up power so that humans would have free will. Another is to cut off the "God is just" corner. After all, God is said to repent of the evil he intended in Exodus 32, and Isaiah says that God "creates both peace and evil." Finally, one may decide to lop off the corner that says that there is undeserved suffering in the world. It may not be obvious why someone is suffering, but that doesn't mean that there's not a good reason. Perhaps we simply cannot see the justice of it as God does. In any case, you can't solve the problem of theodicy without cutting a corner.

What's fascinating to me is that, taken collectively, biblical literature does not solve the problem. Rather, it argues about it, exploring different responses and ultimately affirming the question over any and every solution. It cannot be reduced to a univocal answer.

There are very many biblical texts that raise questions of theodicy. In some cases, a biblical story will raise it subtly, between the lines. Why, for example, does God in the Exodus story "harden Pharaoh's heart" so that Pharaoh refuses the demand to "let my people go," so that God will "get glory" over Pharaoh, leading ultimately to the death of every firstborn in all of Egypt, "from the firstborn of Pharaoh who sits on his throne to the firstborn of the female slave who is behind the handmill, and all the firstborn of the livestock"? Were these firstborns deserving of such a fate? Was the collateral damage justifiable? It seems like a lot of unnecessary loss and suffering for the sake of a more dramatic and glorious flight from bondage.

Questions also well up from the raw experience of personal suffering as it finds voice in Israel's prayer book, the book of Psalms.

> How long, O LORD? Will you forget me forever?
> How long will you hide your face from me?
> How long must I bear pain in my soul,
> and have sorrow in my heart all day long?
> How long shall my enemy be exalted over me?
> (Psalm 13:1–2)

Such texts are categorized by biblical scholars as psalms of lament and complaint, but biblical theologian Walter Brueggemann offers a more provocative term: "psalms of disorientation." He insists that these profoundly challenging voices be allowed to

stand in radical, irresolvable tension with other "psalms of orientation." In psalms of orientation, all is right with the world
and "God sits enthroned over the flood" (Psalm 29:10). God
is altogether good and altogether omnipotent; therefore justice
and order prevail on every level, from body to house to society
to cosmos. In psalms of disorientation, however, that splendid
order of creation so confidently articulated in psalms of orientation is pulled downward into the depths of theological chaos
by poetry that cuts so breathtakingly close to the bone that it
can make a reader dizzy. One of the most stunning is Psalm 88,
which gives voice to a life of undeserved, God-inflicted despair,
loneliness, and depression.

> Your wrath lies heavy upon me,
>> and you overwhelm me with all your waves.
> You have caused my companions to shun me;
>> you have made me a thing of horror to them.
> I am shut in so that I cannot escape;
>> my eye grows dim through sorrow. (Psalm 88:7–9)

Here there is no trace of hope. Yet the psalmist is relentless in
bearing the pain up to an unheeding God.

> O LORD, why do you cast me off?
>> Why do you hide your face from me?
> Wretched and close to death from my youth up,
>> I suffer your terrors; I am desperate.
> Your wrath has swept over me;
>> your dread assaults destroy me.
> They surround me like a flood all day long;
>> from all sides they close in on me.
> You have caused friend and neighbor to shun me;
>> my companions are in darkness. (Psalm 88:14–18)

So the psalmist ceases, desperate and fearful, cowering alone in a world of theological disorientation and divine terror.

Many of us, horrified by this articulation of Godforsakenness, feel the urge to turn away from such raw despair. We are uncomfortable with letting the experience of unanswered suffering have the last word. We want to mute its terrible echo with an assuring answer. But the psalm itself, indeed the Bible itself, doesn't turn away with us. It stays with the voice of pain. Even as it lingers in the hollow silence after Jesus's own lonely cry from the cross, "My God, my God, why have you forsaken me?" In that opening line from another psalm of disorientation, Psalm 22, Jesus himself finds words for his Godforsaken terror on the cross. The German Jewish philosopher Theodor Adorno once wrote, "To let suffering speak is the condition of all truth." The library of the Bible has spaces to let suffering speak and be heard.

Trials of God

Elsewhere in the Bible, we feel as though we've stepped into an ongoing argument about the problem of theodicy. Consider, for example, the explicit disagreement between the book of Job and the book of Deuteronomy. We'll call it Job against Moses.

The book of Deuteronomy in the Torah is essentially a long sermon delivered by Moses, as mouthpiece of God, to the Israelites before they enter the Promised Land. In it he offers a vision of a perfectly moral universe governed by God. All of creation bears witness to the wisdom and justice of God. The justice of the creator God inheres within it. Social order and moral behavior follow from it. Keep God's commandments and you, your society, and your world will thrive and be blessed. Disobey them and everything goes to hell in a handbasket. Do good, be blessed. Do bad, be cursed. Obedience puts you in blessed harmony with the moral universe. Disobedience puts you wretchedly out of sync with it. "I call heaven and earth to witness against you today," declares Moses toward the end, "that I have set before you life and death, blessings and curses. Choose life so that you and your descendants may live."

The book of Job directly challenges the faith in that moral universe. Job suffers not because he has sinned or disobeyed God. In fact, Job is singled out by God precisely because he is so good. The story begins with God saying to the accuser (*hassatan*, "the accuser," often wrongly called by the proper name Satan), who acts as a prosecuting attorney in the divine court, "Have you noticed my servant Job? There is no one else like him on the earth, blameless and upright, fearing God and turning away from evil" (Job 1:8). The accuser replies, "Have you not put a fence around him and his house and all that he has on every side?" (1:10). Good point. After all, how hard is it to be good if you never face adversity? To see if Job will remain righteous even without all his goods, God allows his property to be taken and his children killed. Thus, contrary to Deuteronomy, Job's righteousness singles him out not for blessing but for curse.

When he continues to hold fast to his righteousness, the accuser rebuts, "Skin for skin! A man will give up all he has for his own life. But touch his bones and flesh . . ." (2:4–5). So begins phase two of Job's suffering, as he is "inflicted . . . with terrible boils from the sole of his foot to the top of his head."

This is where the argument with Deuteronomy begins to heat up. The boils that Job gets are precisely, word for word, what Deuteronomy describes as punishment for disobedience: "If you do not obey the LORD your God . . . the LORD will inflict you . . . with terrible boils from which you will never recover, from the sole of your foot to the top of your head" (28:15, 35). Both passages use the same Hebrew verb for "inflict" (*nakah*), and the description of the terrible boils is virtually identical. Clearly, the description of Job's cursed affliction is drawn directly from Deuteronomy, but with a major twist. In Deuteronomy, the curse is the promised punishment for unrighteous, disobedient behavior. In Job, however, it is brought on by Job's exemplary righteousness. Job's exceptional goodness has made him a target for suffering, by the will of God! Whereas Deuteronomy lops off the "people suffer undeservedly" corner of the triangle, the book of Job lops off the "God is just" corner.

In his wretched state, Job rants and rails against the injustice of his suffering, questioning God's goodness in very direct terms. Job's so-called friends scold him for doing so. They defend God's moral universe, and insist that Job must've done something wrong to deserve such misery. They expect God's anger to burn against Job for his blasphemous words. But in the end, it is against them, not Job, that God's anger burns, because they "did not speak rightly about [or to] me as my servant Job has" (42:7). The one who has argued with God has spoken rightly; the ones who defended God have not. In Job, speaking rightly with God is a boldly contentious business.

One of the greatest teachers on Job as a biblical model of a faith that refuses to let go of the struggle with and against God is the Jewish philosopher and Holocaust survivor Elie Wiesel. I first got to know him as a faculty colleague at Eckerd College, where he was a distinguished visiting professor during several month-long winter terms. One might expect such a preeminent scholar and public intellectual to keep his distance from us regular teachers, students, and staff. That was not the case at all. He was always on campus, always happy to meet with students in his office and talk with professors over the copy machine.

Rarely if ever was such conversation light. The first time I met him was at a dinner party hosted by our dean. After a few formal introductions at the door, my wife, Clover, and I sat down on the living room sofa facing him and his wife, Marion (a remarkable force in her own right). I was just about to sit back and take a bite of pita and hummus when he turned to me and asked, "Tim, what will the historian of the twenty-first century say about our time?" I can't honestly remember how I answered. Something about fascination and fear, reflecting how I felt not only about our time but also about the fact that I was actually talking face to face with Elie Wiesel.

In several subsequent winters, it was my great privilege to get to know him as a colleague and friend, and in the process to hear him speak personally about his deep and abiding relationship with biblical tradition. In one conversation, which we published in a book about reading the Bible after the Holocaust, we talked at length about his play, *The Trial of God*, as an interpretation of Job.

The play takes place in a seventeenth-century eastern European village after the massacre of local Jews. It's the eve of Purim, a celebration of the book of Esther, and the last few survivors are holed up in a tavern. The proprietor, Beresh, and his guests decide to put on a Purim play in which they put God on trial for what has happened to their community and to others throughout history. The only problem is that no one is willing to represent God. Then, just when it appears that the case will have to be dismissed, a mysterious man named Sam arrives and gladly agrees to take the role of defense attorney. In the trial that ensues, Beresh is very much the voice of Job, refusing to justify God in the face of this undeserved suffering. Sam, on the other hand, sounds very like Job's so-called friends. Unlike in Job, however, this trial is cut short not by divine intervention but by the bloodthirsty villagers eager to murder the last Jewish survivors. In the final moment of the play, as the mob breaks through the tavern door, Sam pulls off his mask and reveals himself to be none other than Satan.

"In this play, the only one willing to 'do theodicy,' that is, to justify God . . . is revealed as Satan in the final terrible moments. Does this suggest," I asked, "that to justify God in such a situation . . . is in some sense 'satanic' or evil?"

"Satan knew the answer," Wiesel replied. "He has all the answers. Actually Satan speaks like a fanatic. In this play I wanted to show the danger of fanaticism. The fanatic thinks he is justifying God. Never think that you are justifying God. To ask questions of God's justice is all right." There's a difference, he insisted, between asking theodicy questions about God's justice, or lack thereof, and answering them.

"Think of the Hebrew word for question, *she'elah,*" he continued. "There is *'el* (God) in *she'elah.* God is in the question. But to give the answer? Keep asking the question."

Is this not also the lesson of the book of Job? Job's friends are trying to answer for God against Job's accusations, but they are ultimately scolded because they did not "speak rightly" to or about God. Job, after all, is the only one who has insisted on maintaining his questions against all answers.

"God seems to be saying to the friends, 'who are you to answer for me? Who do you think you are?! Who asked you?!' And God takes the side of Job. God does not tell him the truth, but God does take Job's side over against the friends. In a way, God at the end of Job is saying, 'look who I have to defend me!' How pathetic are these defendants! And in *The Trial of God,* it is not Beresh's friends but Satan alone who will be God's champion. Imagine, at the end of *The Trial of God,* God saying, 'look who is my defendant!' As in Job, this shows the pathos of God, the tragedy of God. And so all the questions are there — even God's."

The book of Job is like a fault line running through the Bible.

In it, the moral universe affirmed in texts like Deuteronomy, according to which righteousness equals blessed well-being and disobedience equals cursed suffering, is shaken to its core. It's a book of theological horror.

Yet Job is no more the final word than is Deuteronomy. Neither does the psalmist of disorientation have the final word over the psalmist of orientation. The contradictory voices remain, as do many others that approach this problem from other perspectives and experiences. Contending with this, the most profound of theological questions, the Bible remains entirely unsettled, and unsettling. The argument goes unresolved. The question is canonized, sanctified. God is in the question — and in the argument, even when it is against God.

Weak Rope Theory

The New Testament is no more univocal than the Old Testament. Compare, for example, the empty-tomb stories in the four Gospels. Who went to the tomb and discovered it was empty? In Matthew, they are Mary Magdalene and "the other Mary." In Mark, they are Mary Magdalene, Mary the mother of James, and Salome. In Luke, they are Mary Magdalene, Joanna, Mary the mother of James, and "the other women with them." And in John, Mary Magdalene is the only one. What did they see? In Matthew, they see an angel who looked like lightning come down from heaven and roll away the stone while the guards freeze like dead men. In Mark, they see that the stone has already been rolled away and they find a young man dressed in white sitting inside. In Luke, they see the stone rolled away and two men standing beside them in dazzling clothes. And in John, Mary Magdalene sees only that the stone is rolled away. What did they do? In Matthew and Luke, they go and tell the disciples that Jesus is risen. In Mark, they run away in fear and tell no one. And in John, Mary Magdalene runs back to tell the others that someone has stolen the body. These are just some of the more glaring differences in the empty-tomb stories. There's no obvious way to harmonize them.

Or compare the three different versions of the story of Paul's conversion on the road to Damascus in the Acts of the Apostles. The first is told by the narrator (Acts 9), and the other two are told by Paul to different audiences (to Jewish authorities in chapter 22, and to King Agrippa in chapter 26). Set the three versions side by side. What happened to him? In the first and second versions, a great light descends and shines around Paul, he alone falls to the ground blinded, and Jesus says, "Saul, Saul, why are you persecuting me?" Jesus then commands him to go to Damascus to receive further instructions. In the third version, a light "brighter than the sun" shines around him and his companions, they all fall to the ground, and Jesus says, "Saul, Saul, why are you persecuting me?" but then adds, "It hurts you to kick against the goads." Jesus does not send him to Damascus, but explains then and there what his mission will be. Meanwhile, what did Paul's companions see and hear? In the first version, they remain standing, speechless "because they heard the voice but saw nothing." In the second, it's reversed: they see the light but don't hear the voice. And in the third, they see the light, which knocks them to the ground along with Paul, and apparently hear the voice too. These are only a few of the discrepancies in the three versions. To be sure, there may be literary reasons for them. The narrator's version may be taken as the historically correct account, and Paul's two versions of it may be seen as rhetorically "spun" in order to address his different audiences. Perhaps, too, there were different accounts of that story told among early Christians, and this was a way to incorporate them all within a single narrative.

In any case, the contradictions stand without an obvious way to explain them away.

Another well-known New Testament contradiction concerns what happened to Judas Iscariot after he betrayed Jesus to the authorities. In Matthew, Judas commits suicide by hanging himself, indicating remorse for his act of betrayal. In Acts, by contrast, he trips over a rock and is disgorged, indicating divine judgment. Some seem unable to accept that the Bible could contain such a discrepancy. Thus was born the "weak rope" or "weak bough" theory. According to it, Judas hangs himself, but the rope or branch he uses is weak and breaks before he dies. He then stumbles around, half-asphyxiated, falls on a rock, spills his guts, and dies. So, obviously, both passages are true!

We could go on multiplying examples of biblical polyvocality almost endlessly. Some, like the question of Judas's fate, are simple matters of what happened when: different chronologies of kings and prophets (e.g., discrepancies between Kings and Chronicles), different sequences of events in the Gospels. Others involve different metaphorical images of the divine, which sometimes also imply very different theologies of the character of God: warrior, mother, nurse, jealous husband, loving daddy, rock, still small voice. There are also different names for God: *El, Eloah, Elohim* (literally, "gods"), *El-Shaddai* (often translated "God on high," but more literally "God of breasts"), *Adonai,* and the unpronounceable Tetragrammaton, *Yhwh.* Still others, as we have seen, elaborate very different, mutually incompatible responses to some of the deepest and most fundamental human questions. How did the world begin? Why do innocent people suffer? What is justice? And so on and on.

Some see this rich polyvocality and contradiction as a problem to be solved. Many labor tirelessly to explain away all potential discrepancies, to get it all to say the same thing. Bibles like the

Quest Study Bible and *The Apologetics Study Bible* go to great, tedious, sometimes ingenious lengths to explain them all away. Both of these, by the way, adhere to the weak rope theory, with *Quest* adding the lovely point that the only way Judas's guts could've "burst" was if he'd already been rotting and distending for a good long time before the rope broke. Many other such explainings-away are at least as desperately creative. Desperate, in that they speak to the desire of many Bible readers to establish univocality within a deeply, richly, irrepressibly polyvocal collection of Scriptures. Creative as they are, they nonetheless stifle the rich complexity of biblical literature. They impoverish the text, and the faith that lives and moves and has its being in relation to it.

Is the Bible a Failure?

In many ways, those dedicated to removing all potential biblical contradictions, to making the Bible entirely consistent with itself, are no different from irreligious debunkers of the Bible, Christianity, and religion in general. Many from both camps seem to believe that simply demonstrating that the Bible is full of inconsistencies and contradictions, as I have just done, is enough to discredit any religious tradition that embraces it as Scripture. Bible debunkers and Bible defenders are kindred spirits. They agree that the Bible is on trial. They agree on the terms of the debate, and what's at stake, namely its credibility as God's infallible book. They agree that Christianity stands or falls, triumphs or fails, depending on whether the Bible is found to be inconsistent, to contradict itself. The question for both sides is whether it fails to answer questions, from the most trivial to the ultimate, consistently and reliably.

But you can't fail at something you're not trying to do. To ask whether the Bible fails to give consistent answers or be of one voice with itself presumes that it was built to do so. That's a false presumption, rooted no doubt in thinking of it as the book that God wrote. As we have seen, biblical literature is constantly interpreting, interrogating, and disagreeing with itself. Virtually nothing is asserted someplace that is not called into question or undermined elsewhere. Ultimately it resists conclusion and explodes any desire we might have for univocality.

We don't know, and will never know, many details about the history of the development of biblical literature. No doubt there have been countless hands, scribal and editorial, involved in writing, editing, copying, and circulating the various versions of various texts that eventually were brought together into a canonical collection. Nor do we know very much for certain about the ancient life situations — ritual practices, oral traditions, legal systems — in which these texts had their beginnings. Nor do we know everything about the complex process by which the canons of Jewish and Christian Scriptures took form. What we do know for certain is that the literature now in our Bibles was thousands of years in the making.

Given how many hands have been involved in so many contexts over such a long time in the history of this literature, can we honestly imagine that no one noticed such glaring discrepancies? Can we believe, for example, that the seam between the first and second creation stories in Genesis, as well as the many other seams found throughout the Torah, were not obvious? That if agreement and univocality were the goal, such discrepancies would not have been fixed and such rough seams mended long ago? That creation stories would have been made to conform or be removed? That Job would've been allowed to stand against Moses? That Gospel mix-ups concerning who saw what after Jesus's resurrection would have been left to stand? That Judas would have died twice, once by suicide and once by divine disgorge? And so on? Could all those many, many people involved in the development of biblical literature and the canon of Scriptures have been so blind, so stupid? It's modern arrogance to imagine so.

The Bible canonizes contradiction. It holds together a tense diversity of perspectives and voices, difference and argument — even and especially, as we have seen, when it comes to the profoundest questions of faith, questions that inevitably outlive all their answers. The Bible interprets itself, argues with itself, and perpetually frustrates any desire to reduce it to univocality.

Faith in Ambiguity

I'm reminded of the famous parable of the Grand Inquisitor in Fyodor Dostoyevsky's *The Brothers Karamazov*. The story is told by Ivan, a cynical atheist, to his younger, mystically minded Christian brother, Alyosha. In it, Jesus appears in the city of Seville during the Spanish Inquisition, just as a huge crowd gathers to witness a mass execution. He never says a mumbling word, and yet everyone immediately recognizes him. Throngs gather around him, and he blesses and heals them. A tiny white coffin passes by, and the child within it is revived.

Standing in the cathedral doorway, the Cardinal Grand Inquisitor also sees Jesus, and immediately has him arrested. "Such is his power over the well-disciplined, submissive and now trembling people," explains Ivan, "that the thick crowds immediately give way, and scattering before the guard, amid dead silence and without one breath of protest, allow them to lay their sacrilegious hands upon the stranger and lead Him away." In the evening, the Grand Inquisitor visits Jesus alone in his prison cell, and explains to him that in the morning he will be burned at the stake "as the most wicked of all the heretics; and that same people, who today were kissing Thy feet, tomorrow at one bend of my finger, will rush to add fuel to Thy funeral pile."

The reason, explains the Inquisitor, is that Jesus came to give people freedom, but that's not what they want. What they really want, he says, is to be told what to do and believe, and to be fed. "For fifteen centuries, we have been wrestling with Thy freedom, but now it is ended and over for good."

Are Ivan and his Grand Inquisitor right? Would we rather not be free, to think and question for ourselves? *Sapere aude!* proclaimed the Enlightenment philosopher Immanuel Kant. "Dare to know" or "be wise," to release yourself from your self-incurred tutelage under the authority of others and think for yourself, to trust your own reason and imagination. To be sure, such a calling is both empowering and intimidating. Would we rather be told what to do and think? Do the questions make us nervous? Do we thirst for the answers that will put our restless spirits to rest? Is that what we really want religion to be, or rather do, for us? Is that what we want from the Bible?

A few years ago I had the pleasure of doing an interview with National Public Radio's Michele Norris about my book, *Roadside Religion*. That book tells the story of my family's "blue highways" exploration of roadside religious attractions, from the World's Largest Ten Commandments and Holy Land USA to Precious Moments Chapel and Golgotha Fun Park. Norris knew that I had grown up in a conservative Christian environment, and wondered what kinds of thoughts and feelings these places evoked for me. Her final question was meant to bring our conversation around to this topic.

"As an avowed atheist . . ." Norris began.

"Um, wait. I'm sorry. I'm not an atheist. I'm actually Christian."

"Really!? Your publicity kit says you're an atheist at least twice."

Later, I asked my publicist why the kit described me as an atheist. She said that she got it from the book's introduction, where I wrote that there were days when I could "atheist anyone under the table." That's true. But to say that is not to say that I am an atheist. In fact, what I'd written was, "Although I can atheist anyone under the table on some days, I remain a Christian, and I remain committed to the church . . ."

The interview cleaned up nicely, and the confusion was worth a good laugh. But I think it belies a more significant, popular cultural understanding of what faith is, and what religion is. There is a widely held, simplistic definition of faith as firm belief. To many, especially nonreligious people, faith is seen as absolute certainty despite or without regard to observed facts or evidence. Yet, as anyone trying to live faithfully in this world knows full well, there is no faith without doubt. Doubt is faith's other side, its dark night. Indeed, in an atheisting match, I'd put big odds on the faithful any day. People of faith know the reasons to doubt their faith more deeply and more personally than any outside critic ever can. Faith is inherently vulnerable. To live by faith is to live with that vulnerability, that soft belly, exposed.

Likewise the Bible. The Bible can atheist any book under the table on some pages. It presumes faith in God, yet, as we have seen, it also often gives voice to the most profound and menacing doubts about the security of that faith. The Bible is not a book of answers but a library of questions. How rare such places have become in a society addicted to quick fixes, executive summaries, and idiot's guides. The canon of the Bible is that kind of place.

Ambiguity is the devil's playground. Let it creep into your faith life and all hell will break loose. So some say. For them, faith is essentially a battle to keep up the wall of certitude against the immanent floodwaters of chaos. Uncertainty is a crack in the dam of faith. Elie Wiesel obviously disagrees. His Satan figure, the only one willing to defend God against life's most profound questions, is the Grand Inquisitor's soul brother. Contrary to them, faith deepens not in finding certainty but in learning to live with ambiguity, as we ride our questions as far into the wilderness as they will take us. Biblical literature hosts that journey.

Nothing but a Burning Light

Gospel singer, preacher, and pioneer of the blues Blind Willie Johnson understood the power of the honest question, and he perceived its flame in the Bible.

Johnson was born in poverty in 1897 and blinded at age seven when his stepmother, in a fight with his father, threw lye in his face. He died in poverty in 1945, sleeping on a wet bed in the ruins of his house, which had burned down two weeks before. Thankfully, between 1927 and 1930, he recorded a number of his biblically based blues songs with Columbia Records. These have inspired countless rockers, from Led Zeppelin to Beck. In 1977 his "Dark Was the Night — Cold Was the Ground," a hauntingly inarticulate meditation on the crucifixion, was sent into deep space on the *Voyager 1* as part of the Voyager Golden Record, a collection of music representing the sounds of Earth to any potentially interested extraterrestrials. The time capsule left our solar system in November 2004 and is scheduled to be within 1.7 light years of two nearby suns in about forty thousand years. The closest thing to timeless any musical artist could possibly achieve. Mercy, how we do so often love to immortalize those despised and forgotten in life.

Johnson's uniquely spiritual blues music is driven by the deepest questions, often finding voice through an encounter between biblical tradition and his own life experience, which was well acquainted with sorrow. The Bible peopled his imagination. It was his wellspring of imagery. It empowered him to call this world into question and to envision another. On at least one occasion the powers that be recognized how potentially explosive such an inspired combination of biblical language and lived oppression could be: he was arrested in front of a New Orleans city building for inciting riot simply by singing "If I Had My Way I'd Tear the Building Down," a song about the biblical hero Samson, who tore down the house of the Philistine lords after they had gouged out his eyes. To the officer who arrested him, the ancient story suddenly sounded dangerously contemporary.

In his well-known song "Soul of a Man," Johnson growls out the question he has pursued his whole life, knowing that no one can really help him find the answer: Just what is the "soul of a man?" Indeed, what is soul? It's a question filled to overflowing with other questions. Am I more than my mind? More than my body? More than the sum of my parts? Do I have a soul? Does it live beyond this mortal coil? What am I? Who am I? Why am I here? Such profound questions are often asked, but too often are followed by erudite answers from someone who claims to know. Rarely by someone who honestly does not know. As none of us do.

Johnson recalls his lifelong soul search. He's traveled far and wide, through cities and wildernesses. He's heard answers from lawyers, doctors, and theologians. None have satisfied. In response to each of the answers he's been given, he repeats his question with more forceful, gravelly urgency.

In his quest, he turns to the Bible.

> I read the Bible often. I tries to read it right
> And far as I could understand, nothing but a burning light

Called to preach since age five, steeped in the African American Baptist tradition, this blind sage of spiritual blues knew the Bible inside and out from memory. Yet it gave him no answer, only a more profound mystery: nothing but a burning light.

I first discovered this song when I heard Canadian singer-songwriter Bruce Cockburn perform a cover of it in a concert in Atlanta, Georgia, about a year before I finished graduate school at Emory. The image of "nothing but a burning light" immediately grabbed me, and stayed with me as I began my career as a professor. In fact, it was the title of my final lecture the first time I taught my introductory Bible course, which I called Dead Prophets Society. To me, it is an image of mystery that is both compelling and at least a little dangerous. Warming, burning. Enlightening, blinding. Life giving, dangerous. No angel of the Lord speaking from it, as there was in the burning bush that spoke to Moses. An all-consuming revelation, it sheds light on the absence of answers.

There is indeed a bluesy biblical mysticism here, a solicitation of deep spiritual unrest that opens us to that which is beyond articulation. The failure to find the answer gives way to a more profound revelation, a burning light of unknowing.

In its "failure" to say one thing on anything, in its "failure" as a book of answers or font of univocal truth, the Bible opens itself to mystery. It is faithful not to the answer but to the question that takes you to the edge of knowing. "There is a crack in everything," declares another great songwriter and theologian, Leonard Cohen. "That's how the light gets in."

The Bible by the Side of the Road

The ninth-century Zen master Lin Chi is remembered for saying, "If you see the Buddha on the road, kill him." Meaning kill your attachment to the Buddha. Nurturing an attachment, even to the master of detachment, prevents spiritual growth.

Attachment to the cultural icon of the Bible is similarly debilitating. It's a false image, an idol. If you see it, kill it. The Bible is dead; long live the Bible. Not as the book of answers but as a library of questions, not as a wellspring of truth but as a pool of imagination, a place that hosts our explorations, rich in ambiguity, contradiction, and argument. A place that, in its failure to give clear answers and its refusal to be contained by any synopsis or conclusion, points beyond itself to mystery, which is at the heart of the life of faith.

We might even go so far as to say that the Bible kills itself. It deconstructs itself. Reading it undermines the iconic idea of it as a univocal, divinely authored book and our desire to attach to it as such. As we saw in our exploration of biblical polyvocality, Scriptures have a tendency to exceed the boundaries of orthodoxy and resist closure. The Bible keeps reopening theological cans of worms. It resists its own impoverishment by univocality. In so doing, it fails to give answer, leaving readers biblically ungrounded.

In response, we can buy another values-added Bible and keep the dream alive. If at first we don't succeed, buy, buy again. The Bible biz is at the ready. Or we can give up on the Bible altogether. Very many do, as if it stands or falls based on how well it fits our inadequate idea of it. Or we can begin to let our attachment to that idea die.

8

And I Feel Fine

WHEN I GRADUATED from high school, a former Sunday school teacher and close friend of my family gave me a paperback copy of Harold Lindsell's *The Battle for the Bible,* urging me to read it before leaving for the Lower 48 to begin college at Seattle Pacific University. Considered a fundamentalist manifesto by many, the book argues that Christian faith stands or falls on biblical inerrancy.

In this day of iTunes and Target gift cards, such a graduation gift seems inappropriately serious. But this friend was sincerely concerned about the challenges I would soon be facing. His inscription on the inside cover warned that, "even at a Christian college like Seattle Pacific," there were professors who did not believe in the inerrancy of the Bible and would seek to undermine my faith in it. College, like life, he seemed to be saying, would be a battle for the Bible.

I brought the book with me to college, but I decided not to read it. By that time in my life, there was a still small voice inside me that longed for an alternative to this sort of embattled Biblicism. Although I didn't admit it to my peers or this friend, the battle for the Bible was already well under way. I had lost most of my will to stand guard.

Still, the battle was far from over. I did very well in college, except in the one course I took on the Bible. It was an introduction to the literature and history of the Old Testament. I failed the final exam and got a C-minus overall. Part of the problem was that my former girlfriend, who'd dumped me over Christmas break, was also in the class, and I had a hard time concentrating on the lectures. More than that, however, I found myself struggling with the course content. I'd like to say that it was too conservative in its presumptions about the Bible. After all, by that time, halfway through my sophomore year, I had given up on church, let alone reading the Bible. I thought of myself less as a Bible-believing Christian than as a poetry-reading mystic.

Truth is, my problem wasn't that the course was too conservative. In fact, it was exactly what my former Sunday school teacher had worried it might be, and what I thought I wanted. A well-respected biblical historian and very popular teacher, Professor Frank Spina modeled depth and complexity in his understanding and abiding appreciation of the Bible — what it is, where it came from, and how to study it in a faithful yet academically responsible way. He adeptly drew our attention to the differences in the two creation stories in Genesis, refusing to explain them away as mere seeming contradictions. He encouraged us to ask whether biblical accounts of the Hebrew people's liberation from bondage in Egypt and their conquest of Canaan in the books of Exodus and Joshua were historically accurate, and offered us alternative scholarly theories that fit better with the archaeological record and other ancient documents. Throughout the course, he challenged our simplistic ideas and preconceived notions.

Looking back now, I can see that the main reason I earned a low grade in the course was that I wasn't quite ready to embrace what it was offering. Although I'd abandoned the biblical faith of my youth, I retained its basic, iconic understanding of the Bible. I hadn't changed my idea of it. I had simply rejected it as such.

In my case, it took a very different sort of introduction to the Bible for me to begin to let go of my preconceived, all too familiar idea of it. It was in a course on English Romantic poetry, and the voice that broke through was that of the visionary print-maker and eccentric genius William Blake. ("That explains a lot," more than one colleague has remarked. I always take it as a compliment.) Blake wrote of encounters with prophets and devils, whom he liked very much, and with moralists and angels, whom he resented even more. He declared moral goodness oppressive and reason a false idol. He wrote "Proverbs of Hell" that praised excess over prudence and desire over reason. He lamented any lack of imagination, closing the "doors of perception," keeping us from seeing the infinite in everything. I wasn't always sure what to make of his provocative proclamations and strange visions. But I was drawn to the impassioned volatility of his religious imagination. My sense in studying his works was that he had been somewhere I had never been but wanted to go. His imagination seemed radically other than my own. Yet he passionately identified with Christianity and claimed that his inspiration was none other than the Bible.

Two lines that Blake wrote in his *Laocoön*, a collage-like meditation on art and religion, hit me especially hard: "If Morality was Christianity, Socrates was the Savior" and "The Old & New Testaments are the Great Code of Art."

For Blake, Christianity was not about morality but art, by which I think he meant the ongoing process of making and re-making, visioning and revisioning, of changing the world by changing one's way of seeing, opening the "doors of perception." To be creative was to be in the image of God; creativity is God in and with us. The Bible, moreover, was not to him anything like the moral guide and book of answers that I'd grown up with. It was, rather, "the Great Code of Art."

For me, studying religion is about making the strange familiar and the familiar strange. It's about encountering religious beliefs and practices that initially appear unfamiliar, foreign, other, and coming to understand how they can be true for those who embrace and live by them. It's about getting to know the context within which they make sense. But it's also about encountering those religious beliefs and practices that seem familiar to us in new and surprising ways, whether interpreting them according to new theories and methods or comparing them to less familiar religions. In that process, we often find that the familiar becomes strange. As we become familiar with the strange — as we begin to see ourselves in the stranger — we also may begin to see the stranger in ourselves. A sense of otherness takes root in our own familiar.

I never went so far as to join the Church of William Blake (yes, there is such a thing). But for me, studying how Blake saw the Bible began to estrange me from what I thought I knew about it. A thousand Sundays hence, I am still drawn to his vision of the Bible as a code of art. Not a book of moral guidelines or answers, "Basic Instructions Before Leaving Earth," but a body of literature whose spiritual value lies in its power to inspire new creations, new ideas, new ways of seeing ourselves and our world. Not the final word, the end of the discussion, but a locus of genesis, a deep wellspring of creative meaning-making, with no final Word in sight.

There are, moreover, resonances between Blake's great code of art and my library of questions. As code of art, the Bible not only is art, but it inspires artistic creation in those who study it. Likewise, as library of questions, the Bible not only raises questions, but also inspires readers to raise new ones in relation to it. And both ways of thinking about the Bible value process over conclusion: art is about the making more than the made, and questioning is about the asking more than the answering. The most profound questions, those that burn at the heart of the religious life, are those that live beyond all the answers given them. And there is indeed an art to asking those kinds of questions. The Bible is a pool of imagination in which to pursue that art. It hosts the human quest for meaning without predestining a specific conclusion. For those wanting "real answers, real fast," I recommend Socrates.

Cracking the Binding

With my own students, I often enjoy sharing what I call "word snacks," little etymological explorations of words that perhaps have become too familiar. I find that looking into the early family life of a word rekindles latent meanings that can be enlightening and even inspiring. So it is with the word "religion."

Most say that the Latin origin of religion is in *religare*, from the verb *ligare*, "to bind" or "attach." *Religare* therefore means "to re-bind" or "re-attach." With this origin in mind, we have a sense of religion as a kind of binding. Religion is about being bound and re-bound to a set of beliefs, doctrines, institutions, and scriptures. It's about identifying oneself with a particular tradition, and with a larger body of likewise religiously bound people. That's religion in terms of the binding.

But the ancient philosopher Cicero suggested that the meaning of religion goes back to a different Latin origin, *relegere*, from the verb *legere*, "to read" (from whence we get words like "lecture" and "lectionary"). *Relegere* is therefore "to re-read" or "read again." Take this as the origin and we have a sense of religion that is less about the binding and more about the ongoing process of rereading. It's about reinterpreting sacred scriptures and other religious traditions in order to make them speak meaningfully to new horizons of meaning.

Our aim here is not to decide which is the true origin, but to reflect creatively on what each might suggest about religion, and in what sense the Bible is a religious text. Instead of choosing one origin or the other, I suggest that we think of religion in terms of both *religare* and *relegere,* both rebinding and rereading. Thus: religion is about being bound together as a community and being bound to a library of scriptures that we are bound to reread and reinterpret in relation to new and unique horizons of meaning. In this light, religion is not simply a binding system of beliefs or set of doctrines but a *process of rereading,* reexamining, reinterpreting a scriptural tradition that we have inherited and that gives us a sense of identity and context. The religious life is a communal practice of reading again, of opening the Bible in ways that crack its binding, so to speak, and open it to new understandings, new interpretations. Or, to put it in terms we used earlier, it calls for a reinvestment of sacred capital: out of the product and into the process, thereby privileging the vital, ongoing relationship between readers and texts, a relationship that is dynamic, transient, and creative.

In fact, the Bible itself models this kind of rereading. Recall, for example, how the book of Job rereads the book of Deuteronomy as a way to raise questions about why the good suffer and the wicked prosper, and what it means to speak rightly to and about God. Recall as well how different creation stories draw images from others, creating new visions of cosmic and human origins and, in the process, new ways of conceiving the relation between creator and creation. And recall how different literary strands from different periods in Israelite and Judean history were sewn together by later editors, reread into larger narratives like the Torah. We find evidence of similar editorial processes of rereading and reinterpreting throughout the Jewish Scriptures.

The New Testament literature likewise is shaped by rereading. All its writings are fundamentally concerned with rereading

Jewish Scriptures in order to understand the meaning of Jesus's life, death, and resurrection. Again and again, the Gospels quote Jewish Scriptures that they reinterpret as "fulfilled," that is, filled out, by Jesus's words and actions. Moreover, they ground Jesus's authority in his own rereadings of Jewish Scriptures. Jesus is presented, first and foremost, as a biblical interpreter. We saw this very clearly in the story of Jesus reading from the Isaiah scroll in his hometown synagogue in the Gospel of Luke. Another good example is the Sermon on the Mount in the Gospel of Matthew (chapter 5), in which Jesus repeatedly quotes passages from the Torah and then reinterprets them in radically new ways. "You have heard that it was said, 'An eye for an eye and a tooth for a tooth,'" he declares, quoting a line that appears three times in the Torah. "But I say to you, Do not resist an evildoer. But if anyone strikes you on the cheek, turn the other also; and if anyone wants to sue you and take your coat, give your cloak as well; and if anyone forces you to go one mile, go also the second mile. Give to everyone who begs from you, and do not refuse anyone who wants to borrow from you." Here and throughout the Gospels, Jesus does not simply cite Scripture as though it were a self-evident, self-interpreting source of authority. He rereads it, drawing out new, often highly provocative meanings, "fulfilling" it in a way that gives it new form for a new day. What would Jesus do? Reread. The Bible tells me so.

So too Paul's letters, which often reread Jewish Scriptures in surprisingly creative ways, drawing entirely new meanings from them in the process. We saw an example of this in his letter to the Galatians, where he rereads a fairly mundane regulation about how to handle a corpse, along with other passages, in order to develop his own insight into the meaning of Jesus's crucifixion as it relates to their particular community.

So too throughout the New Testament. The book of Reve-

lation alone has well over two hundred references and allusions
to Jewish Scriptures. Indeed, one is hard-pressed to find a few
hundred words in a row from the New Testament where there
is no reference to or interpretation of a passage from the Old
Testament.

Loose Canon

There are many more examples of biblical passages rereading
other, earlier ones. The Bible grew into its present form as new
roots and branches grew from older ones. The Bible is rereading
all the way down. It is a library whose various titles are in vital
conversation with one another. They do not all agree on any of
the most important questions, but they are engaged with one another in a dynamic relationship of interpretation and argument.

The Bible is, moreover, an unfinished conversation, a work
in progress. To say that biblical texts reread and reinterpret
other biblical texts is not to say that the Bible as a whole is self-
interpreting, and therefore closed off from our own rereadings. It
does not interpret itself in such a way as to tell us what it means.
It does not tell us the right way to read it. It does not provide
the keys to its own right interpretation. Rather, in its rich, unresolved polyvocality, it leaves open innumerable, perhaps endless
possible readings.

Here we may find inspiration in Jewish tradition. Rabbi ben
Bag Bag, a second-century sage, is remembered for saying of the
Torah, "Turn it and turn it, for everything is in it." Another Jewish legend says that every one of the six hundred thousand people
who were present at Mount Sinai for the giving of the Torah saw
a different face or facet of it. From early on, Rabbinic Judaism
rooted itself in the faith that the Torah is an inexhaustible font of
meaning. The Torah is not so much in the world as the world is

in the Torah. It anticipates its own infinitude of interpretations. Seen in this light, the Torah is a loose canon, insofar as it remains open to innumerable rereadings.

I suggest we think of the Bible in a kindred way. The Bible does not stand alone. Its canon is closed, but only loosely so. The ever-growing body of biblical interpretations and other creative works inspired or otherwise provoked by the Bible are part of it, like new wings and annexes to the library (and some of these new spaces get a lot more traffic than the older ones). In its hosting of disagreement, the canon of the Bible remains open, inviting us to enter, explore, and add our voices to the ongoing conversation.

The Bible creates community by providing space for community to happen. It offers storied worlds and theological vocabularies around which people can come together in conversation about abiding questions. It calls for creative, collaborative participation. This is true especially for Christians. It is "our" library of questions and pool of imagination, the place we gather to read again in order to find meaning in new situations. In its many voices, perspectives, and contradictions, it both embraces the diversity of voices among us and provides a context in which we can affirm unity within that diversity — not by agreeing about what it means but by joining in the creative, meaning-making process of interpretation that it hosts.

Here again we may find insight from Jewish tradition's understanding of Torah. One legend says, "When the Holy One, blessed be he, gave the Torah to Israel, he gave it only in the form of wheat, for us to make flour from it, and flax, to make a garment from it." The idea is that God depends on the community to fulfill biblical meaning. The Torah is incomplete without its interpreters who make something new of it. God rejoices to see what meanings come from the creative, generative labors of the people. Everything is there, this tradition proclaims, and it is the call of the Jewish people throughout history to discover as many meanings as possible.

It is no coincidence, by the way, that Jacques Derrida, who gave us the phrase "impoverishment by univocality," was Jewish and had a deep and abiding appreciation for the interpretive traditions of Rabbinic Judaism.

Back to the Future

What might this process of rereading look like in practice? Let me offer three illustrations that give a sense of the range of possibilities, from the Internet to the kitchen table to the church pew.

Earlier we considered the impact of the digital revolution on the cultural icon of the Bible, how the end of print culture will also mean the end of the Word as we know it, that is, the end of the idea of the Bible as a book, *the* Book, and so on. By the same token, I believe that this revolution also opens new possibilities for engaging Scripture in vital, virtual communities that privilege process over product and questions over answers. Three dimensions of reading and writing in our emerging digital, networked media culture are especially suggestive. First, this culture is *hypertextual,* meaning that any text within it, including Scripture, is linked to a vast, practically infinite network of other texts, images, and other digital media. These are all present as an excess of potential relationships. Texts overflow, spilling into others. The line between text and context is always permeable and negotiable.

Second, digital network culture is *processual.* Complex relations within it are always in the process of formation, deformation, and reformation. There is no end game. Everything is impermanent — adaptable, combinable, editable, cut-copy-and-pastable.

Third, digital network culture is *collaborative*. Not only are texts connected to one another in ongoing, ever-changing networks. So are the people reading, writing, and creating meaning within those networks.

Although still largely unrealized, the potential implications of these three dimensions of the digital network revolution for biblical interpretation are not hard to see. Loosed from its binding in the book, the canon of Scriptures loses its tight closure. Biblical words and phrases are easily linked up with other texts, both biblical and extrabiblical. Individual biblical writings are easily removed from the larger canonical whole to float independently. Smaller snippets of biblical texts are copied, edited, and pasted into new contexts, thereby creating relationships between them and previously unrelated texts. Likewise, other texts can easily find their way into the biblical canon. Interpretations and marginal comments may be inserted, for example.

To some, this may look like doomsday, the end of the Word set in the context of the end of the world. And yet, ironically, it also looks very like the scriptural culture of early Christianity. Indeed, scriptural culture *after* the book may have much in common with scriptural culture *before* the book. There, as we saw, Christian communities were theologically and culturally diverse, with no central organization. Scattered throughout the Roman Empire, specific groups were connected to others through more or less informal networks. Different communities had different collections of scriptures, written in different languages and stored in different media forms, and they copied and shared them within these networks. Their *testimonia* essentially created new scriptural texts from older sources.

As in early Christianity, moreover, the ongoing process of biblical engagement in digital networked culture is beyond anyone's authority or control. There is no central administration.

It's about participation in a social world where readers are writers and consumers are producers. Here meaning and value are created collaboratively within constantly changing networks of communication and community. Nor is there any end in sight. Everything is impermanent, inconclusive. Everything is subject to revision and reformulation.

Living Conversations

The second illustration may seem more old school, but it is equally suggestive of the power of the Bible, as a library of questions and pool of imagination, to generate new meanings in new contexts and thereby affirm both unity and diversity in communities whose members engage one another around it. It comes from a public television series hosted by Bill Moyers called *Genesis: A Living Conversation*. Each of its ten hourlong sessions brings together a handful of people, some scholars, some writers, from different religious and nonreligious backgrounds, around a single short story from the book of Genesis. The format is very simple. They sit in a circle and talk about the story, keeping their comments and questions grounded in the details of the text.

As each conversation progresses, one has the feeling that there are at least as many versions of the story as there are people in the room. Nonetheless, the different voices and readings stay connected to each other through respectful, even if sometimes a little contentious, conversation. In the end, there is no agreement or adjudication by Moyers, no final word on what the story means or how to understand it. But there is a much richer, deeper appreciation for the biblical story, the questions it raises, and how those questions relate to the particular experiences of those who have participated.

The tremendous success of the *Genesis* series testifies to the generative power of biblical stories, which turn out to be far less familiar than we thought they were: Adam and Eve, Noah and the Flood, and so on. It also testifies to the desire among people from a variety of religious and nonreligious backgrounds to engage in open conversation in which the whole is greater than the sum of its participants. It speaks to the power of biblical texts to spark lively, meaningful, mind-changing encounters.

I often show a video of one of the sessions to my students as a model for how we might engage this literature. When it's over, they don't want to talk about the celebrity scholars, authors, and artists who said their piece on screen. They want to talk about the biblical story. They want to continue the conversation. In fact, I find that this model for biblical discussion works better with people who are not scholars, who are not used to speaking with authority about biblical literature. They tend to have less investment in a text meaning one thing and not another, and they are more open to surprise.

No matter what kind of people are gathered around the biblical text — a class of college students, a group of friends on a Thursday night, or participants in a Sunday-morning adult-education class at church — and no matter what biblical text is the focus of conversation, two simple ground rules are important. First, the biblical selection needs to be small, never more than a page, and preferably less. Second, no comment or question is off-limits so long as it emerges from specific details of the passage at hand.

People who've never experienced this kind of open-ended conversation around such a small piece of biblical text often worry that they'll run out of things to talk about, that there's not enough there to sustain much of a discussion. But such concerns are quickly dispelled. On the contrary, people are inevitably surprised when they run out of time. It feels like they've barely scratched the surface. Which is true. When it comes to biblical literature, the closer you look, the more you see.

Seeds to Go Around

Our last example of what it looks like to practice what I'm preaching comes, appropriately enough, from the pulpit.

Last year, our church developed an adult-education program inspired by the "living conversation" model I just described. Around the same time, my wife, Clover, and her pastoral colleague, John Lentz, began asking how they might bring some of the same participatory spirit of biblical interpretation into the worship service. How to get away from the traditional, one-way mode of sermonic communication, in which the preacher tells the congregation what she or he believes the Bible is saying, and they passively receive it?

In that spirit, Pastor Lentz recently "preached" on Jesus's parable of the sower in the Gospel of Matthew. He began with a few brief introductory remarks to set up the passage. Parables, he explained, are like extended metaphors, in which something familiar, like a story about planting seeds, is compared to something unfamiliar, like the kingdom of God. In fact, scholars believe that the parable was Jesus's signature mode of teaching. Which is interesting because, like all metaphorical thinking, parables offer poetic meaning that is not easily nailed down in a simple equation of this equals that. In fact, Jesus's parables often seem to confuse and complicate rather than clarify and simplify, even for his disciples. With this particular parable in Matthew, there's actually an interpretation that follows. But that explanation wasn't originally part of the teaching. It was added later. As a pastor, John proposed that we focus on the parable alone, to let it stand without explanation, to see what we can see. "So now, as we hear this familiar parable of the sower, imagine its words are being sewn on you."

A member of the congregation read the passage.

> Listen! A sower went out to sow. And as he sowed, some seeds fell on the path, and the birds came and ate them up. Other seeds fell on rocky ground, where they did not have much soil, and they sprang up quickly, since they had no depth of soil. But when the sun rose, they were scorched; and since they had no root, they withered away. Other seeds fell among thorns, and the thorns grew up and choked them. Other seeds fell on good soil and brought forth grain, some a hundredfold, some sixty, some thirty. Let anyone with ears listen! (Matthew 13:2–9)

After a minute of silent reflection, John invited people in the congregation to share their own first impressions of the parable. A well-liked gentleman with a booming voice who regularly participates in adult-education classes spoke first, summarizing the "Sunday school" version many people know. It's about God planting seeds of grace and salvation in different people, he explained. Some people, maybe one in four, have "good soil" and the seed thrives in them; in most, however, it doesn't take.

"Are you familiar with that message?" John asked the congregation. Nearly everyone nodded. "Well, how does it make you feel?" People began to perk up. Several scooted forward in their seats.

"I must be one of those bad guys with bad soil," one man said.

"I worry, what have I done with the seed in me?" a woman called out.

"Where's my seed?" a high school boy asked. Others laughed and nodded.

These honest first responses quickly broke open the text and the congregation. Both began to open up. New possible meanings, rereadings, began to emerge. Maybe each of us has all kinds of soils in us. Have the birds gotten a bad rap? After all, they don't just take seeds away. They spread them to new places. Seeds have lots of chances to take. Surely Jesus's agriculturally minded audience would've known that.

What about the one sowing the seeds? Shouldn't he know where and where not to sow? Is he being rational, practical? He's just scattering seeds all over the place, with no discretion. His actions seem downright wasteful and excessive. If we think of the sower as God, what does that say? Maybe that God is not stingy or even careful about where he scatters the seeds? That divine grace is lavishly, uneconomically, improvidently broadcast all over the place.

And what if *we* are the sowers? What does the life of faith look like from that angle? We too can be carelessly, wastefully free. As we talked, and as the excitement of the congregation grew more and more palpable, I imagined children playing in heaps and heaps of seeds, tossing them into the air like balls in a McDonald's play area. An image of the kingdom of God.

John had wisely trusted that simply hosting a gathering of these people and this text would produce new fruit, and he remained open to whatever surprises that process might bring. By the end of the "sermon," John's role had changed from preacher to facilitator. There was no wrapping up, no bringing it all back to a single point. The open-ended process of rereading had itself become a sacramental moment, a means of receiving and sharing seeds of grace. The many voices remained present in all their diversity of insight and experience, echoing in and through the final "amen."

Word Without End

The great rabbi Yosef Chaim once described the din of students reading, interpreting, and debating passages of Torah in their house of study as words rising through the roof and up to heaven. The indecipherable racket of the many voices interpreting Scripture was like a hymn of praise to God. He imagined God glorying in the ongoing, noisy process of interpretation, the cacophony of meanings without end.

In kindred spirit, what if we were to think of the Word of God not as bound between two covers of a book but as that endless noise of interpretation, an inconclusive process that we are invited to join? What if that cacophonous hymn, rising up across time and space from digital networks, living rooms, lunchrooms, churches, and bus stops is the living Word of God? An endless, inarticulate din of talking, arguing, reading, and rereading in the library of questions. The Word as we *don't* know it. The Word as we live it. Word without end.

Acknowledgments

THIS BOOK HAS BEEN the greatest challenge of my life as a scholar and writer, and I have never relied more heavily on more people. I am especially grateful to friends and colleagues who generously offered critical insights and support at many stages in my research and writing process, especially Robin Craig, Bill Deal, Pam Eisenbaum, Ed Gemerchak, Barry Hartz, John Lentz, Tod Linafelt, Brent Plate, Jean Reinhold, Lou Rice, Jana Riess, and Tom Zych. I have also benefited greatly from opportunities to present my work in progress to thoughtfully engaged audiences at Maryville College, the Iconic Books Symposium at Syracuse University, St. Andrew's College of the University of Saskatchewan, the Rocky Mountain–Great Plains meeting of the American Academy of Religion, the Tel Mac Theory Lunch and Praxis Breakfast in Diaspora, the Whitehead Salon, Pioneer Church, and Forest Hill Church.

Thanks also to many people variously involved in the Bible-publishing business, some named, most not, who offered stories and information that helped me make my own sense of that fascinating world, and to friends and friends of friends who shared a wealth of personal biblical experiences, including Patti and Bill

Munk, Mel and Cliff Taylor, Darlene and Chuck Gilbert, Peggy and Carl Johnson, and especially Stephanie Ramos.

I could not have completed this book without generous assistance from Case Western Reserve University, especially: a Foreign Travel Grant from the Baker-Nord Center for the Humanities for research in Rome; a Library Opportunity Grant from the Kelvin Smith Library to acquire market research data on Bible sales; a sabbatical during which I completed drafts of the early chapters; enthusiastic help from Sue Hanson, head of Special Collections at Kelvin Smith Library; administrative assistance from Sharon Skowronski and Lauren Gallitto in the Department of Religious Studies; and collegial support from my department chair, Peter Haas. I am also grateful for hospitality during several visits to the archives of the American Bible Society in New York, especially from Liana Lupas, curator of the Scripture Collection, and Jacquelyn Sapiie, Library Services supervisor.

I do most of my writing at local cafés and diners, and am pleased to acknowledge them here: Amy Joy Donuts, Arabica, Big Al's, Dink's, Eat at Joe's, Inn on Coventry, Michael's, Tommy's, and Yours Truly.

In the course of research and writing, I have had innumerable occasions to recall my deep gratitude to my professors and mentors, especially Walter Brueggemann, David Gunn, and Carol Newsom, whose scholarly integrity, love of biblical studies, and willingness to share power and opportunity with those fortunate enough to be their students will always be my aspiration.

Many thanks to my editor, Andrea Schulz, who has steadfastly believed in me and in this book, from genesis to revelation, and to her smart and savvy editorial associates, especially Lindsey Smith, Christina Morgan, Melissa Dobson, and Lisa Glover. Thanks also to my literary agent, Gail Ross, and her associate, Howard Yoon, for their keen interest, friendly professionalism, and good-humored patience throughout the process.

As ever, I am especially grateful for Clover Reuter Beal, best colleague, Presbyterian shaman, and love of my life, for listening, reading, challenging, enlightening, and keeping faith.

Finally, I offer my heartfelt thanks to my mom, Geraldine Kandler Beal, to whom I gratefully dedicate this book. As I write, she is about to begin a Master of Theology program at her alma mater, Whitworth University (class of 1956). A source of much pride and joy, to be sure! Still, in my book, she has been a master of theology for as long as I can remember.

Notes

1. The End of the Word as We Know It: A Personal Introduction

Some scholars of religion may balk at my integration of personal religious history in this book, not to mention my explicit religious interest in its argument. Such admixtures may seem to them like a monstrous hybrid of religion and the academic study of it. For a nonspecialist introduction to scholarly debates about the relationship between religion and the study of it, see Charlotte Allen, "Is Nothing Sacred? Casting Out the Gods from Religious Studies," *Lingua Franca* (November 1996), 30–40. The best scholarly treatment of it, in my opinion, is Russell T. McCutcheon, "A Default of Critical Intelligence? The Scholar of Religion as Public Intellectual," *Journal of the American Academy of Religion* 65 (1997), 443–68, when taken along with the response by June O'Connor, "The Scholar of Religion as Public Intellectual: Expanding Critical Intelligence," *Journal of the American Academy of Religion* 66 (1998), 897–909. Their central question is, What is the role of the scholar of religion in public life? McCutcheon's answer is that she or he should be a "critical rhetor" who "exposes the mechanisms whereby [religious] truths and norms are constructed, demonstrating the contingency of seemingly necessary conditions and the historical character of ahistorical claims" (p. 453). I agree that such an approach is important, and I see my own efforts to historicize the cultural iconicity of the Bible, for example, to expose its constructedness and the processes of its deconstruction, now under way, as that kind of work. I include my own personal religious history in that context in part to expose and critically examine my own insider/outsider position in relation to this construction. Yet I also agree with O'Connor that McCutcheon's approach, which sees religion strictly as a mode of authorization, is not the only one appropriate to scholars of religion. Other approaches, which operate from different theories of religion, call for different strategies in order to empower the public to think critically, and self-critically — "to open wide the drapes," as O'Connor puts it, "giving viewers and readers access to the production of religions past and present but also to the production of theories about religions," that is, exposing and contextualizing the different ways we as scholars understand and critically examine them (p. 904). In any case, I hope that the elements of religious autobiography in this book will serve those aims. One of my inspirations since graduate school has been Hélène Cixous, in her aptly titled Oxford Amnesty Lecture, "We Who Are Free, Are We Free?" trans. Chris Miller, *Critical Inquiry* 19 (1993), 203, where she writes, "The prisons precede me. When I have escaped them, I discover them: when they have cracked and split open beneath my feet."

For a critical assessment of the limits of theorizing religion strictly as a mode of authorization, that is, a kind of "locative social labor" that ignores its dislocative, disfiguring dimensions, see Tyler Roberts, "All Work and No Play: Chaos, Incongruity and Différence in the Study of Religion," *Journal of the American Academy of Religion* 77 (2009), 84; and Mark C. Taylor, "Refiguring Religion," *Journal of the American Academy of Religion* 77 (2009), 105–12. My own understanding of the unstable interdependence of order and chaos, orientation and disorientation, in biblical theology is best articulated in my *Religion and Its Monsters* (New York: Routledge, 2002), and in my introduction to *Reading Bibles, Writing Bodies: Identity and The Book* (New York: Routledge, 1996), 1–15.

The Pew Forum's survey report, *Many Americans Uneasy with Mix of Religion and Politics*, released August 24, 2006 (http://pewforum.org/publications/surveys/religion-politics-06.pdf), indicates that 35 percent of respondents agree with the statement "The Bible is the actual word of God and is to be taken literally, word for word"; another 43 percent agree with the statement "The Bible is the word of God, but not everything in it should be taken literally, word for word." Thus 78 percent understand the Bible as, in some sense, the Word of God. The Gallup Poll data from 2007 correlate closely with the Pew data (see www.gallup.com/poll/1690/Religion.aspx). On the popular view that "the Bible is

totally accurate in all of its teachings," see www.barna.org. On the popular view
that it contains "all or most of the basic questions of life," see Alec Gallup and
Wendy W. Simmons, "Six in Ten Americans Read Bible at Least Occasionally," October 20, 2000 (http://poll.gallup.com). The Pew Forum's 2006 survey also asked, "Which should be the more important influence on the laws
of the United States? Should it be the Bible or should it be the will of the
American people, even when it conflicts with the Bible?" Thirty-two percent
of all respondents said that the Bible should take precedence. Among white
evangelicals, the number was 60 percent; among Catholics, 23 percent; and
among white mainline Christians, 16 percent. Even 7 percent of those identifying themselves as secular said that the Bible should take precedence over the
will of the people in this matter! The question itself presumes that the Bible is
a book having a coherent position on matters of law and order.

"The Bible" as I discuss it in this book refers to the Christian Bible in
its various forms, but not to the Tanakh, or Hebrew Bible, which I refer to
as "Jewish Scriptures" (I also use this name for other translations, including
Greek versions of the Septuagint). Jewish Scriptures have a very different literary and cultural history, from which Christians have much to learn. Even the
idea of the Jewish "Bible" is a fairly recent development in the history of Judaism, in many ways responding to the growing centrality of the Christian Bible
within Protestant culture. See esp. Abigail Gillman's forthcoming history of
the German Jewish Bible from the late eighteenth century (Chicago: University of Chicago Press, 2011).

A "cultural icon" is not the same as an icon per se. An icon is a particular
material thing; a cultural icon is not. It does not, indeed cannot, have a particular visual or material form. It is, rather, an immaterial, amorphous, inarticulate
condensation of cultural meaning and value, a symbol whose outline is vague,
impossible to pin down to a particular image or thing. The image of the closed
black leather book, for example, is a common one for the cultural icon of the
Bible, but the Bible's cultural iconicity is not inextricably tied to that image. It
could be brown or red, zippered or clasped, indexed or plain, open or closed,
and so on. Indeed, this visual-material vagueness is essential to a cultural icon's
power. It gives it a flexibility that allows more people to identify with it; it allows it to stretch farther before breaking. Therefore, I mean to distinguish
between particular biblical icons, whose iconicities are tied to their particular
material forms and are created and maintained by particular rituals, and what

I am calling the cultural icon of the Bible. To be sure, many particular iconic Bibles help create and maintain the Bible's cultural iconicity. Think, for example, of a monument to the Ten Commandments in a courthouse, or the Bible used at the swearing-in ceremony of Presidents Lincoln and Obama. Yet the Bible as a cultural icon cannot be reduced to any one of them.

My understanding of the Bible as a cultural icon, as distinct from the particular images of particular iconic Bibles, such as the Gutenberg Bible or Lincoln's Bible, may be helpfully unpacked in dialogue with the excellent discussion by Dorina Miller Parmenter, "The Iconic Book: The Image of the Bible in Early Christian Rituals," *Postscripts: The Journal of Sacred Texts and Contemporary Worlds* 2, nos. 2–3 (2006), 160–89, which I discovered late in the writing of this book. Parmenter focuses on particular biblical icons, which she defines as visible material objects that mediate a transcendent reality. Their iconicity depends, moreover, on particular ritual performances that imbue and maintain their mediatory role between the material and spiritual realms (see also James W. Watts, "The Three Dimensions of Scriptures," *Postscripts* 2, nos. 2–3 [2006], 135–59, which argues for three interrelated dimensions of Scriptures in particular cultural contexts: the semantic, the performative, and the iconic).

John W. Nevin, "Early Christianity," *Mercersburg Review* 3, no. 6 (November 1851), 549. This passage is Nevin's summary of the emerging consensus view of what he calls the "Puritanic Bible" movement, which was claiming to go back to earliest Christianity's reliance on Scriptures. His argument, very like mine, was that the movement's image of early Christianity is not historically accurate. It was a myth of an ideal, pristine origin.

Constitution and address "To the People of the United States" by the American Bible Society, May 8, 1816, courtesy of the American Bible Society archives.

My abbreviated history of the rise of the icon of the Bible vis-à-vis the Bible missionary movement and fundamentalism is especially indebted to Peter J. Wosh, *Spreading the Word: The Bible Business in Nineteenth-Century America* (Ithaca, NY: Cornell University Press, 1994), and Peter J. Thuesen, *In Discordance with the Scriptures: American Protestant Battles over Translating the Bible* (New York: Oxford University Press, 1999).

Julius Wellhausen, *Prolegomena to the History of Israel,* trans. A. Sutherland Black and Allen Menzies (Edinburgh: Allen and Charles Black, 1885), first published in German in 1878. William Robertson Smith popularized Wellhausen's work among English readers through his article "Israel" in the *Encyclopaedia Britannica*. A minister in the Free Church of Scotland, Smith, like Rev. Charles Briggs, was tried for heresy and accused of publishing "opinions which are in themselves of a dangerous and unsettling tendency in their bearing on the doctrines" of the church with regard to Scripture. See W. Robertson Smith, *Additional Answer to the Libel with Some Account of the Evidence That Parts of the Pentateuchal Law Are Later Than the Time of Moses* (Edinburgh: David Douglas, 1878).

On the importance of small-group Bible study to the rise of American fundamentalism, see George M. Marsden, *Fundamentalism and American Culture: The Shaping of Twentieth-Century Evangelicalism, 1870–1925* (New York: Oxford University Press, 2006), which shows how the fundamentalist movement and its dispensational theology "did not develop in seminaries but in Bible conferences, Bible schools, and, perhaps most importantly, on the personal level of small Bible-study groups where the prophetic truths could be made plain" (pp. 61–62). See also the subsequent note on recent anthropological studies of evangelical Bible-study groups by Malley and Bielo (chapter 2).

My treatment of the rise of the parachurch evangelical movement and its consumerist orientation is especially indebted to Joel A. Carpenter, *Revive Us Again: The Reawakening of American Fundamentalism* (New York: Oxford University Press, 1997).

In his foreword to Harold Lindsell's *Battle for the Bible* (Grand Rapids, MI: Zondervan, 1976), Harold Ockenga, who was the first president of Fuller Theological Seminary, claimed to have coined the term "neo-evangelicalism" in a 1948 convocation address: "While reaffirming the theological view of fundamentalism, this address repudiated its ecclesiology and its social theory. The ringing call for a repudiation of separatism and the summons to social involvement received a hearty response from many Evangelicals."

The Way: The Living Bible Illustrated (Wheaton, IL: Tyndale House Publishers, 1972). Sales data courtesy of Tyndale House Publishers. Tyndale House Foundation is a nonprofit organization created to support missionary efforts. All royalties for *The Living Bible* (over 41 million copies sold) and Tyndale's more recent New Living Translation (over 15 million sold to date) have been donated to the foundation. In fact, Tyndale donates all royalties for all its Bibles.

On the evangelical Christian culture industry, see esp. Daniel Radosh's insightful, thoughtful, and subtly sympathetic *Rapture Ready! Adventures in the Parallel Universe of Christian Pop Culture* (New York: Scribner, 2008).

Oswald Chambers, *My Utmost for His Highest* (New York: Dodd, Mead and Company, 1935), first published in Great Britain in 1927.

Annie Dillard, *Teaching a Stone to Talk: Expeditions and Encounters* (New York: Harper & Row, 1982), 19.

2. The Greatest Story Ever Sold

The NPR story is Barbara Bradley Hagerty, "Understanding the Gospel According to Huckabee," February 8, 2008, www.npr.org/templates/story/story .php?storyId=18821021.

On declining biblical literacy, see research by the Barna Group (www .barna.org); the Bible Literacy Project (http://bibleliteracy.org); the Gallup Poll (www.gallup.com); and George Gallup Jr., *The Role of the Bible in American Society* (Princeton, NJ: Princeton University Press, 1990). See also Gary M. Burge, "The Greatest Story Never Read: Recovering Biblical Literacy in the Church," *Christianity Today,* August 9, 1999; David Gibson, "America's Favorite Unopened Text: The Bible Is the Least-Read Best-Seller of All Time," www.beliefnet .com/story/57/story_5746_1.html; and Stephen Prothero, *Religious Literacy: What Every American Needs to Know—And Doesn't* (San Francisco: HarperSanFrancisco, 2007). Congressman Westmoreland appeared on *The Colbert Report* on June 14, 2006; the interview is available at www.colbertnation.com.

The Baylor University study is *The Baylor Religion Survey* (Waco, TX: Baylor Institute for Studies of Religion, 2005).

National Endowment for the Arts, *Reading at Risk: A Survey of Literary Reading in America,* June 2004 (www.nea.gov/pub/ReadingatRisk.pdf). The report is based on the literature segment of the Census Bureau's *Survey of Public Participation in the Arts* (2002), which surveyed over seventeen thousand adults about literary reading over the previous twelve months. The decline in general literacy may not be quite so dramatic as this report suggests. Note that 9.2 percent of people reported that they used the Internet to learn about, read, or discuss novels, poetry, or plays. In much of the report, use of the Internet is associated with use of TV, music, and video games, over literary reading. Also note the growing popularity in recent years of narrative nonfiction, memoirs, and histories that most would consider literary but that don't fit into the survey's categories of novels, poetry, and plays.

As noted, Bible sales data are closely guarded by publishers. The figure of

$770 million for 2007 was first published in Stephanie Simon, "Selling the Good Book by Its Cover," *Los Angeles Times,* December 25, 2007, and was derived from calculations by the Evangelical Christian Publishers Association (ECPA) in collaboration with a major Bible publisher. I presume that the number is based on that company's sales data for 2007 and the ECPA's estimate of its share of total Bible sales for the year. So, for example, if this company sold $231 million in Bibles and had 30 percent of the market, the total for that year would calculate to $770 million. The final numbers are accepted by the ECPA, which does its own extensive market research on Bible publishing. The report of $609 million in sales for 2005 was an estimate made by Zondervan in Cindy Crosby, "Not Your Mother's Bible," *Publishers Weekly,* October 30, 2006. The estimate for 2008 of $823.5 million is from the Book Industry Study Group (BISG), as reported in Sarah Skidmore, "Bible Publishers Go Niche in Hopes of Gaining Readers," *USA Today,* October 7, 2008. Note that the BISG estimate for 2007 was $795.2 million, which is slightly higher than the ECPA estimate, but included sales of prayer books and hymnals as well as Bibles.

The larger publishing industry has not kept pace with the Bible business. Although general book sales continue to grow, there are signs of slowing. From 2002 to 2006, the Association of American Publishers estimated a compound growth rate in book sales of 2.4 percent, whereas it estimated an annual rate of 4.7 percent in the period from 1997 to 2004. This more recent estimate, moreover, includes dramatic growth in the area of electronic books. When nontraditional book formats (e-books, standardized test manuals, etc.) are removed, growth appears even more modest.

The Nelson sale is reported in "Thomas Nelson Board Votes to Take Company Private," press release, February 21, 2006 (www.thomasnelson.com). Before its buyout, Thomas Nelson was a publicly traded Standard & Poor's Small-Cap 600 company whose net revenues had grown every year for twenty-five years. At the time of the buyout, its stock value was fifty-fold its original valuation. Nelson has been especially successful in creating and promoting its own proprietary translations of the Bible. These include the popular New Century Version (NCV) and the New King James Version (NKJV), which tries to retain some of the literary whiff of the King James Version of 1611. It has sold more than 25 million copies since its introduction in 1982. The NCV is used in most of Nelson's more trendy Bibles.

Market share data on publishers is from ECPA research for 2005. Both

Nelson and Zondervan claim slightly higher percentages than ECPA reported to me. Zondervan has held North American publishing rights to the New International Version (NIV) translation of the Bible since 1973. Created by the International Bible Society, the NIV is the most popular Bible translation since the King James Version. It has been published under nearly nine hundred different titles and has sold more than 215 million copies.

On religion and consumer culture, see esp. Vincent J. Miller, *Consuming Religion: Christian Faith and Practice in a Consumer Culture* (New York: Continuum, 2005).

Two recent anthropological studies of Bible-study groups are particularly helpful in revealing how such groups help shore up the iconic meaning of the Bible that I have been describing, even while they provide a space for negotiating and, at least temporarily, overcoming the sense of disconnection between that iconic idea and actual experiences of reading Bibles. Brian Malley, *How the Bible Works: An Anthropological Study of Evangelical Biblicism* (Walnut Creek, CA: AltaMira Press, 2004), argues that, among evangelicals, calling oneself a "literalist" is less about making a specific argument about the biblical text than it is about identifying with conservative evangelical Christianity over against "liberal" or "mainstream" forms. Thus, we might say, they are expressing adherence to a particular cultural iconicity of the Bible without necessarily working out a particular argument or position that supports it. James S. Bielo, *Words upon the Word: An Ethnography of Evangelical Group Bible Study* (New York: New York University Press, 2009), moves the discussion forward by exploring how presuppositions or "textual ideologies" about the Bible (e.g., as "literal Word of God" and practical guide to how one should conduct one's life) are supported by particular "textual practices" in group Bible studies that discourage disagreement.

3. Biblical Values

On the Bible in magazine form see Angie Kiesling, "Tuning In to the Teen Soul," *Publishers Weekly*, March 11, 2002; and Ann Rodgers, "iPod Bibles, Bible-Zines? You Name It, They've Got It," *Pittsburgh Post-Gazette*, April 8, 2007, which reports that Nelson had sold 2 million Biblezines. Thomas Nelson has also developed program tie-ins that are turning some Biblezines into the centerpieces of larger cultural movements. The biggest one to date is the Revolve Tour, a national stadium tour of musicians and inspirational speakers geared toward teen and tween girls created by Women of Faith, Inc. In 2005 and 2006, the Revolve Tour attracted more than 120,000 attendees. Fourteen tour dates were scheduled for the 2007–2008 school year. Women of Faith, by the way, is a for-profit division of Nelson, which purchased it in 2000.

The edition of *Refuel* cited is subtitled *Old Testament Epic War Battles* (Nashville, TN: Thomas Nelson, 2005).

Information on Nelson's "felt needs" research comes from a personal interview with Wayne Hastings on October 7, 2008. Hastings oversaw this research program at Thomas Nelson and has been the primary spokesperson for its results. The quotation from Hastings on buying as an emotional decision is from "Consumers Have Needs," http://waynehastings.blogs.com, June 11, 2007. See also *How to Sell Bibles: Basics of Great Retail* (Nashville, TN: Nelson Bibles, n.d.; available online at www.thomasnelson.com).

Nelson is promoting a new way of organizing Bible displays in stores according to its categories of felt needs (rather than according to translations). This approach is less appealing to Zondervan, whose NIV has huge brand recognition as the all-time best-selling modern Bible translation. Nelson's interest in promoting its new system is driven not only by consumer needs but also by its own felt need for a competitive advantage.

Customer reviews of *Becoming, Explore, Refuel,* and *Real* Biblezines were taken from Amazon.com.

Data on the total number of editions of the Bible sold in 2004 and 2005 is from the Evangelical Christian Publishers Association.

On niche Bibles, specifically those marketed to African Americans, see Carrie Mason-Draffen, "Word! The Good Book Finds New Niches," *Black Issues Book Review,* March-April 2005.

It perhaps goes without saying in today's consumer world that most niche Bibles are gendered. I half-expect bookstores to start organizing their Bibles like Toys "R" Us organizes its toys, into pink and blue rows. The not-so-subtle message is that the Bible has something different to say to women than it does to men.

The story of David, Bathsheba, and Uriah is found in 2 Samuel 11–12. On Samson, see esp. my teacher and colleague David M. Gunn's brilliant essay, "Samson of Sorrows: An Isaianic Gloss on Judges 13–16," in Danna Nolan Fewell, ed., *Reading Between Texts: Intertextuality in the Hebrew Bible* (Louisville, KY: Westminster/John Knox, 1992), 225–53, which sees Samson as caught in a drama of "divine control and human freedom," as were King Saul and the Pharaoh of the Exodus narrative, and which ultimately highlights potential Christological dimensions in his character and story.

A clear and useful introduction to the range of modern translations and the approaches behind them is David Dewey's *A User's Guide to Bible Translations: Making the Most of Different Versions* (Downers Grove, IL: InterVarsity Press, 2004). Dewey's introduction is more pastoral and less critical of functional-equivalence translations.

"Now let me alone . . ." Exodus 32:10, New Revised Standard Version. Unless otherwise noted, the NRSV is the translation used in quoting Bible passages throughout this book.

The Hebrew expression *mashtin beqîr*, "one that pees against a wall," appears in 1 Samuel 25:22, 34; 1 Kings 14:10, 16:11, 21:21, and 2 Kings 9:8. Interestingly, *mashtin*, "one who pees," also sounds very like *mishteh*, which is a drinking party (related to the verb *shatah*, "drink").

Kenneth Taylor is quoted in Harold Myra, "Ken Taylor: God's Voice in the Vernacular," *Christianity Today*, October 5, 1979; other Taylor quotes are from a biographical video at www.kennethtaylor.com.

On biblical translation as an "over-living" of an original, see esp. Tod Linafelt's brilliant study of the translational history of Lamentations in *Surviving Lamentations: Catastrophe, Lament, and Protest in the Afterlife of a Biblical Book* (Chicago: University of Chicago Press, 2000).

On mangas, see the exhibit by the Kyoto International Manga Museum (www.kyotomm.com). Sales data is from Calvin Reid, "New Report Finds Manga Sales Up; Anime DVD Down in '07," *Publishers Weekly*, December 7, 2007. Reid's figures are from research by Milton Griepp, president of ICv2. In recent conferences, Griepp has noted that manga sales doubled from $100 million to $200 million between 2003 and 2006. Manga serials are collected and bound into larger books called *tankōbon*, which would be best translated by our term "graphic novels." In American publishing, *manga* refers to what Japanese would call *tankōbon*.

NEXT and Tyndale plan to release four more biblical mangas like *Manga Messiah*. Each will focus on a different corpus of biblical narrative. At the bottom of each page in these biblical mangas are references to the specific verses that the artists are representing. This not only works as a kind of citation system, indicating that the artists want to be accountable for their creative interpretations; it also encourages readers to go and read the actual passages. With respect to Tyndale's more conservative approach to this format, as compared with that of Zondervan and Nelson, one has to wonder if it and NEXT's not-for-profit approach to Bible publishing is the distinguishing factor.

Volume 1 of Zondervan's *Manga Bible*, cited here, is *Names, Games, and the Long Road Trip* (Genesis–Exodus), written by Young Shin Lee, created by Brett Burner, and illustrated by Jung Sun Hwang (Grand Rapids, MI: Zondervan, 2007).

The British-Nigerian graphic artist Siku's *The Manga Bible: From Genesis to Revelation*, published by Galilee Trade, a Christian inspirational division of Doubleday, appeals to teenage and young-adult audiences with somewhat darker, edgier graphics and themes (war and apocalypse, for example). Although this manga Bible purports to cover the entire Bible, from Genesis to Revelation, it is by no means comprehensive. It does not include any biblical text in translation, and it is very selective in what parts of the biblical canon to include. It really is Siku's own graphic canon within the canon, connecting a number of biblical themes and stories together in order to tell a grand, overarching narrative of the history of the world, from creation to apocalypse.

On Bibles that attempt to tap more liberal, progressive markets see Priests for Equality, *The Inclusive Bible* (Plymouth, U.K.: Rowman & Littlefield, 2007). Another popular example, to which I myself was a contributor (on the book of Esther), is Harper's *Renovare Spiritual Formation Bible*, ed. Richard Foster, Dallas Willard, Eugene Peterson, and one of my mentors, Walter Brueggemann (republished by HarperOne in 2009 as *The Life with God Bible*). It includes notes and essays by a range of scholars and pastors and aims to foster biblical study that crosses conservative-liberal lines. Its central theme is what Foster calls "the with-God life," which sees the whole of the Christian canon of Scripture as "the unfolding story of God's plan for our loving relationship with our Creator." I find the book of Esther as a challenge, even a contradiction, to such an understanding of the biblical canon, insofar as the presence of God in its story is entirely uncertain. Indeed, the book of Esther can be read as a story about the "without-God life." I wrote my introduction and notes to Esther with this challenge in mind. To their credit, the editors allowed my perspective on Esther as a countervoice to faith in the with-God life to stand (albeit alongside more with-God-affirming reflections from other contributors).

Paul Caminiti is quoted in Stephanie Simon, "Selling the Good Book by Its Cover," *Los Angeles Times*, December 25, 2007.

4. Twilight of the Idol

Marshall McLuhan, *Understanding Media: The Extensions of Man* (1964; Cambridge, MA: MIT Press, 1994), 7–21. It is interesting to note that McLuhan himself converted to Catholicism in his early twenties. We may wonder whether the more religious aesthetic orientation of his own liturgical and devotional practices within that tradition influenced his understanding of the inseparability of meaning and its material embodiment. Kenneth A. Myers, *All God's Children and Blue Suede Shoes: Christians and Popular Culture* (Westchester, IL: Crossway Books, 1989), sees the evangelical impulse to adopt and adapt to popular culture as a woeful disregarding of McLuhan's famous dictum.

Stories behind the development of *The Way* are from correspondence with former editors of *Campus Life* who participated in the project. They did not ask for or receive credit for their work.

Brian Scharp is quoted in Stephanie Simon, "Selling the Good Book by Its Cover," *Los Angeles Times,* December 25, 2007.

Customer reviews of Biblezines were quoted from Amazon.com, accessed October 3, 2008.

On different forms of social and cultural capital, see Pierre Bourdieu, "The Forms of Capital," trans. Richard Nice, in *Handbook of Theory and Research for the Sociology of Education,* ed. John G. Richardson (Westport, CT: Greenwood, 1986), 241–58. My concept of sacred capital is not reducible to Bourdieu's cultural capital, or to his later concept of symbolic capital, as it does not necessarily or at least exclusively relate to one's relative social status or power.

For more on the digital revolution as the larger setting for biblical brand dilution see Timothy Beal, "The Rise of the Information Society," *Religion in America: A Very Short Introduction* (New York: Oxford University Press, 2008), 93–99.

Walter J. Ong, *Orality and Literacy: The Technologizing of the Word* (New York: Methuen, 1982), 129–32.

On Internet-based reading and writing, it's interesting to note that, according to the 2004 National Endowment for the Arts report *Reading at Risk,* the decline in traditional literary book reading does not correlate with a decline in creative writing. In fact, according to the report, the number of people doing creative writing grew by 30 percent between 1982 and 2002, even as literary reading declined. If the report had been able to survey Internet-based activities, especially among younger people, in greater detail, I suspect it would have found that writing activities in that context were increasing dramatically. Indeed, in the context of the emerging network society, reading and writing are becoming harder to distinguish from one another. They often take place simultaneously.

Timothy Beal, *Biblical Literacy: The Essential Bible Stories Everyone Needs to Know* (San Francisco: HarperOne, 2009).

Bible Illuminated: The Book, New Testament (Sweden: Förlaget Illuminated, 2008). Publishing details are taken from "Your questions answered in this FAQ," October 28, 2008, at www.illuminatedworld.com. The Good News Translation used in the English edition is a 1992 revision (using more inclusive language) of the American Bible Society's translation, Today's English Version. Given the intentionally provocative approach of Illuminated World, it's interesting to note that this translation has attracted criticism from some fundamentalists on account of one of its chief translators, Robert Bratcher, who, in 1981, said that only willful ignorance or intellectual dishonesty could account for the doctrine of inerrancy. I suspect that this background was seen as a plus by Söderberg and company.

Though less provocative than the *Bible Illuminated,* I commend *The Voice* New Testament translation (Thomas Nelson, 2008; whole Protestant Bible forthcoming) as another project of defamiliarization with "the Word as we know it." Done collaboratively by a diverse group of scholars, ministers, and creative writers, this text often presents dramatically new rewritings of the biblical text, based on work with the original languages, that can be evocative of multiple meanings. Unlike the typical disambiguating, depoeticizing approach of most functional-equivalence translations, its effect is often to estrange the reader from traditional biblical language. Despite the claim from Nelson marketers that *The Voice* has "captured the mood and voice of the original New Testament writers," I recommend it as an experiment in creative translation as a form of poetic biblical interpretation.

5. What Would Jesus Read?

For a fuller discussion of the social worlds of reading and writing in early Christianity and Judaism in the context of Greco-Roman literary culture, see esp. Harry Y. Gamble, *Books and Readers in the Early Church: A History of Early Christian Texts* (New Haven, CT: Yale University Press, 1995), on which much of my discussions in this and the next chapter depend. See also James L. Kugel and Rowan A. Greer, *Early Biblical Interpretation: Two Studies of Exegetical Origins* (Philadelphia, PA: Westminster Press, 1986).

Although it is highly unlikely that Jesus or his disciples ever saw Jewish Scripture or any other literature in codex form, it is possible that they were familiar with the use of codices as notebooks for keeping records and even writing down the words of teachers. Saul Lieberman, *Hellenism in Jewish Palestine: Studies in the Literary Transmission, Beliefs, and Manners of Palestine in the I Century* BCE–*IV Century* CE (New York: Jewish Theological Seminary of America, 1962), argues that, despite later rabbinical requirements that Scriptures be put only on scrolls, codices may actually have been a Jewish innovation that was then picked up by Christians. Perhaps Jesus's own disciples used simple codex notebooks as a customary way to record their rabbi's teachings.

On scroll making, see Pliny the Elder, *Natural History*, chap. 13; Bruce M. Metzger, *Manuscripts of the Greek Bible: An Introduction to Paleography* (New York: Oxford University Press, 1991), 14–18; and Gamble, *Books and Readers in the Early Church*, 44–48. Later rabbinical law requires that Torah scrolls be made of parchment from kosher animals, etc. One must use caution, however, in projecting those later regulations onto first-century Jewish scriptural culture in all its diversity, especially in the Diaspora.

On the scroll of Isaiah, see Francolino J. Gonçalves, "Isaiah Scroll," *The Anchor Bible Dictionary*, vol. 3, 470–72; D. Barthélemy and J. T. Milik, *Discoveries in the Judaean Desert, I: Qumran Cave 1* (Oxford: Oxford University Press, 1955).

James Kugel, "Early Interpretation: The Common Background of Late Forms of Biblical Exegesis," in Kugel and Greer, *Early Biblical Interpretation*, traces the emergence of Judaism as a scriptural-interpretive culture. By the early first century, he argues, studying Scripture was the "fundamental religious activity" of Judaism.

Most archaeological data on the architecture of early synagogues comes from the third and fourth centuries and cannot be applied reliably to first- or even second-century Judaism. During that time, we have only general references to the Jewish *proseuché* (Greek for "place of prayer") and *synagogē* (Greek "gathering place") with no specific information about space, architecture, etc. See James F. Strange, "Synagogues, Ancient Times" in *The Encyclopedia of Judaism*, ed. Jacob Neusner, Alan J. Avery-Peck, and William Scott Green (Leiden: Brill, 2005).

In addition to the passage in Luke, other early Jewish references to synagogue services include Josephus, *Against Apion*, Book 2, and Philo, *On Dreams*, Book 2, both of which describe only two activities during weekly meetings: reading and explicating Scripture. Some argue that these were the exclusive activities of synagogue meetings, at least in Palestine. See the discussion and assessment of scholarship on the issue in Gamble, *Books and Readers in the Early Church*, 208–11 and 322–23.

With respect to the order of events in an early Christian service, in chapter 67 of his *First Apology* (c. 150 CE), Justin Martyr describes his community gathering on Sunday to read together "the memoirs of the apostles or the writings of the prophets . . . for as long as time permits," followed by interpretative discussion and Communion.

On oral cantillation of Scripture in early Christian culture, see the discussion in Gamble, *Books and Readers in the Early Church*, 225–27, and the extensive references in his notes. The Talmud passage is from Tractate Megillah 32a. "Tunefulness" is a translation of *n'ymh*. Nehemiah 8:8 describes the leaders reading the scripture of the law "with interpretation," which may mean not that they read and then commented on it but that they chanted it in a way that interpreted its meaning for the hearers. On the origins of biblical chant, see James Kugel, *The Idea of Biblical Poetry: Parallelism and Its History* (New Haven, CT: Yale University Press, 1981), 109–16.

Gamble, *Books and Readers in the Early Church*, 25, quotes Barnabas Lindars's study of quotation practices in early Christian writings as an "active and ingenious enterprise."

With respect to early Christian scriptural collections, although the earliest known Christian *testimonia* manuscripts date to the third century, it is probable that they were used much earlier. See esp. Martin C. Albl, *And Scripture Cannot Be Broken: The Form and Function of the Early Christian Testimonia Collections* (Leiden: Brill, 1999). Albl argues that quotations from Scripture in the Gospels may well have been taken from authoritative *testimonia* collections.

Kim Haines-Eitzen, *Guardians of Letters: Literacy, Power, and the Transmission of Early Christian Literature* (Oxford: Oxford University Press, 2000), shows that Christians in the second and third centuries did not hire professional copyists but used "private networks" of scribes, including women, who were not only producing the texts but also using them. This system was in contrast to the larger Greco-Roman literary culture, in which scribal work was seen as a menial task for a lower professional class to carry out. Within early Christian scribal culture, therefore, literacy and power were closely related. Scribes influenced the development of Christian orthodoxy and the canon. They were, as Haines-Eitzen puts it, "theologically invested" (16–18). See also Anthony Grafton and Megan Williams, *Christianity and the Transformation of the Book: Origen, Eusebius, and the Library of Caesarea* (Cambridge, MA: Belknap Press, 2006), which shows how the scholarly Christian culture of the third and fourth centuries (thanks especially to Origen and Eusebius) contributed to the development of the library and the rise of the book.

On textual criticism and the question of a common original source in Jewish Scriptures, especially in light of Dead Sea Scrolls discoveries, see Emmanuel Tov, "Textual Criticism (OT)," *The Anchor Bible Dictionary*, vol. 6, 393–412. P. E. Kahle, "Untersuchungen zur Geschichte des Pentateuchtextes," *Theologische Studien und Kritiken* 88 (1915), 399–439, was the first to argue that there was no "Ur-text" (single original text), but rather multiple versions of Jewish Scriptures (*Vulgärtexte*) from the earliest times. He did so based on rabbinical quotations and differences among Aramaic, Greek, and Hebrew versions known before the discoveries at Qumran. Tov partially disagrees with Kahle and his followers, arguing that there was an Ur-text, which he defines as the "finalized literary product which incorporated the last recognizable literary editing of the book." Yet he recognizes that other versions (earlier editions, for example) would not have disappeared at that point, and so there were, even then, multiple versions. Moreover, he sees subsequent generations of scribes making various changes, intentional and unintentional, to that Ur-text, so that the period of the early first century was one of great textual variety.

Another example of the discrepancies common among various ancient Hebrew manuscripts is found in the Great Isaiah Scroll (1QIsa-a), discussed earlier. Differences between it and the standard text of Isaiah (the "received" Masoretic Text, based primarily on the Leningrad Codex) seem particularly appropriate to the sectarian community at Qumran. Compare, for example, Isaiah 8:11 in the two versions. The Masoretic Text has "he *corrected me* [from verb root *ysr*, 'correct'] so that I would not follow the path of this people." 1QIsa-a, however, has "he turned me away [from the verb *swr*, 'turn'] from following the path of this people." The latter lends a more separatist meaning to the text. This verse is also found in another text, 4QFlor 1:15 (a *testimonia* text), to describe how God separated the Qumran community from the mainstream.

On New Testament textual criticism and working with Greek manuscripts, see Metzger, *Manuscripts*; and Eldon Jay Epp, "Textual Criticism (NT)," *The Anchor Bible Dictionary*, vol. 6, 412–35.

Mark 1:2 quotes from Malachi 3:1 and Isaiah 40:3 but treats them as a single quotation from Isaiah. Isaiah 40:3 is quoted alone and attributed to Isaiah in Matthew 3:3 and Luke 3:4. Some later manuscripts of Mark have the quotation attributed to "the prophets" rather than to "the prophet Isaiah." Most scholars believe these to be scribal corrections.

Concerning Luke's quotation of Isaiah in the synagogue scene, note too that there is no single edition of the Septuagint. There must have been as many variants among Greek translations as there were among Hebrew manuscripts in the first century.

As precedent for early Christian liberty with scriptural citation and paraphrase, see "A Postscript to the Book: Authenticating the Pseudepigrapha," in *Reading Bibles, Writing Bodies: Identity and The Book*, ed. David M. Gunn and Timothy Beal (London: Routledge, 1997), in which Kyle Keefer argues that early Jewish interpreters, as evidenced in the Pseudepigrapha, often paraphrased and even remixed various passages of Jewish Scripture from memory in highly "re-creative" ways that reflected a "low" view of the canon. In his conclusion, he suggests that the same was true for early Christian writers and scribes.

The idea that there never was a single original of most texts now in the New Testament is not new among scholars. As early as 1965, for example, in his presidential address to the Society of Biblical Literature, Kenneth W. Clark asked "if there really was a stable text at the beginning," or at least whether it "remained stable long enough to hold a priority." The address was published a year later as "The Theological Relevance of Textual Variation in Current Criticism of the Greek New Testament," *Journal of Biblical Literature* 85 (1966), 1–16. Such an argument from evidence is of course a major challenge to the foundations of biblical fundamentalism, which locates biblical inerrancy in the "original autographs" to which all the variants are believed to point.

"All scripture is inspired by God . . .": 2 Timothy 3:16. Most scholars agree that both 1 and 2 Timothy, along with Titus, were not actually authored by Paul himself but are later, "deutero-Pauline" epistles. Their literary style, vocabulary, and theological orientation are different from the main body of Pauline writings, and Marcion's canon (c. 140 CE) does not include them. Nearly all those who use this passage to argue that the Bible itself guarantees its own inspiration, however, attribute it to Paul. In referring to its author as Paul, I am following their logic for the sake of argument. In any case, whether written by Paul or not, 2 Timothy dates to an era well before Christian conceptions of the New Testament canon and the Bible had taken form. Another later text, 2 Peter 3:16, refers to Paul's letters, but does not attribute canonical status, let alone divine inspiration, to them.

Easter letter: Athanasius, *Festal Letter* 39 (for 367 CE).

Eusebius of Caesarea, *Ecclesiastical History,* vol. 3, chap. 25. His categories are somewhat ambiguous, leading many to divide what I consider to be the second category (*antilegomena,* "disputed") into two categories, "disputed" (*antilegomena*) and "spurious" (*notha*), a term he uses after his reference to 1–2 John: "Among the spurious books must be reckoned *also* the Acts of Paul . . ." With most scholars, I consider this to be a continuation of his list of disputed texts. Before moving onto his last category (heretical), he summarizes: "Now all these would be among the disputed books [*antilegomena*]; but nevertheless we have felt compelled to make this catalogue of them, distinguishing between those writings which, according to the tradition of the Church, are true and genuine and recognized, from the others which differ from them in that they are not canonical, but disputed, yet nevertheless are known to most churchmen."

In 397 CE the Council of Carthage listed the books of the full Christian canon, including the Old Testament and Apocrypha, insisting that these alone are to be read in church as sacred scriptures. See Henricus Denzinger, *Enchiridion Symbolorum et Definitionum* (Würzburg: Sumptibus Stahelianis, 1854), 11–12. But note that we find subsequent editions of the Vulgate Bible that include scriptures not included in this list, including a gospel harmony and the Letter to the Laodiceans. These suggest that the canon was still not solidly fixed and closed even after the Council of Carthage.

6. The Story of the Good Book

On the Mithraeum at Santa Prisca see Hans Dieter Betz, "The Mithras Inscriptions of Santa Prisca and the New Testament," *Novum Testamentum* 10 (1968), 62–80.

For discussions of early second- and third-century manuscript evidence for the rise of the Christian codex, see Gamble, *Books and Readers in the Early Church,* chap. 2; and Larry W. Hurtado, *The Earliest Christian Artifacts* (Grand Rapids:

Eerdmans, 2006), 43–93, 209–29. An exhibit of P46, the early (c. 200) codex of Pauline writings, is available at www.lib.umich.edu/reading/Paul/index
.html. Saul Lieberman, in *Hellenism in Jewish Palestine*, argues that the early Christian adoption of the codex was not necessarily in contradistinction to Judaism. In fact, it could well have had its beginnings in notebooks kept by Jesus's
disciples for recording personal notes on his teachings. Furthermore, although
there is very little data on Jewish scriptural culture outside Palestine during
the time when codices were gradually taking over scrolls, it's entirely possible
that Diaspora Jews as well as Christians were using Greek codices for their
Scripture.

The different holders of pages from Codex Sinaiticus have cooperated
to produce an online exhibit of the entire surviving manuscript: www.codex-
sinaiticus.net.

"sacred Scriptures . . . written on prepared parchment . . ." Eusebius, *Ecclesiastical History*, vol. 4, chap. 36.

Jerome, *Preface to the Four Gospels*, addressed to Pope Damasus (c. 383 CE). An
excellent account of Jerome's Vulgate and its subsequent history is available in
Christopher De Hamel, *The Book: A History of the Bible* (London: Phaidon, 2001),
12–39.

Desiderius Erasmus, *Novum Instrumentum omne* (Basel: Johann Froben, 1516).
A copy of the Complutensian Polyglot Bible may be found in the Library of
Congress's Rare Book and Special Collections Division as *Biblia polygotta* (Alcalá
de Henares, Spain: Arnaldi Guillelmi de Brocario, 1514–17). My treatment of
both works is based on examination of the copies held in the Scripture Collection of the American Bible Society. I also had access to a copy of Erasmus (1535
edition) in the Special Collections of Kelvin Smith Library at Case Western
Reserve University.

My review of early English Bibles, beginning with the Geneva Bible, is
based on two primary sources: personal examination of the Scripture Collec-
tion of the American Bible Society, which is the largest collection of English
Bibles in the United States; and T. H. Darlowe and F. H. Moule, *Historical
Catalogue of the Printed Editions of Holy Scripture in the Library of the British and Foreign
Bible Society* (London: The Bible House, 1903–11). Another valuable resource
is Margaret T. Hills, ed., *The English Bible in America: A Bibliography of Editions of the
Bible & the New Testament Published in America 1777–1957* (New York: American Bible
Society, 1961).

Luther's reference to James as "an epistle of straw" (*eine recht strohende Epistel*) is in his 1522 foreword to his translation of the New Testament (*"Vorrede auf das Neue Testament"*), and his questioning of the inspiration of Revelation is in his foreword to that book (*"Vorrede auf die Offenbarung S. Johannis"*). He places these books, along with Hebrews and Jude, at the end of the New Testament, out of canonical order. On Luther's disparaging, sometimes blatantly anti-Jewish treatments of Esther, see Timothy Beal, *The Book of Hiding: Gender, Ethnicity, Annihilation, and Esther* (London: Routledge, 1997), 6–12.

". . . encloses thought in thousands of copies": Ong, *Orality and Literacy*, 129.

James I's complaint about seditious notes in the Geneva Bible is from William Barlow, *The Summe and Substance of the Conference . . . at Hampton Court* (London, 1604).

For a masterfully written, highly readable history of English Bibles after Gutenberg, culminating with the King James Version, see Alisdair McGrath, *In the Beginning: The Story of the King James Bible and How It Changed a Nation, a Language, and a Culture* (New York: Doubleday, 2001). On the post–King James proliferation of Bibles (despite the royal copyright restrictions), including discussions of value-added illustrated Bibles, Bible commentaries, and thumb-sized Bibles, see esp. De Hamel, *The Book*.

Examples of early King James Version Bibles containing typographical errors are: *The Holy Bible . . . With Marginal notes, shewing Scripture to be the best Interpreter of Scripture* (probably Amsterdam, 1682); and *The Holy Bible* [aka the Wicked Bible] (London: Barker and Assigns of Bill, 1631).

Michael Sparke, *Scintilla; or A Light Broken into Darke Warehouses,* in Darlowe and Moule, *Historical Catalogue,* 189–94.

Examples of Bibles on the market by 1800: *The Souldiers Pocket Bible . . .* (London: G. B. and R. W. for B. C., 1643); *The Christian Soldier's Penny Bible. Shewing from the Holy Scriptures, the Soldier's Duty and Encouragement . . .* (London: R. Smith, 1693); Jeremiah Rich, *Whole Book of Psalms in Meter According to the Art of Short-writing* (London: Jeremiah Rich, 1659); *Solomons Proverbs, alphabetically collected out of his Proverbs and Ecclesiastes, for help of Memory. With an additional Collection of other Scripture-Proverbs out of the Old and New Testament . . .* By H. D. [Henry Danvers] (London: 1666); Symon Patrick, *The Books of Job, Psalms, Proverbs, Ecclesiastes, And the Song of Solomon, Paraphras'd: With Arguments to each Chapter, And Annotations thereupon* (London: J. Walthoe, 1727), a reprint of one of the volumes of Symon's Bible; William Mace, *The New Testa-*

ment in Greek and English. Containing the Original Text corrected from the Authority of the most Authentic Manuscripts . . . (London: J. Roberts, 1729); William Whiston, *Mr. Whiston's Primitive New Testament* (Stamford and London: W. Whiston, 1745); *The Family Testament, and Scholar's Assistant: calculated not only to promote the reading of the Holy Scriptures in families and schools, but also to remove that great uneasiness observable in children upon the appearance of hard words in their lessons, and by a method entirely new . . .* (2nd ed.; London: T. Luckman, 1767); John Brown, *The Self-Interpreting Bible* (3rd ed.; London: W. Flint, 1806); Matthew Talbot, *An Analysis of the Holy Bible, containing the whole of the Old and New Testaments: collected and arranged systematically, in thirty books . . .* (Leeds: Edward Baines, 1800; and London: Thomas Conder, 1800).

On the history of the American Bible Society, see Peter J. Wosh, *Spreading the Word: The Bible Business in Nineteenth-Century America* (Ithaca, NY: Cornell University Press, 1994). On its British counterpart, see Leslie Howsam, *Cheap Bibles: Nineteenth-Century Publishing and the British and Foreign Bible Society* (Cambridge: Cambridge University Press, 1991).

In its Thirty-third Annual Report of the American Bible Society (1849), the Printing and Publishing Department reported, "it was thought that the Society had reached the extremity of its cheapening and multiplying the leaves of the Tree of Knowledge and of Life." In 1852 the ABS's Committee on Versions reported nearly twenty-four thousand variations among six copies of the KJV that it compared (courtesy of the American Bible Society archives).

Novel nineteenth-century Bibles include *The Holy Bible . . .* miniature facsimile edition (Glasgow: University Press for David Bryce and Son, 1896). Pocket-sized red leather Bibles for Civil War soldiers were published by the American Bible Society in New York (New Testament only, 1862) and by William H. Hill in Boston (whole Bible, 1863). Lifeboat Bibles from World War II include: *The New Testament for Lifeboats and Rafts* (New York: American Bible Society, n.d.); *The New Testament for Life Boats and Rafts* (Toronto: The British and Foreign Bible Society of Canada and Newfoundland, n.d.); and *Scriptures: Protestant, Catholic, Jewish* [including fascicles of the Psalms and Gospels], with no publication data given on the outside of the sealed package. Novel versions of the biblical text are Andrew Comstock, *Δe Nw Testament ov ør Lwrd and Sevyur JDizus Krist* (Filadelfia: A. Komstok, 1848); Julia E. Smith, *The Holy Bible: Containing the Old and New Testaments Translated Literally* (Hartford: American Publishing, 1876), on which see Hills, *The English Bible in America,* 290–91; and C. K. Ogden, *Stories from the Bible Put into Basic English* (London: Kegan Paul, 1933).

The Illuminated Bible . . . Embellished with sixteen hundred historical engravings by J. A. Adams, more than fourteen hundred of which are from original designs by J. G. Chapman (New York: Harper & Brothers, 1846).

Colleen McDannell, "The Bible in the Victorian Home," in *Material Christianity: Religion and Popular Culture in America* (New Haven, CT: Yale University Press, 1995), 67–102. The quotation about Bible reading as breastfeeding is from p. 80. McDannell notes the slow decline of the family Bible phenomenon beginning in the 1870s and continuing through World War I, as American popular culture gradually distinguished itself from Victorian ideals. I obviously disagree, however, that this decline meant that publishers subsequently "simplified their content and form" so that the Bible no longer functioned as an iconic sacred object but "returned to being a compilation of sacred scriptures" (p. 101), especially over the longer term of the twentieth century. With the rise of an individualistic evangelical consciousness, the cultural meaning of the Bible and Bibles as sacred objects remained central to patriarchal family values (especially sexuality and gender roles) but was tied more solidly to issues of personal salvation and sanctification, especially as it relates to Christ-like moral behavior.

Peter J. Thuesen, "Some Scripture Is Inspired by God: Late-Nineteenth-Century Protestants and the Demise of a Common Bible," *Church History* 65 (1996), 609–10; see also *In Discordance with the Scriptures: American Protestant Battles over Translating the Bible* (New York: Oxford University Press, 2002). My abbreviated version of the story of the Revised Version and the Revised Standard Version is drawn primarily from Thuesen's account.

"A master stroke of Satan": the quotation from Hux is in Thuesen, *In Discordance,* 97.

7. Library of Questions

Jacques Derrida, "Living On," trans. James Hulbert, in *Deconstruction and Criticism,* ed. Harold Bloom (New York: Seabury, 1979), 73. The French phrase is *appauvrissement par univocité.*

I am translating *yehi 'or* (Genesis 1:3) as "there is light" rather than the more familiar "let there be light," which treats the verb as a jussive. Both are correct, but "there is light" better conveys the sense that God is literally speaking light into existence.

There are irreducible multivalences in other words in the Genesis story as well. 'adam, for example, which appears initially with the definite article (ha'adam), means "the human." After the woman is created from it, however, it appears both as the proper name Adam (without a definite article), and as the male human (with a definite article). Even one of the names for God, 'elohim, is polyvocal: although it is a plural noun literally meaning "gods," it is often used as a singular noun, with singular verbs (e.g., "then 'elohim said . . ."). Complicating things, however, is the fact that on two occasions in these stories, God speaks in the first person plural: "And God [elohim] said, 'let us make human-kind in our image, according to our likeness'" (Genesis 1:26); "Then the LORD God [yhwh 'elohim] said, 'See, the man has become like one of us'" (Genesis 3:22). Interestingly, in each of these instances (and also later, in Genesis 11:6), what's at issue is the degree to which God and humans are alike and different. It's almost as if God's own identity is less stable in those moments. On this is-sue, see esp. the groundbreaking essay by David M. Gunn and Danna Nolan Fewell, "Shifting the Blame: God in the Garden," in *Reading Bibles, Writing Bodies: Identity and The Book*, eds. Timothy Beal and David M. Gunn (New York: Rout-ledge, 1996), based on a paper originally delivered by Gunn at a meeting of the Society of Biblical Literature in 1990.

On Job 38 and the divine speech from the whirlwind, see Timothy Beal, *Re-ligion and Its Monsters* (New York: Routledge, 2002), chap. 4.

Mark Twain's "Bible Teaching and Religious Practice" is in his *Europe and Elsewhere* (New York: Harper & Bros., 1923), 387–93.

On Richard Hoskins's *Vigilantes of Christendom* (Lynchburg: Virginia Pub-lishing Company, 1990) and the Phineas Priesthood, see Timothy Beal, "The White Supremacist Bible and the Phineas Priesthood," in *Sanctified Aggression: Legacies of Biblical and Post-biblical Vocabularies of Violence*, ed. Jonneke Bekkenkamp and Yvonne Sherwood (London: T & T Clark, 2003).

Passages in which God is identified primarily with liberation, reminding Is-raelites that they, too, were once slaves: Deuteronomy 15:15; 16:12; 24:18, 22; cf. 6:20–25; 26:5–9; Exodus 23:9; Deuteronomy 10:18; 14:29; 16:11–14; 24:17–21; 26:12–13; 27:19; cf. Isaiah 1:17; 9:17; Jeremiah 7:6; 22:3; and Amos 2:6–8. Paul's liberative proclamation is Galatians 3:28.

Amos on abuses of law and order: Amos 2:6–8, for example, is a strong in-dictment on injustices committed against the poor and powerless by the rich and powerful, including the priesthood. But Amos does not want the destruc-tion of the *institutions* of social privilege and power themselves. Rather, he de-

mands that power be used "justly" by them, that is, according to the legal tra-
ditions of justice-as-social-order. In fact, the abuses of justice described by
Amos can be read in direct reference to laws now found in Torah (e.g., Exodus
22:25–27; Deuteronomy 24:10–14; cf. 21:7–11; Leviticus 19:20–23). The old
Protestant dichotomy of prophet versus priest simply does not hold in Amos.
See esp. Timothy Beal, "Specters of Moses: Overtures to Biblical Hauntology,"
in *Constructs of Ancient Israel: The Bible and Its Social Worlds,* ed. David M. Gunn and
Paula McNutt (New York: Continuum, 2002).

Adrienne Rich, "Power," in her *The Dream of a Common Language* (New York:
Norton, 1978).

Walter Brueggemann, "The Book of Psalms," in his *An Introduction to the Old
Testament: The Canon and Christian Imagination* (Louisville, KY: Westminster/John
Knox, 2003), 277–91. See also Walter Brueggemann, *Theology of the Old Testament: Testimony, Dispute, Advocacy* (Minneapolis, MN: Fortress, 1997), esp. 400–
403 on "maintaining the tension" between "Israel's core testimony" and "Israel's countertestimony" about God.

The only differences between Job 2:7 and Deuteronomy 28:35 are pronom-
inal: in Job, the curses are happening to Job, whereas in Deuteronomy, they will
happen to "you," that is, Moses's audience. For more on the book of Job's contention with the moral universe of Deuteronomy, see Timothy Beal, "Facing
Job," in *Levinas and Biblical Studies,* ed. Tamara Eskenazi and Gary A. Phillips (Atlanta, GA: Society of Biblical Literature, 2004); and Beal, *Religion and Its Monsters,* chap. 3.

Elie Wiesel and Timothy Beal, "Matters of Survival: A Conversation," in
Strange Fire: Reading the Bible after the Holocaust, ed. Tod Linafelt (New York: New
York University Press, 2000). The conversation took place on March 19, 1999,
in St. Petersburg, Florida. The play referred to is Elie Wiesel, *The Trial of God
(as it was held on February 25, 1649, in Shamgorod): A Play in Three Acts,* trans. Marion
Wiesel (New York: Random House, 1979).

Fyodor Dostoyevsky, "The Grand Inquisitor," excerpted from *The Brothers
Karamazov,* trans. H. P. Blavatsky, *Theosophist* 3 (November 1881).

Interview from NPR's *All Things Considered* (June 20, 2005), is available at
www.npr.org.

"Although I can atheist anyone under the table . . .": Timothy Beal, *Roadside
Religion: In Search of the Sacred, the Strange, and the Substance of Faith* (Boston: Beacon,
2005), 22.

Blind Willie Johnson, "Soul of a Man," with backup vocals by Willie B. Harris (Columbia Records, 1930).

Leonard Cohen, "Anthem," *The Future* (Sony Music Entertainment, Inc., 1992).

8. And I Feel Fine

Harold Lindsell, *The Battle for the Bible* (Grand Rapids, MI: Zondervan, 1976).

William Blake, *Laocoön*, in *Milton: A Poem, and the Final Illuminated Works*, ed. Robert N. Essick and Joseph Viscomi, vol. 5 of *Blake's Illuminated Works*, gen. ed. David Bindman (Princeton, NJ: Princeton University Press, 1993).

Religare and *relegere* are themselves etymologically related: to read (*leg* stem) is to connect (*lig* stem) letters and words together into a meaningful utterance.

My description of rereading in Hebrew Scriptures is influenced by Michael Fishbane's concept of "inner-biblical exegesis" as presented in his highly influential work, *Biblical Interpretation in Ancient Israel* (Oxford: Clarendon Press, 1985). Fishbane argues convincingly that biblical texts and traditions in ancient Israel "were not simply copied, studied, transmitted, or recited. They were also, and by these means, subject to redaction, elucidation, reformation, and outright transformation" (p. 542). The Hebrew Scriptures grew as earlier texts were reinterpreted in new contexts. See also Timothy Beal, "Glossary" and "Ideology and Intertextuality: Surplus of Meaning and Controlling the Means of Production," in Danna Nolan Fewell, ed., *Reading Between Texts: Intertextuality in the Hebrew Bible* (Louisville, KY: Westminster/John Knox, 1992).

I understand biblical interpretation as a "fusion" of two horizons — the horizon of the text and the horizon of the reader who encounters it — on which, see Hans Georg Gadamer, *Truth and Method*, 2nd rev. ed., trans. Garrett Barden and John Cumming, rev. trans. Joel Weinsheimer and Donald G. Marshall (New York: Crossroad, 1993); and William E. Deal and Timothy Beal, "Hans Georg Gadamer," in *Theory for Religious Studies* (New York: Routledge, 2004).

Matthew 5:38–42. The phrase "eye for eye, tooth for tooth" appears in Exodus 21:24, Leviticus 24:20, and Deuteronomy 19:21. Note that Jesus's next scriptural quotation in the Sermon on the Mount (5:43) diverges from the standard Hebrew editions of today: "You shall love your neighbor" does appear in our versions of Leviticus 19:18, but "and hate your enemies" does not. It appears that Jesus and/or the Gospel of Matthew may have been drawing from a different edition of Torah.

NOTES   225

Ben Bag Bag is quoted in *Mishnah Pirkei Avot* 5:22.

The image of Torah as wheat and flax is in *Seder Eliyahu Zuta,* chap. 2.

On the ways digital network culture is transforming society, see Manuel Castells, *The Rise of the Network Society,* vol. 1 of *The Information Age: Economy, Society and Culture* (Malden, MA: Blackwell, 1996); summarized in Timothy Beal, *Religion in America,* 93–99.

Genesis: A Living Conversation with Bill Moyers, DVD (Hamilton, NJ: Films Media Group, 1997). The idea for this PBS series came from Rabbi Burton L. Visotzky, a professor at Jewish Theological Seminary in New York, who, in 1987, began hosting a monthly discussion group focused on stories from Genesis. The dozen or so members included a number of writers with various religious and nonreligious backgrounds, along with Jewish and Christian scholars. Moyers's interest was sparked by a newspaper story about Visotzky's group written by Eleanor Blau, "Writers and Editors Ponder the Bible," *New York Times,* March 6, 1989.

The image of the words of Torah interpretation rising through the roof of the *bet-midrash* to heaven is in the *Ben Ish Chai,* a collection of sermons by Yosef Chaim (1832–1909).

Index

CPSIA information can be obtained
at www.ICGtesting.com
Printed in the USA
LVHW021458140123
737176LV00005B/44